Nostalgia for the Modern

POLITICS, HISTORY, AND CULTURE

A series from the International Institute at the University of Michigan

SERIES EDITORS: George Steinmetz and Julia Adams

SERIES EDITORIAL ADVISORY BOARD: Fernando Coronil, Mamadou Diouf, Michael Dutton, Geoff Eley, Fatma Müge Göcek, Nancy Rose Hunt, Andreas Kalyvas, Webb Keane, David Laitin, Lydia Liu, Julie Skurski, Margaret Somers, Ann Laura Stoler, Katherine Verdery, Elizabeth Wingrove

Sponsored by the International Institute at the University of Michigan and published by Duke University Press, this series is centered around cultural and historical studies of power, politics, and the state—a field that cuts across the disciplines of history, sociology, anthropology, political science, and cultural studies. The focus on the relationship between state and culture refers both to a methodological approach—the study of politics and the state using culturalist methods—and a substantive one that treats signifying practices as an essential dimension of politics. The dialectic of politics, culture, and history figures prominently in all the books selected for the series.

Nostalgia for

ESRA ÖZYÜREK

THE MODERN

State Secularism and

Everyday Politics

in Turkey

Duke University Press ✳ Durham and London ✳ 2006

Printed in the United States of America on acid-free paper ∞

Designed by Katy Clove

Typeset in Quadraat by Keystone Typesetting, Inc.

Library of Congress Cataloging-in-Publication Data

appear on the last printed page of this book.

Duke University Press gratefully acknowledges the

support of the Institute of Turkish Studies, which

provided funds toward production of this book.

Portions of chapter 2 previously appeared in "Wedded to the Republic: Public Intellectuals and Intimacy Oriented Publics in Turkey," in *Off Stage/On Display: Intimacies and Ethnographies in the Age of Public Culture*, edited by Andrew Shryock. 101–30. Stanford: Stanford University Press.

Portions of chapter 3 appeared in "Miniaturizing Atatürk: Privatization of the State Imagery and Ideology in Turkey," *American Ethnologist* 31(3): 374–91.

To my parents, Sünter and Mustafa Özyürek

Contents

Acknowledgments

Abbas Kiorastami, the most gifted filmmaker of our times, once said in an interview that he makes films in order to connect to people. I believe that the single most worthy reason for going through the painfully long process of writing an ethnographic monograph is also the same. I am grateful to this book for being the mediator of my most meaningful relationships in life and the transformer of already existing ones.

Nearly every single issue I explore in this book was introduced to me for the first time during my undergraduate education at Boğaziçi University in Istanbul. Yeşim Arat, Faruk Birtek, Belgin Tekçe, Nilüfer Göle, Leyla Neyzi, Nükhet Sirman, Ayşe Öncü, and Taha Parla put seeds of intellectual curiosity in my young mind. My after-class discussions with Ari Adut, Ayşe Gül Altınay (Karayazgan), Ayfer Bartu, Tansel Demirel, Dicle Koğacıoğlu, Halide Velioğlu, Nazan Üstündağ, and Nilgun Uygun in the dark, smoky cafeterias on campus turned out to be among the most interesting intellectual exchanges I would ever have. The larger intellectual community of Boğaziçi spread around the world is the primary addressee of my thinking and writing.

The University of Michigan proved to be the perfect place to pursue my interests. There I had the chance to become part of one of the biggest and most brilliant cohorts in anthropology. My conversations with Penelope

Papailias, Carla Daughtry, Mani Limbert, Theresa Truax, Jeff Jurgens, Jim Herron, Setrag Manukian, Laura Kunreuther, Janet McIntosh, Rachel Heiman, and Karen Strassler have been an endless source of inspiration. Without Ellen Moodie I probably would not have been able to go through graduate school or complete this manuscript. The Young Turks of Ann Arbor provided me with the right kind of intellectual and emotional support to write and stay sane. I am mostly thankful to Aslı Gür, Aslı Iğsız, and Cihan Tuğal. My mentors Bruce Mannheim, Müge Göçek, and Alaina Lemon gave the best combination of support and challenge any student could ever hope for. Andrew Shryock's arrival in the department during my writing stage was one of the greatest academic gifts I have received. His gentle but astute criticisms of my work, always framed in a great sense of humor, pushed me to produce the best work I ever could.

My wonderful colleagues—including Dwight Reynolds and Mayfair Yang at the University of California, Santa Barbara; Bob Hayden and Nicole Constable at the University of Pittsburgh; and Joel Robbins, Nancy Postero, and Elana Zilberg at the University of California, San Diego—provided me with invaluable intellectual and friendly company during the final stages of writing. My position at UCSD came with the most precious gift of Keith McNeal's heart-warming camaraderie.

George Steinmetz and Julia Adams generously pointed to the book hidden in the dissertation. Lara Deeb, Levent Soysal, and one anonymous reviewer read the whole manuscript and helped me crystallize my arguments. Sharon Torian and Reynolds Smith of Duke University Press patiently assisted me in jumping through the numerous hoops of academic publishing.

My research was based on my lifetime connections in Turkey. I am grateful to everyone who made the time to talk, think, and explore with me. Of those, my cousin, friend, and editor Asena Günal has been one of my greatest supporters and critics through my research and writing process. She patiently answered my endless questions over e-mail and kept me updated on the Turkish intellectual scene by regularly sending new books that came out. Most important, she encouraged me to write in Turkish and take part in the Turkish language intellectual dialogue. The positive feedback and encouragement I received from scholars based in Turkey became one of my main sources of motivation.

This project allowed me to connect with my parents Sünter and Mustafa

Özyürek in new ways since many of my questions and analyses of Turkish political culture have been shaped through my conversations and arguments with them. My primary reason for undertaking this project was to understand them better. I chose to come to the United States for graduate school in the first place so that I could be close to my sister Aslı Özyürek. As a scholar, I strive for her ability to think big, never tire of asking new questions, and pursue them without relinquish.

The greatest reward I received in my life as a result of coming to the United States to pursue this project was meeting my partner Marc David Baer. I developed all my ideas in this book as I debated with him. For more than a decade he kept sharpening my arguments, giving them historical depth, and converting my sentences written in Turkish grammar to proper English. Without his day-to-day loving support, critical involvement in my project, and, most important, sense of humor, I cannot imagine having completed this work.

Introduction

"This time," my mother said, her voice suddenly serious, "you will find Turkey very different."

It was the summer of 1997. She and my father had just picked me up from the Atatürk Airport in Istanbul. I was back again after my final year of graduate coursework in the United States. During our two-hour ride through endless traffic to their apartment on the other side of the Bosporus, my parents kept on pointing. They pointed to veiled women drivers in cars. They showed me the countless new mosque complexes on the fringes of the city. They read out loud Islamist car stickers such as "Peace is in Islam." All the while, they went on and on about the policies of the Islamist Welfare Party, whose coalition had ruled the country from 1995 until a few months before my return to Turkey. They were not perfectly happy that a discreet military intervention into politics had banned the party, but my mother especially was relieved that political Islam had been contained, at least for the time being.

When we arrived at their apartment, I told them that I was too tired to talk any more. I tried to reorient myself into their place and life by quietly wandering through the rooms. I scanned the walls to see if they had hung new paintings. I rifled the drawers where they stuffed recent snapshots. I caressed the new clothes they had bought. I studied the shelves on which they stacked their latest books.

I noticed some curious things among all the items and images. What first attracted my attention was that Atatürk, the founding father of modern Turkey—literally father Turk—dead nearly sixty years by then, seemed to be everywhere. I noted pictures of a standing Atatürk on coffee tables and in bookshelves, there were mugs and key chains with pictures of Atatürk, and six different pins had been fixed onto four different coats belonging to my mother and father. I noticed that they had also read several books on Atatürk's and other early Republican citizens' lives: A Life with Atatürk (Gökçen 1994); The Blonde Zeybek: The Last Three Hundred Days of Atatürk (Dündar 1998); Atatürk's Gallery of Lovers (Yesilyurt 1997).[1] What surprised me most were pictures from a 1930s-style ballroom dance party they had attended with little red paper Turkish flags in their hands. My mother had doffed a stylish black hat, and a piece of tulle covered the upper part of her face, but my father wore one of his usual navy blue suits with a bright red tie. In the following days, as I strolled through the city and visited relatives and old friends, what kept intriguing me was not the veiled drivers, but the repeated appearance of Atatürk and nostalgic references to the 1930s in homes so familiar to me.

Although I could not make much sense of these new developments taking place in my parents' or friends' lives at the time, I soon realized that it was not only the Islamists who changed but also secularist citizens like themselves, devoted to early Republican principles, who were transforming the way they experienced and displayed their ideological commitments. It seemed that the Republican ideology and imagery, once marking the public sphere, had suffused domestic space in a new way.

This book explores new everyday expressions and emotive affiliations associated with neoliberal political culture. It investigates rapidly shifting boundaries between what is considered public and private, political and apolitical, legitimate and illegitimate. It focuses on the way grounds of the political field and state-citizen relations are transforming in a peculiar but globally connected way in Turkey.[2] In the late 1990s, the memory of a strong, independent, self-sufficient state and its secularist modernization project that dominated the public sphere through the past century was challenged by the rise of political Islam and Kurdish separatism, on the one hand, and the increasing demands of the European Union (EU), the International Monetary Fund (IMF), and the World Bank, on the other. In the past decade, Islam, which the secular Turkish Republic had limited to the private sphere after its founding in 1923, gained visibility in public places (Öncü 1995; Göle 1996; Bartu 1999; Çınar 1997; Navaro-Yashin 2002) and became part of party politics (Gülalp 2001; Tuğal 2002; White 2002). Concurrently, Kemalism, the publicly official ideology of the secularist, modernist, and developmentalist Turkish Republic founded by Mustafa Kemal Atatürk in 1923, was moving to the private sphere—yet without deserting the public. Ordinary citizens promoted the ideology, carrying its symbols to private domains such as businesses and homes, and developed a nostalgic attachment to the founding days. In other words, as religion increasingly became "public" (Casanova 1994), secular state ideology underwent privatization.

In this study I trace the much neglected second set of changes. I analyze how secular state ideology, politics, and symbolism found a new life and legitimacy in the private realms of the market, the home, civil society, life history, and emotional attachment just as political Islam began to occupy the public sphere and a newly hegemonic neoliberal symbolism defined the civic and private spheres as the latest exalted centers of power. More specifically, I explore how and why the symbolism of neoliberalism, which aims to substitute the market for both society and the state, is being popularly translated into new contexts with strong state ideologies and nostalgic memories of state-led modernization projects.[3] Most of the countries once deemed to belong to the second or third world—having recently adapted the neoliberal policies of a liberalization of the markets, the privatization of state enterprises, and structural adjustment—have experienced state-led modernization projects. How, then, do they take up the new conceptual and organizational transformation that sees the state not as the agent but the inhibitor of the latest kind of modernization project to be adopted? I ask how and why local political leaders and actors who worked under the strong-state ideology now translate the history and symbolism of state-led modernization into the conceptual framework of the new hegemony of market-led modernization.[4] And how do ordinary citizens adopt these concepts into their everyday lives?

What I explore in this book is the unexpected integration of the neoliberal symbolism of privatization, market choice, and voluntarism with that of the etatist, nationalist, and modernist ideology of Kemalism in the 1990s. I argue that the Kemalist political, intellectual, and army elite, as well as their citizen supporters, utilized market-oriented symbols of neoliberalism, along with powerfully authoritarian measures, in order to defend their ideology and position in opposition to political Islam. This symbolism, I suggest, allowed Kemalist citizens to carry the symbols, practices, and emotional affiliations with the Turkish state outside the conventional and public boundaries of the state, there giving Kemalism a new home and legitimacy in the private. In that respect, state ideology and imagery in Turkey became "privatized" in multiple meanings of the word.

Elizabeth Povinelli (2002) reminds us that liberalism travels well and gives way to novel meanings and practices when in diaspora. Be it multiculturalism in Australia, neoliberalism in Chile (Paley 2001), or the creation of a market economy in Eastern Europe (Bockman and Eyal 2002), liberalism in its late form has become a powerful model of modernization that non-Western and postcolonial societies intimately related to at the turn of the twenty-first century. Turkey offers a particularly interesting place to study the peculiar manifestations of neoliberalism since it has been one of the earlier and most steady testing grounds for the policies of deregulation and structural adjustment prescribed by the World Bank and the IMF in the 1980s.[5] These new policies contradicted the earlier model of state-led modernization based on self-sufficiency and independence. The neoliberal symbolism of the market and privatization rapidly traveled to spheres of life outside the economy such as civil society, the domestic sphere, history writing, and emotional expression. Hence it radically transformed the political field by introducing new boundaries and key concepts such as voluntarism, choice, and privacy. Everyday actions establish the hegemony of these concepts outside the field of economy, and by doing so, they privatize politics and can thus also be called "popular neoliberalism," the topic of this book.

THE PRIVATIZATION OF POLITICS

The process that I define as the privatization of state ideology is far from unique to Turkey, although it takes a particular form there. Scholars of contemporary societies agree that the definition, practice, and location of politics have changed around the globe at the turn of the millennium. Social order is maintained by new rationalities, strategies, and technologies. Political actors and lay citizens alike carry the newly hegemonic ideology of neoliberal privatization into political and social realms. International aid agencies and political advisors encourage governments in Turkey and elsewhere to leave their responsibilities to nongovernmental organizations and private companies and to redefine the role of the state as a "consumer state" rather than a "citizen state." In such states, Philip

McMichael (1998, 95) argues, "governance . . . has become evaluated according to how effectively states adopt market-oriented economic policies," even though this process leads governments to lose the freedom to pursue national redistributive and macroeconomic policies.

A number of scholars have interpreted the latest transformations in the political field in quite negative terms. Jean and John Comaroff (2000, 232), for example, argue that neoliberalism actually kills politics by prioritizing the economy and defining political relations in terms of self-interest. Others have even termed the West's contemporary moment as "post political" because the decision-making process is delegated to technocrats (Žižek 1999, 198), or as "anti-political" because the neoliberal ideology empties the public sphere and defines society as a "self-propelled and self-sustaining machine driven by market competition" (Schedler 1997, 5). In this context, these thinkers argue, politics has come to be seen not only as unnecessary but also as "nothing other than a parasitic, rent-seeking activity" (5).

In this study, rather than deny the existence of politics in the neoliberal order of things, I argue that the end of the twentieth century produced a new kind of politics—or a new governmentality, to use Michel Foucault's (1991) language—that allowed new imaginations of the public, the state, and the state-citizen relationship. As the symbolism of the market, of privacy, and of voluntarism as located outside the state are increasingly becoming hegemonic, the symbolic center of politics is not dismantling but shifting from public institutions to such things as civil society (Cohen and Arato 1992; Hann and Dunn 1996) consumer activism (Yudice 1995), and faith-based organizations (Casanova 1994). The public sphere is becoming intimate as private matters of sexuality, morality, and family values have become key issues to be discussed in public (Berlant 1997; Beck 1997; Bauman 2001; Plummer 2003). In this new public sphere, Lauren Berlant argues, citizenship appears "as a condition of social membership produced by personal acts and values" (1997, 5). Accordingly, politics is conceptualized as something that does not take place in relation to a shared public and does not recognize a shared public good.

In countries like Turkey, where state ideology and symbolism occupied a central role in the local political field for centuries, the concept of a shared public sphere is still imperative. Yet the global ideology of neoliberalism and the local controversy between Islamism and secularism make privacy and intimacy vital to politics and citizenship in a particular way. In the 1990s increasing numbers of Islamists, Kurdish nationalists, and liberal intellectuals argued that the oppressive reforms of the Turkish state were creating a secular public ideology and ritual not effectively integrated with beliefs and practices of domestic life, ethnic identity, or religious belief. Since that time a new configuration of the personal, domestic, sentimental, and consumerist practices of commitments to Republican values have been put into practice and publicly displayed by secularist political activists, civil society organizations, and the mass media, as well as lay citizens, as proper models of citizenship. Such dedication has manifested itself through novel practices such as consuming symbols of the Turkish state, developing nostalgic sentiments for the early Republican days, and paying attention to the life histories of elderly citizens who transformed their private lives through the Turkish reforms. This book explores the publicly displayed private expressions through which visible sections of Turkish society personally relate to the state and its founding principles in ways that they had not done before. It suggests that personalized expressions of politics, or such expressions that take place in the private sphere, have become the new basis of citizenship and legitimate political participation, as well as a novel rationale for governmentality.

A crucial lesson we learn about contemporary politics from a close examination of the Turkish case is that the popularization of neoliberal symbolism in the political public sphere cannot simply be understood as a displacement of personal issues. Scholars who study the transformation of the public and private spheres in the United States and Europe explain the rise of new kinds of political and public discussions focusing on private issues as a result of new reproductive technologies such as test-tube babies or cybersex (Plummer 2003), the increased individualization of social life during the postindustrial phase (Beck 1997; Bauman 2001; Putnam 2000), or the growing power of corporations (Marden 2003). Whether they evaluate these developments as positive or negative, most scholars assume that the emergence of new private concerns or intimacies precedes their colonization of the public sphere (Bauman 2001; Marden 2003). My analysis of the privatization of state ideology in Turkey instead suggests that political agents deliberately create and display novel privacies and intimacies in order to represent freely internalized, and hence voluntary and legitimate, political positions. These actors transform the old and create new meanings for the private spheres according to the newly shared priorities of neoliberal ideology.

At another level, my work on the privatization of politics is an attempt to demonstrate how the different "privates" of economic, civil, domestic, or personal life are actually connected to and shape each other. It is important to note that by pointing to a privatization in politics I wish to suggest neither the existence of a well-recognized distinction between the private and the public nor that political affairs by definition belong to the latter area. To the contrary, my analysis of the shifts between what is considered private and public are inspired by feminist scholars who have successfully demonstrated that the line between the two spheres has always been under negotiation (Suad 1997; Landes 1998; Benhabib 1998; Gal 2002; Gal and Kligman 2000). In this book I demonstrate that local political actors reshape their definitions of the public and private, as well as of the political and the apolitical, as they engage with the broader social, political, and discursive transformations in which they find themselves situated. I also consider it central to this study to pursue how these actors define, reify, and transform the representation of the state as they valorize seemingly irrelevant realms of the private—such as the nonstate ownership of businesses, family life, or domestic organization—in opposition to the state.

A discussion of the private sphere and hence privatization is impossible without paying tribute to Jürgen Habermas's (1989) definition of the public sphere. In his seminal work about the development of the bourgeois public sphere, Habermas points out that multiple meanings are associated with the phrase, ranging from an event open to all, to a sphere of commodity exchange, to state authority. What Habermas does not pay equal attention to in his work is the multiply conceptualized and dynamically functioning nature of the private sphere. In his creatively imagined discussion, he argues that the public sphere "grew out of the audience-oriented subjectivity of the conjugal family's intimate domain" (28), but he does not discuss how the public sphere in turn shaped and formed the private sphere again, especially once there was an audience formed to observe the displays taking place in the internal domain.

At the turn of the new century, the *public* seemed to carry a more uniform meaning for Turkish citizens, namely, that of state authority.[6] A multiplicity of meanings lay in the *private sphere* since it included any field conceptualized as outside the direct involvement of state power and hence one in which individuals engaged in activities freely and voluntarily. My ethnographic research demonstrates that Turkish citizens did not think in terms of a tripartite public/private model that differentiated between the market, civil society, and the state (Cohen and Arato 1992). According to Turkish political activists, any sphere outside the commonly accepted boundaries of the state organization is considered private, and hence represents the voluntary engagement of citizens. That is why seemingly disparate areas such as individual life history, the domestic sphere, family, the market, civil society, and private property were all considered as constituting the private and thus related to each other. Furthermore, any activity taking place in one of these spheres was considered as more in tune with the neoliberal ideal of free expression—and hence more legitimate and modern.[7] This novel criterion for political legitimacy gave way to innovative conceptualizations of both political actions and private spheres, rather than a well-defined public simply growing out of a preconstituted private.

THE ROLE OF NOSTALGIA

In this study I focus on the "structure of feeling" (Williams 1977) of nostalgia as one way in which what used to be considered public and political has become privatized in post–Cold War Turkey. I argue that nostalgia and privatization are among the powerful driving forces behind neoliberal ideology, which turns objects, relations, and concepts into commodities and transforms political expression by converting it to an issue of personal interest. In the past several years, scholars have studied privatization and taken note of emergent forms of nostalgia in postsocialist countries, usually without connecting the two phenomena to each other (Berdahl 1999; Rofel 1999; Boym 2001). This book traces the development of interconnections between nostalgia and privatization as they shape and transform a local political culture at the "margins of Europe" (Herzfeld 1987).

Nostalgia, a term that originally named the symptoms of homesick Swiss soldiers in the seventeenth century (Lowenthal 1985), is now a widespread feeling shared by millions of people at the margins of the Western world. From Islamic activists in Afghanistan (Roy 1994) to discontented postreform workers in China (Rofel 1999) and disillusioned Kemalists in Turkey longing for the 1930s,[8] large groups of people yearn for bygone days and imagine a pristine past in which each individual society united around a common goal. A widely held belief about nostalgia is that because modernity could not fulfill its promises for a better and freer life, people marginalized during the modernization process now look back at the past fondly. According to Andreas Huyssen (1995), modernity ended with the end of hope for tomorrow. Since then, people have looked for their utopias in the past rather than in the future. Another popular explanation for the new orientation toward the past holds the modern age's rapid social and technological transformations responsible. According to Pierre Nora (1996), modern people have lost an embodied sense of the past, so that their only access to earlier periods occurs through archived, alienated, or dutifully followed histories. In his words, "Memory is constantly on our lips because it no longer exists" (1).

Although dissatisfaction with modernization projects that did not deliver on their promises could serve as a viable explanation for the spread of nostalgia across the globe, I favor another perspective, namely, that nostalgia has been an integral part of modernity. Svetlana Boym (2001) argues that nostalgia and progress are merely alter egos of each other because, she claims, both concepts emerged as a result of radical transformations in the concept of time as unilinearly progressive and thus unrepeatable and irreversible. Longing for a past lost became possible only by concentrating on a future that had yet to arrive. Boym provides a perceptive account of the development of nostalgia in the nineteenth and twentieth centuries. But what about the recent explosion of nostalgia at the turn of the twenty-first century, I ask, the nostalgia coming after the utopias had vanished? How is recent nostalgia related to the neoliberal modernity in which it flourishes?

Market-oriented modernization projects aim to carry every possible object or relationship into a market regulated by a Smithian "invisible hand." In the late stage of capitalism we live in, the biggest challenge is to constantly create new commodities for consumption. Nostalgia, in this context, becomes a convenient desire that can transform public concepts such as the national past or identity into personalized commodities. Kathleen Stewart (1988) has already noted that nostalgia runs with the economy of which it is part. This is truer than ever for late capitalism. Marilyn Ivy, for example, demonstrates how nostalgia has become a crucial part of Japanese capitalism by creating the desire necessary for consumption. This is maintained through having "a nostalgia for a Japan that is kept on the verge of vanishing, stable yet endangered (and thus open for commodifiable desire)" (1995, 65). At the turn of the twenty-first century, nostalgia privatizes and, by doing so, commodifies images and concepts once seen as public and thus nonmarketable by previous capitalists around the world.

Nostalgia plays another specific role in Turkey's current relationship with Europe. Since the eighteenth century scholars have defined temporality, a constant sense of newness, as a central aspect of modernity.[9] Contemporary scholarship has discussed the experience of alternative modernities in the non-West as a sense of repetition (Mitchell 2000), of lagging behind (Bhabha 1994), or of longing for the future (Göle 2001). But what of countries like Turkey, which have been modernizing for generations, where not only Western modernity but also local modernization projects have been repeated as ideal models? What of places that became modern but then went "unmodern"? Based on her study of a textile town in Java called Laweyen, Suzanne Brenner (1998) argues that modernization is not a straight path but can also have reverse trajectories. Also, what once was considered modern can at one point come to be seen as traditional or simply nonmodern. Like the residents of Laweyen, many Kemalists have also suggested that Turkey stopped moving forward and has even gone backward in the past several decades and let slip away the stage of modernity it had earlier achieved, especially after political Islam came to power.

At the turn of the twenty-first century, European and American advisors had completely different criteria for the modernity by which they asked Turkey to abide. Although European leaders had approved of the authoritarian model in the 1930s as setting Turkey on the right track, in the 1990s they were increasingly critical of the Turkish state for being too intrusive. They accused Turkish politicians and bureaucrats of limiting political freedom, violating human rights, and oppressing ethnic minorities. As European Union officials asked for a smaller state—particularly for a reduced political role for the army—at the political level,[10] the primarily American-controlled IMF and the World Bank asked for a smaller state at the economic level.[11] They wanted Turkey to privatize state enterprises, decrease state subsidies and protection for agriculture, and lower the state contribution to social security.

With the vivid memory of the 1930s as a modern past utopia in which the citizens united around their state, many contemporary nationalist-modernist citizens do not recognize modernity in the European present. They are discontent with the new criteria of modernization that the European Union imposed on Turkey, becoming resistant to persistent criticisms of the way Turkey has handled the Kurdish issue and human rights violations. Such direct involvement of the European Union in what are considered internal affairs conflicts with the memory of Turkish modernization in the 1930s, achieving as it did its success through an all-powerful and homogenizing state that suppressed local identities, demands, and economies. At the end of the 1990s, many Kemalist citizens and politicians argued that being part of the European Union would lead to a loss of sovereignty. Ironically, at that point, it was only the Islamist politicians who favored membership in the European Union, hoping that the new laws Turkey would be required to adopt would create an atmosphere allowing them political activism and the freedom of religious expression.[12]

In a circumstance in which Kemalist Turks could locate modernity neither in the present or future of Turkey nor in the present of Europe, they sought it in the single-party regime of the 1930s. After all, the strength of the Turkish Republic was founded in part on its defeat of the European occupying forces after World War I. At first sight, such a nostalgic vision of modernity looks like a complex irony, an unexpected reversal that modernity theorists could not foresee. However, I argue that it is merely a different expression of non-Western modernity that locates modernity in the non-present. Contemporary Turkish modernists experience the present as the decay of a former modernity and have chosen as their model for repetition the Turkish past of the 1930s. Furthermore they know that being part of a European present, or more precisely, the European Union, would not make the Turkish state stronger, as it did in the 1930s, but weaker. At the same time, however, by invoking nostalgic feelings toward Kemalism, they have marked this ideology as something that does not belong to the present practices of Turkey, but to those of the past, thus remaining unattainable.

Before I discuss how nostalgia has worked to privatize politics in the Turkish case, I will explain how the concept of state-led modernization in Turkey gave way to a nostalgic modernity as the driving factor of political discourse.

In his foundational 1958 monograph on modernization theory, *The Passing of a Traditional Society*, Daniel Lerner considers the Turkish case as an ideal model. For him, rapid transformation in a Muslim country becomes proof that "the same basic model [developed in the West] reappears in virtually all modernizing societies on all continents of the world, regardless of variations in race, color, creed" (46). Although Lerner bases much of his proof on one village, which rapidly developed thanks to its proximity to the newly founded capital of the country, he is right to suggest that Turkish modernization is uncommon in being a self-initiated and rapidly developed project. Unlike many third world modernization projects, the Turkish one did not start in a formally colonial or postcolonial setting.[13] Rather, it was initiated by the Ottoman Empire's elite and reached its climax during the authoritarian regime of the early Turkish Republic.

The Ottomans introduced the first measures of modernization in the eighteenth century following the weakening of the empire by its European enemies, the Habsburgs and Romanovs.[14] After a major defeat by the Russians in 1774, Sultan Selim III, who had shown interest in the Western world as a prince, adopted some Western models in the military (Göçek 1987; Zürcher 1998). The aim of these reforms was to make the central Ottoman state stronger against both European enemies and internal semi-independent local power holders. France was Selim's source of inspiration, and French advisors established new models of medicine and schooling, in addition to military organization. The following generations of the Ottoman elite kept adopting certain aspects of European ideas, practices, and symbolisms that they believed made them better equipped to fight their enemies (Hanioğlu 1995; Deringil 1998). While doing so, they did not merely imitate European ways but made the new ways of thinking and acting, such as centralized education, their own (Fortna 2002; Gür 2002).[15] Because of economic difficulties or disputes regarding which aspects of European ways of life should or should not be adopted not all their reforms succeeded. Yet they opened new ways of thinking and organizing the relationship between the state and its subjects.

Şerif Mardin (1962) argues that the Ottoman elite conducted such modernization measures not for the sake of being Western, but rather to protect the strength of its state. He claims that the idea of "the priority of the state" motivated the nineteenth-century Ottoman officials and intellectuals to adopt enlightened despotic methods borrowed from Europe. They were, according to him, uniformly concerned with the idea of saving the state, rather than with promoting democracy. Similarly, he argues, Ottoman soldiers organized the national liberation war against the imperial powers in order to save their state. That is why Mardin (1997) suggests that the state as an institution was little changed from the Ottomans to the Turkish Republic.

Mardin's approach to modern Turkish history highlights the close link between modernization and the state in Turkey. Since the eighteenth century, many Ottoman and Turkish reformers saw modernization as the key for a strong state. Moreover, most of the time, they considered it crucial even if the masses were not content with top-down reforms. The foundational years of the Turkish Republic can be interpreted as a time when the state had the full strength to adopt modern ways developed in Europe in many aspects of life. The reformers believed this transformation would make the state stronger, especially vis-à-vis the West.[16]

Following the defeat of the Ottomans at the end of World War I, the Allies partitioned the empire and the Greek army invaded the country. Despite the wishes of the sultan and the government in Istanbul, Mustafa Kemal Atatürk and his comrades started an uprising in Anatolia, where they organized armed forces to fight against the Greeks and the Allies. Mustafa Kemal's army defeated them, abolished the sultanate, and founded the Turkish Republic in 1923, replacing the six-hundred-year-old Ottoman Empire. Under the leadership of Mustafa Kemal the authoritarian single-party regime engaged in a series of reforms to modernize the country immediately after the military victory.

Both West European and Soviet models of modernity inspired Turkish officials to secularize the country by placing religion under the strict supervision and control of the state (Toprak 1981; Tapper 1991; Davison 1998) and limiting its expressions to the public sphere.[17] They discarded the symbols and institutions of Muslim rule such as the office of the caliph, religious orders, lodges, tombs, and religious schools. Swiss, French, and Italian law replaced Muslim law in the courts. The ruling elite officially declared the republic secular in the constitution of 1937. It complemented these reforms with symbolically important others such as changing the alphabet from Arabic to Latin script, expunging Arabic and Persian vocabulary from Turkish, and importing French and German terms in its place. They also banned Islamic clothes and the fez, changed the day of rest from Friday to Sunday, and adopted the European calendar to fit European norms. Kemalist cadres attempted to replace the Islamic religion with a civil religion organized around new rites and rules (Turan 1991; Tapper and Tapper 1991; Yavuz 1999; Gülalp 2005). Cutting off ties with the Islamic Middle East and emphasizing the pre-Islamic central Asian culture of the Turks helped the new regime to fulfill its nationalist ideology in transition from an empire to an Anatolia-based nation-state (Copeaux 1998).

The foundation of all these reforms during the early years of the republic was Kemalism, named after Mustafa Kemal Atatürk. The six principles of this ideology, represented in the six arrows of the Republican People's Party (RPP) emblem, are nationalism, republicanism, statism, populism, revolutionarism, and secularism. Scholars critical of this ideology agree that Kemalism is an elitist, centralist, statist, and positivist ideology that sees people as objects of the Westernizing state (Parla 1991; Robins 1996; Zürcher 1998). Such Jacobin top-down ideas about modernizing society constituted a continuation of similar trends developed in Ottoman society during the nineteenth century. Taha Parla (1985) argues that a Durkheimian corporatist understanding of society promoted by Ziya Gökalp at the end of the nineteenth century formed the basis of Kemalist ideology. On the one hand, this ideology aimed to combine Turkish nationalism with the science and technology of the postliberal Western society of the 1930s (Parla 1992). On the other hand, it aimed to create a homogenous society deprived of class conflicts and ethnic and religious differences (Bali 2000; Yıldız 2001) and unified around its omnipotent and omnipresent father/ leader (Delaney 1995). Differentiating itself both from liberalism and socialism, Kemalism situated itself as a third-road ideology, a form of third world developmentalism (Seufert 2000).

Although they accepted Kemalism as the official ideology of the Turkish Republic in 1935, state officials did not publish any text that formally defined its features.[18] Some scholars argue that it is the indeterminacy of Kemalist ideology that has allowed it to remain alive in changing political contexts over the past seventy-five years (Zürcher 1998). Since his death, Atatürk's ideology has served as the major legitimating symbol for almost any Turkish political movement from the right (Bora and Taşkın 2001) to the left (Alpkaya 2001; Kazancıgil 2001) ends of the political spectrum, even those with radically different aims.[19] Atatürk's exclusive association with the foundation of Turkey as an independent nation, with centralized state power, and with modernization reforms makes it necessary for any political group with goals for Turkey to associate themselves with the founder at one level or another.

Beginning in the 1980s, and especially in the 1990s, integration with the world economy, a resurgence of both Islamic fundamentalism and Kurdish nationalism, as well as increased corruption at all levels of the state threatened the foundational principles of the Turkish Republic as a fully independent, homogenous, secular, and paternalistic state. Many Kemalist intellectuals and citizens have suggested that things began to turn wrong for Turkey much earlier; particularly in 1950, when the Democrat Party won the first free elections. Starting from this period, the Turkish state not only became more populist but it was also integrated into the world political and economic system following World War II (Keyder 1987). It became part of NATO, benefited from the Marshall Plan, participated in the Korean War, and a decade later started the process of entering the European Union. However, until the 1980s Turkey still had a largely closed economy with heavy taxes on imported goods to protect local industries. Import-substitution industrialization was the official state policy of the 1960s and 1970s and aimed to protect domestic industries from competition. Yet the increased oil prices during the 1970s and the dependency on foreign technology and know-how put the Turkish economy into a debt cycle.

The economic liberalization program of the 1980s aimed to attract foreign capital to the country by lowering wages and stripping workers of their basic social rights and radically decreasing import taxes (Cam 2002; Coşkun 1997; Togan and Balasubramanyam 1996). Turkish capitalists who wanted to open up to the world market supported these changes, put into practice through the strict measures of the two-and-a-half-year-long military rule between 1980 and 1983. The military government borrowed money from the IMF under the Credit for Transformation program in 1980, but went beyond the suggested measures by implementing a tax reform that would reduce the deficit and transformed the banking system to attract foreign capital and decrease wages (Balazs 1990). The post-1980 period led to increasing political and economic relations with the United States, leading to cooperation during the Gulf War, and intensifying relations with what was then the European Community (Müftüler 1995).[20]

In the 1990s many nationalist politicians and intellectuals expressed discontent with the increasing intervention of the IMF and the European Union into the Turkish economy and political and human rights–related issues, respectively. Moreover, the privatization programs suggested by the IMF and the World Bank led to corruption at all levels of the state (Baran 2000; Gülalp 2001). In this new phase the resurgence of Kurdish separatism as an armed guerilla faction and of Islamic fundamentalism as a local but transnationally supported movement further increased the threats to the nationalist and secularist principles of Kemalism. The perceived Islamist threat was quieted by an indirect intervention of the Turkish military in politics in 1997.[21]

NOSTALGIC KEMALISM

In the new international order of which Turkey was a part in the 1990s, the basic reference points of nationalist and Kemalist ideology—the boundaries of the national economy, state, and East and West—were changing. Thus nostalgia for the first ten years of the republic became meaningful at a time when its foundational principles came under threat. The seventy-fifth anniversary celebrations in 1998 organized by civil society organizations depicted a 1930s utopian past in which all Turkish citizens were imagined as having fully internalized the goals and policies of the modernizing Turkish state. People with different political ideologies expressed a nostalgic longing for the foundational years of the republic. This utopia produced a model for contemporary citizens to emulate in the present.

Although nostalgic Kemalism expressed an intense desire for the 1930s in Turkey, it also marked the end of the hegemony of Kemalist principles in their classical sense. Nostalgic discourse defined the foundational years as the childhood of the nation, when everything was pure and citizens were gathered around the authority of their father (see my chapter 2). Recognizing it as such, nostalgic citizens knew that the foundational era was irretrievably gone, similar to a childhood. Kemalism was no longer all powerful and hegemonic, but rather a fragile ideology in need of citizens' protection. At this point, Kemalist citizens carried their ideology, ritual, and symbolism into the privacy of their foundations and homes in order to prevent it from being contaminated by corrupt state officers who, they believed, no longer acted according to Kemalist principles.

The timing of modernist nostalgia or nostalgic Kemalism also has demographic and class-based components. Seventy-five years after the foundation of the republic, almost none of its founders were still alive. Even people who as children had experienced the mythologized early years of the republic were passing away by 1998. Unlike those marking the tenth and fiftieth anniversaries, most of the seventy-fifth-anniversary celebrators had not lived through the foundational years of the republic, but had only heard about them through their grandparents or schoolteachers. The lack of real witnesses made it easy to portray these days as a utopian past, conveniently neglecting any difficulties.

The most fervent promoters of nostalgia were the ones heavily influenced by the economic liberalization of the 1980s. The early republic had created its own bureaucratic elite, one financially supported at the expense of other groups in society. More important, these bureaucrats had symbolic power and authority over the masses.[22] In the 1980s the Turkish government changed its priorities from supporting civil servants to supporting export-oriented businesspeople by lowering tariffs, giving them tax breaks, and ignoring the illegal trade arrangements they made. The early Republican elite and their children suffered from the latest transformations in multiple ways. First, the changing economic structure moved them from upper-middle class status to the lower middle class by diminishing the value of their salaries. Second and more important, they lost their monopoly over public space and their respectable position. Thus the nostalgia for the 1930s also symbolized the real loss of the Turkish bureaucratic elite, of civil servants, and of the parties such as the Republican People's Party that represented their interests.

Like any other form of nostalgia, the Kemalist kind took place in and as part of the present moment (Connerton 1989; Lambek 1996; Thomson 1990). Nostalgic citizens used the new legitimacy of privatization as they organized outside the institutional boundaries of the state and established private foundations to propagate the "original" ideology of the Turkish Republic. In the late 1990s, for the first time in Republican history, dozens of independent foundations and organizations with a total of more than one hundred thousand members nation-wide—organized beyond the traditional boundaries of the state and outside government offices—promoted Kemalist ideology.[23] This privatized version of Kemalism, defined by some scholars as neo-Kemalism, shows parallels to its classical form, but it also differs dramatically. Like classical Kemalism, it promotes nationalism, secularism, and modernization, yet it is organized by independent groups of individuals who define themselves as outside the state organization even when they receive extensive help and support from the army (Erdoğan 2000). In 1998, Türkan Saylan, the committed leader of the nation-wide Support for Modern Living Association, defined the followers of the new organizations such as hers as "educated young people who have remained quiet and individualistic until now, but have discovered the hidden power, namely, the power of Mustafa Kemal, within them" (qtd. in Erdoğan 2001, 588).[24] According to her, these people are motivated by "a platonic love [for the state] that leads them to dominate the state from outside" (qtd. in Bora and Kıvanç 1995, 779). Despite the commitment of these individuals to many of the classic principles of Kemalism, it is significant that they underline their location as outside the state institution and define their primary engagement with Atatürk as one of enduring love. By so doing, they have both personalized the official ideology and have marked the end of a period in which the modernist state elite monopolized Kemalist ideology.

NOSTALGIC MODERNITY

Through its focus on the shift from state-centered to market-inspired modernity in Turkey, this study contributes to the emergent literature on alternative modernities by introducing a temporal dimension. The reintroduction of an interest in non-Western modernity has been a welcome focus in anthropology since the 1990s. Since the radical critique of modernization theory in the 1970s, scholars, and especially anthropologists, have stayed away from the term *modern* for fear of being associated with the previous paradigm. The recent return to the concept, in a framework very different from the previous one, seemed almost inevitable since modernity is central to the way people around the world interpret their own behavior, projects, and aspirations, as well as those of others.

In contrast to the temporal focus of modernization theory, which concentrated on progress through time, alternative-modernities literature is mainly concerned with the spatial variation of modernity around the world.[25] Despite its obvious value for appreciating the diversity of modernities in the present, this body of literature veers too far away from temporality and overlooks the dynamic histories of both Western and non-

Western modernities, as well as how they have shaped each other through time. Even the very term *alternative modernities* assumes one normal, unchanging, and standard (read Western) modernity, making other modernities its alternatives (Mitchell 2000). In the past two hundred years, Turks have to come to terms with radically different understandings of Western modernity as they tried—sometimes willingly, sometimes perforce—to adopt some of its changing aspects. Faced with rapidly changing measures of being modern and the memory of their own experiences, modernizationist Turkish citizens today must reconcile the memory of the state-led modernization project of the 1930s and the hegemony of a market-inspired modernization in the 1990s.

This study demonstrates that in addition to the dynamic nature of Western modernities, local historical factors also prove crucial in shaping non-Western modernities. The recent understanding of modernity in Turkey has been shaped through internal struggles as much as through dialogue with the West. Even in its most centrally managed phases, the Turkish modernization project was marked by "many uncertainties, occasional reversals, and periodic shifts in its speed and priorities" (Kasaba 1997, 20). In its later stages changing discourses of transnational modernity gave new discursive tools of legitimacy to competing local groups with competing interpretations of what constitutes being modern. In the 1990s Islamist and secularist groups utilized different discourses of modernity in order to prove themselves modern—and thus legitimate—portraying others as non-modern. For example, while Islamist groups used discourses of democracy and human rights to point to their suppression, secularist groups took advantage of Western laws such as a French court's decision against veiling in the French school system and interpreted it as a universalist declaration. At other times, nostalgic Kemalists privately consumed Kemalist symbols, thus gaining legitimacy in the neoliberal political semiotics that prioritize privatization and consumption over central production and distribution. Nostalgia for Kemalist modernity formed a crucial part of the latter process. It helped privatize a public past through personalized feelings of nostalgia, love, and desire to protect the regime.

Thus a nostalgic take on modernity, which can also be called nostalgic modernity, is a political ideology, as well as a discursive and a sentimental condition. It refers neither to a contained form of modernity nor to its dissolution. It is instead a moment or even a temporarily held perspective in the Turkish political field. It will inevitably keep evolving and giving way to new forms of modernity as it engages in a dialogue with Western modernities and the emergent forms and ideologies of modernity in Turkey.

NEW POSSIBILITIES FOR POLITICAL ANTHROPOLOGY

Regardless of how we interpret the meaning of political transformations in Turkey or in the world, they elicit new fields of inquiry and require updated methods of analysis. Since the middle of the twentieth century political scientists have been developing increasingly sophisticated statistical models and analyses to study political participation, electoral results, government structures, political parties, and legislatures.[26] As the definition of politics is changing, such studies unfortunately become less useful in reflecting changes on the ground. In Ulrich Beck's language, "we look for politics in the wrong place, with the wrong terms, on the wrong floors of offices and on the wrong pages of newspapers" (1997, 99). For example, in the United States, only a small fraction of people vote.[27] By contrast, in countries of what were once called the second and third worlds, citizens formerly unable to participate in free elections now vote to elect their leaders. Yet the new international agreements these countries are pressured to sign, such as NAFTA (North American Free Trade Agreement) and MAI (Multilateral Agreement on Investments), or the high interest on debt they have to pay in order to receive financial aid deprive them of their sovereignty in terms of making their own laws or conducting redistributive policies. In yet other places again—such as Afghanistan, Iraq, or Palestine—elections take place in conditions that are anything but free. Furthermore, an increasing number of political actions can no longer be labeled deliberative practices. In Peter Marden's words, "Political space is seen to suffer from the intrusion of performative forms of representation" (2003, 235). People prefer attaching flags or stickers to their cars to having open discussions in town hall–style meetings.

What kind of a genealogy can anthropologists follow in their discipline if they want to study new political discourses, practices, and affiliations shaped and transformed by late liberalism? American anthropology has not traditionally been interested in political structures and cultures. British anthropology founded the subfield of political anthropology in the 1940s, but scholars merely concentrated on the tribal structures of stateless societies. Their structuralist-functionalist approach mainly served the British colonial administration by locating indigenous leaders and power structures. More important, political anthropologists legitimated colonial rule by defining the colonized as chaotic.[28]

A second wave of interest in political structures took place almost half a century later on the other side of the Atlantic. In the 1980s, North American anthropology started to shift its long-lasting attention from the colonized toward the colonizer. Coupling this change with the influence of Michel Foucault's work on knowledge and power, an increasing number of scholars paid attention to colonial administrations.[29] This body of literature creatively brought anthropological and historical approaches together to problematize the West, scrutinize the workings of the colonial state, and understand the resistance of indigenous populations.[30]

In the 1990s anthropologists started to pay attention to postcolonial states as well. The recent work focuses on the way local people relate to and interpret postcolonial state institutions.[31] Ethnographies of the state brought a fresh approach to our understanding of the forms and discourses of legitimation for institutional power. It appears intriguing that state ideologies started to attract anthropological attention at a time when many political scientists and sociologists, international political advisors, and local politicians began attributing a smaller role to the state in the globally connected and translocally governed world (Omae 1995; Sassen 1996; Jessop 1999). Today, political acts of decision making, execution, or redistribution are increasingly considered more legitimate if they take place outside the institutional boundaries of the state and thus within market mechanisms (King 1987; McMichael 1998; Chang 2002) and by citizen groups organized outside political parties (Beck 1997; Putnam 2000). Neoliberal ideologies flourish in debt-dependent countries in which international lending organizations and political advisors encourage and/or coerce governments to transfer their responsibilities of national development, the redistribution of wealth, poverty alleviation (Rankin 2001; Elyachar 2002), risk sharing (Erikson et al. 2000), security (Musah 2002), health, education, and even of the distribution of water (Bakker 2003) to nongovernmental organizations and private companies. State institutions are not disappearing, but their functions and privileges (Steinmetz 1999), as well as their relationship with citizens (Fourcade-Gourinchas 2002; Paley 2001) are radically transforming.[32] In other words, states are still alive and well, but the ways in which they define and legitimate themselves are rapidly changing. Thus, if anthropologists want to study the local understandings of politics, they need to redirect their focus outside the institutional boundaries of the state.[33]

Some anthropologists have already urged us to adopt new objects of study and research methods in order to respond to recent transformations such as the increasing pace of transnational movements and the end of the Cold War. Recent suggestions include "multi-sited ethnographic research" (Marcus 1989, 1991, 1995, 1998), transnational anthropology (Appadurai 1996), and a focus on the "new international order of the post–Cold War (Borneman 1998). The new political anthropology I advocate in this book aims to better grasp and respond to recent changes in power relations and in the semiotics of political legitimacy of late liberalism. It is motivated by the above suggestions, but it also goes beyond them. I propose that in the new millennium, anthropologists are uniquely equipped to understand the newly hegemonic culture of neoliberalism in the fields of economy, society, and politics. As the definition of politics transforms, anthropologists inevitably find themselves talking about the same topics with political leaders, advisors, and policy makers. These include family relations and ideologies, the body, religion, structured emotions, and consumption. Voting patterns, the consolidation of democracy, or political participation seem increasingly less important in contemporary political discussions, both from the perspective of political activists and analysts. Politics is moving toward anthropology at a much faster speed than anthropologists are moving toward politics. This new kind of politics is taking place in spaces and actions that used to be considered as private or intimate. Yet they are directed toward a public audience and are aimed at influencing relations of governance, as well as the limits of the rights and duties of citizens. Hence anthropologists who aim to understand the power dynamics of the neoliberal order need to develop new sensibilities concerning the relationship among intimate matters, the market, and formal politics.

As citizens and officials emphasize the private, they also redefine, renew, and recreate it. More important, they connect diverse fields of the private and the personal with each other. The only way to understand ways of being in the new "privates" involves moving back and forth among domestic practices, mundane conversations, intimate sentiments, market activities, and civil society organizations. Anthropological curiosity about the ordinary, everyday, and homely now takes us to new places. Most important, it allows us to understand the pervasiveness and limits of neoliberalism in transforming local relations of governance and emotive affiliation.

FIELDWORK AND FAMILY WORK

Studying transformations in the political field and its expressions in intimate zones was not easy, particularly because both the public and the private I wanted to explore were constantly shifting and converting each other. During my research between 1998 and 1999 in Istanbul and Ankara, I went back and forth between a series of life-history interviews with firsthand witnesses of the republic, participation in Kemalist activities, and following discourses in newspapers and on television. In between, I participated in public celebrations of the seventy-fifth anniversary; visited museums and exhibits; spoke to sponsors, organizers, and visitors; studied home decoration in dozens of Kemalist apartments; and had ongoing conversations with friends and acquaintances about the latest political developments in the country.

As my argument began to crystallize, my parents and some Turkish friends with whom I exchanged ideas suggested that the whole focus of my research was a little off. They proposed that I look at structural transformations in the state in the late 1990s, especially at the increasing role of the military in decision-making processes, alongside the decreasing role of government. Others thought I should talk about the way in which government networks form part of privatization bids. There is no doubt that looking closely at policy making and macroeconomic processes would give a broad sense of how the categories of the private and the public are being negotiated both in political and economic terms. However, my study suggests that it would be impossible to understand the full range of implications of privatization in people's lives with such macro-oriented studies. Because of their very nature, the market-based economy and politics take shape in and in turn reshape the way people organize their domestic space, decorate their walls, narrate their life stories, and feel about political developments. A fuller understanding of neoliberal symbolism and practice in its diversity requires the researcher to have multiple sensitivities and foci of attention, not only toward larger discourses concerning the market but also with regard to how citizens as consumers act in and experience the privatization of Turkey's political economy.

The most important component of this research, however, was my being a member of a devoted Kemalist family. I am the granddaughter of a parliamentarian of the single-party regime and the daughter of two staunch Kemalist and social democrat activists affiliated with the Republican People's Party.[34] During my research about transformations in the Kemalist ideology in Turkey I had to explore and unlearn many of the basic assumptions on which I was raised. I could do both of these only through critical engagement with my parents, who initially had taught me about these values in the first place.

I first noticed transformations in Kemalist ideology and practices over the years by having intimate conversations with my parents, observing the new political icons they displayed at home, and joining them in political activities that looked different from the ones in which I participated when I was younger. Their influence on the project was not limited to an initial inspiration or a grasp of a wider phenomenon. They simply made my research possible through providing me with contacts, informing me about political activities they themselves were attending, alerting me to interesting television programs, preparing folders of newspaper clippings for me, and, most important, talking to me for hours about my ideas. Stacks of lira bills they frequently stuffed in my coat pockets when I was not looking paid for unexpected research expenses.

Both of my parents have been closely involved with my project during the writing process as well. I discussed all my points with them in sometimes heated conversations. They were concerned about my ideas, not only because they were intrigued by my interpretations but also because they thought that my critical stance toward Kemalism—both in its privatized and public forms—could influence them in somewhat direct ways. After the 1999 general elections I wrote an article in *Birikim*, a magazine equivalent to the *Nation* in the United States, about the first veiled Turkish parliamentarian and the process by which she was stripped of her citizenship. When they learned of the article, my parents were concerned that they would lose face if their political allies noticed their daughter's "support" of a political figure they adamantly opposed. When the journal appeared, they chose to frame their dislike of my article in terms of poor writing and my argument's lack of analytical sophistication. Such an evaluation stood in contrast to the usual praise I receive from my parents for my pieces in Turkish. That day they penalized me by canceling a dinner plan we had made earlier. Half jokingly, my father told me that he would call up the Islamist Virtue Party and give them my number so that I could be their honorary lawyer. My mother was more direct in voicing her concern about her political career in the RPP. In the end, I do not think anyone in their party read my article, or made the connection they feared.

Despite her concern about my ruining her relationship with other party members, my mother actually enjoyed taking me to party meetings. I was pleasantly surprised to see the intense, complicated, and sometimes antagonistic relationships my mother has been engaged in. Her friends, who are upset about the lack of attention they receive from younger people, were happy to have me around even if they did not fully agree with my views. Toward the end of my research I established my own friendships with the women RPP members I met through my mother. My mother was proud when they later praised her for raising a "sweet and smart" daughter.

It is most likely that this study became a tool for me to negotiate daughter-parent relations and establish myself as an adult in some ways. At the same time, the intimate and truly personalized nature of my study provided me with an otherwise unavailable window into the privatization of politics among Kemalists in Turkey. I hope these aspects add richness to the research and do not cloud my interpretation of Turkish political culture.

ORGANIZATION OF THE STUDY

Each chapter in this study covers a different form in which official ideology and politics were carried outside of the conventional realm of the state in Turkey during the late 1990s. The first two chapters focus on the personalized understanding of the foundational history and the official ideology of the Turkish Republic. The third and the fourth chapters study the introduction of the market-based ideas of privatization, spontaneity, and free will into the celebration of the Turkish Republic and the commemoration of its founding father. The final chapter analyzes the way Islamists perceived these developments and in return created their own nostalgic approach toward the foundational past in order to have legitimate access to the political center.

Chapter 1, "The Elderly Children of the Republic: The Public History in the Private Story," studies the recent interest in the private lives of the first-generation Republican citizens who took an active role in establishing the Republican revolution in the country. This generation became the symbol of an embodied republic because they publicized their private lives and selves according to the modernist principles of the new regime. Both the elderly Republicans who narrated their lives and others who circulated these stories were interested in recalling the early republic as a nostalgic utopia in which each individual in the nation was united in harmony with the public reforms of its state. Such nostalgic narratives stood against the contemporary criticism of the 1930s as oppressive. At the same time they pointed to the end of the early Republican era.

Chapter 2, "Wedded to the Republic: Displaying the Transformations in Private Lives," analyzes three museum exhibits on the early republic organized by private institutions. As the organizational nature of these exhibits made a statement about private involvement in celebrating the public, their content made historical statements about how Turkish citizens embraced the Republican ideology in the privacy of their lives as early as the 1930s. All three exhibits concentrated on transformations in the private lives of the individuals in areas away from the oppressive authority of the state.

In the late 1990s, Turkish consumers purchased pictures of Atatürk, the founder of modern Turkey and the most potent symbol of the Turkish state, as a popular commodity and displayed them in homes and private businesses. In chapter 3, "Miniaturizing Atatürk: The Commodification of State Iconography," I argue that Kemalist citizens utilize new concepts such as voluntary support in order to reconcile the memory of Atatürk's state-led modernity of the 1930s with recent international pressure for a market-based modernity. As citizens try to mask the authority of the Turkish state with consumer choice, the market makes the symbolism of the Turkish state more ubiquitous by carrying it to spheres heretofore impenetrable to the state.

Chapter 4, "Hand in Hand with the Republic: Civilian Celebrations of the Turkish State," looks at how the organization of Republic Day celebrations (exemplifying the novel idea of a civilian celebration during the seventy-fifth anniversary in 1998) aimed to demonstrate the popular and democratic support for the founding ideology of the state. Based on the idea of the free market, rather than of state planning, the celebrations were organized by civil society organizations and emphasized spontaneity in the festivities. The kind of civilian and personalized enthusiasm the Republicans wished to generate in the parades was, ironically, a clearly defined and homogenizing one. Rather than encouraging free and increased political participation, civil celebrations created space only for limited and carefully crafted kinds of expressions in line with the founding principles of the Turkish Republic.

The final chapter, "Public Memory as Political Battleground: Kemalist and Islamist Versions of the Early Republic," pays attention to the wider context of the negotiations of the limits of politics and its legitimacy by studying the competition between secularists and Islamists over the history of the Turkish Republic. It explores the structural similarities between the two positions that legitimate each other yet are used differently to move between the public and private spheres. It shows that defining the nature of the nostalgic memory of the 1930s also constitutes a public struggle about who will rule the Turkish Republic, and according to which principles.

CHAPTER 1

The Elderly Children of the Republic

The Public History in the Private Story

In 1998, during the seventy-fifth anniversary of the Turkish Republic, an autobiography written by Mina Urgan—a relatively unknown, elderly, retired female professor of English literature—became a best seller in Turkey. Although her previous books on Shakespeare and the history of English literature had sold merely a couple of thousand copies over the years, The Memories of a Dinosaur went through one hundred authorized reprints and countless pirated versions, selling half a million copies in a year.[1] In her book Urgan declares herself a devoted Kemalist and narrates her life story growing up in the early years of the republic to become a university professor and leftist activist. Raised with the idealistic values of the young republic, she defines herself as a dinosaur, a species that does not fit the profit-seeking mentality of contemporary Turkey. On the cover of her book, Urgan appears sitting comfortably but also thoughtfully in an armchair in her crowded library. A careful look reveals her holding a small cigar. Her short, gray, uncovered hair, white shirt, and black vest make her look quite masculine compared to other women of her generation.

Urgan was not the only elderly, educated, urban Kemalist woman who gained public attention that year. Many other members of her generation, born in the young republic and playing a role at the forefront of the Kemalist revolution, wrote their memories and described their personal experiences of the founding years of the Turkish Republic (Turan 1993; Abadan-Unat 1996; Uçuk 1995; Denktaş 1998; Moran 2000; Aksan 2001).[2] There was an increasing interest even in early Republicans who were not talented enough to write their life histories (Ergun 1997; Z. Arat 1998; Gümüşoğlu 2001; Öztürkman 1999).[3] The image of the elderly woman Republican with her unabashedly gray, uncovered hair and a serious expression on her unmade face suddenly became a common image in the mainstream media serving a secularist clientele.

Celebrating the stories and images of the elderly was a novelty, especially in the context of a national celebration. Since the early days of the Turkish Republic, youth as a collective body had been emblematic of the new nation and its utopian idealism (Neyzi 2001). The youth, once ordered as the guardians of the new republic by Atatürk, had now grown old and began vanishing at the republic's seventy-fifth anniversary. Worse, they were taking the belief for the possibility of a brighter future away with them. A nostalgic attention to these people at the very end of their lives attests to the fact that the present youth in Turkey do not have similar utopias. A belief in the future is now only a relic of the past, something to be admired from the distance without bringing it to the present moment.

Despite their old age, the members of this generation were called "children of the republic." Born in the golden age of the single-party regime and raised by the founding father, these people represented the lost childhood of the Turkish Republic. During the seventy-fifth anniversary of the Turkish Republic, younger generations turned toward these eternal children to hear their life stories in which they combined their own childhood with that of their country. In studying these double childhood narratives, I followed Annette Kuhn's advice and did not take them literally. Instead, I saw them as "recourse to this past [as] a way of reaching for myth, for the story is deep enough to express profound feelings in the present" (Kuhn 1995, 1). I examined these narratives in order to understand the shared emotions—such as loss, love, and desire—in the present about the past, even if the stories did not provide valuable information about the past.

I consider the life-history narratives of elderly citizens not for their referential value but as speech acts (Austin 1975). More than four decades ago, Austin argued that some utterances "do things" rather than simply "say things." His famous examples of what he called "performative utterance," despite his dislike of the term, include saying "I do" in a marriage ceremony, or "I give the name of Queen Elizabeth to this boat." Similarly, as my narrators and their listeners continuously reiterated the unoriginal narratives of the early Republican era, they engaged in a socially meaningful political action: they critiqued contemporary Turkey while simultaneously declaring their support for the foundational principles of the republic. Although the verbal performances of the early Republicans were set apart from daily life and ordinary talk, such performances have effects in the real world (Lemon 2000). As part of these speech acts, both the narrators and their listeners jointly inscribed, edited, and circulated a nostalgic account of the foundational past that was legitimized through the personal experiences of the elderly Republicans.

As many scholars of nostalgia agree, this particular structured feeling toward the past is a strategy that serves the present both in terms of legitimating and delegitimating its parts (K. Stewart 1988; Rosaldo 1989; Ivy 1995; Rofel 1999). What makes each moment of nostalgia unique is the role it plays in relation to the present. The list of virtues that belonged to the golden days of the republic took shape in dialogue with (and as a critique of) the political situation in contemporary Turkey. The elderly teachers created their narratives in relation to a "co(n)text" (Silverstein and Urban 1996, 1), the readable or unreadable background to textual fragments of culture, in which these narratives circulate. In the late 1990s, the dominant narratives competing with the semi-official narrative about the foundation of the republic included the Islamist, Kurdish, nationalist, and the liberal so-called second Republicanist narratives.[4] Although these narratives make different claims about the past and the future, they share the common point of criticizing the early days of the republic as authoritarian and oppressive. The personal stories of the first-generation Republicans competed with these critiques in demonstrating that individuals willingly and personally embraced Kemalist policies. As they depicted those days as a lost utopia, they also critiqued the present regime, which they believed remained far from fulfilling the goals set by the founding father.

As I studied the content of the narratives closely, however, I found that the first-generation Republicans did not always tell the privatized version of the official ideology the younger Kemalists sought to hear. The elderly Republicans, socialized to immerse their private selves in the public, resisted a personalized interpretation of the early Republican era and its ideology. Rather, they perceived themselves as embodiments of the public-

and future-oriented nature of the Republican project, which no longer had a place in the self-interest–seeking mentality of neoliberal modernity.

Despite their gray hair, the first-generation Republicans who took active roles in public are still called children or daughters of the republic. This name refers to their association with the mythologized early Turkish Republic, itself as a child of the country's founding father. At the same time, the name establishes an intimate connection between the vanishing generation and the rest of the citizens who can provide these departing children with the protection of familial intimacy and public memory. This name also forever infantilizes an entire generation and by doing so points to unfulfilled expectations set in the 1930s toward the utopia of a fully modern and Westernized Turkey.

The elderly children of the republic could not grow up to be adult citizens because their unfulfilled dreams belong to a future that never arrived in Turkey. In a life-history interview, Nilüfer Gürsoy, the daughter of a minister from the first Republican parliament, declares that she still waits for the realization of her childhood dreams seventy-five years later: "I hope for the accomplishment of that great progress I lived in as a child. I also wish not to be distracted from that vision [because] I comprehended the importance of this process much later."[5] Despite her advanced age, Gürsoy sees herself as a child of the republic and refers to the early Republican goals as parts of a grand project that exceed her (still) childish mind. These goals were set by adult founders, in this case, actually her parents. Yet at the end of her lifetime, none of these goals seem accomplished, nor do they appear replaceable by any other aspiration.

Similarly Cahit Kayra (2002), a retired high-level bureaucrat born in 1917, says in his autobiography, "Dreams are usually about the future. Mine are the other way around. I wish I were a member of the 1908 generation and had died in the 1930s" (16). By the 1908 generation Kayra refers to the Young Turks who played an active role in the 1908 constitutional reform that curbed the power of the Ottoman sultan and then established the Turkish Republic in 1923.[6] This generation imagined a different future for the country and implemented a modernization project. Kayra wishes he had died when Atatürk passed away, leaving the country without a leader. As a member of the first-generation Republicans who inherited Atatürk's mission, Kayra feels deeply disturbed by what he perceives as a recent divergence from the accomplishments and goals of the early republic. "When we were taking part in sweeping transformations around the country," he says, "we could never imagine that after a few decades the Anatolian notables would tragically take the country backwards" (34).[7] As the other unguided citizens moved backward in time, the first-generation Republicans could not achieve full adulthood since their lives were devoted to a public project. For Kayra, the 1920s and 1930s appear closer to the future than today, a backward-oriented present. That is probably why Kayra wishes he was part of an earlier generation that marched straight on their path under Atatürk's leadership.

Imaginations of the Republic (Cumhuriyet'in hayalleri), a well-circulated 1998 documentary, displays the first-generation Republicans as the embodiment of failed futuristic dreams. As one elderly citizen after another appears on the screen to tell in a shaky voice how he or she used to be enthusiastic about the prospects for the republic, the viewer gets the sense that Republican imaginations are doomed to disappear with the first generation. In the documentary, Mina Urgan says, "The most important characteristic of the [early] republic is that it was a period of hope. We believed all the unimaginable utopias were about to be realized before our eyes. This gave our generation such a hope that it still keeps us going." Yet the decaying images and nostalgic narratives of the elderly Republicans remind us of the fact that the first generation in fact does not belong to the present, but to a failed future of the past, one once promising. By naming the section in which the narrators talk about early Republican hopes the "Fairy Tale of the Happy-Land" ("Mutluluk ülkesi masalı"), the documentary makers set the early republic in a fairy-tale time-space that vaguely connects with the present context in which the viewers listen to the narratives.

ELDERLY REPUBLICANS AS LIFETIME TEACHERS

Despite the fact that the devoted first-generation Republicans see themselves and are seen by others as eternal children, they are also perceived as the teachers of contemporary generations. An alternative way to look at the same phenomenon is to argue that specifically because they were marked as children, the first generation, and especially women, found it most appropriate to dedicate their lives to the education of children.[8] At the same time, they proved key to the Republican project since they were to replace the family, relatives, neighbors, and religious teachers in educating the new generation and inculcate them to the nationalist and secularist teachings of the new regime (Atay 2004). Of the relatively small number of vanguards at the forefront (and the beneficiaries) of the Republican revolution, retired schoolteachers attracted most of the attention. These teachers, trained by the new education system of the republic in order to spread its ideology, were considered ideal representatives of this vanguard group. Shortly after he founded the Turkish Republic, Mustafa Kemal Atatürk started an education campaign and adopted the name "Head Teacher" (Başöğretmen). He paid utmost attention to training a new generation of teachers who would both be ideal citizens themselves and also teach new generations how to become the same. The teachers' role in establishing the republic was so important that they were called the "soldiers" of the "education army," who would fight the war with ignorance much like Turkish military soldiers fought with the imperialists (Altınay 2004). Most important, the new generation of teachers would embody the principles of the new state, which educated, disciplined, and watched over its citizens.

Women educators were simultaneously the most prevalent objects and subjects of the Republican reforms.[9] In their bodies, women teachers united what Homi Bhabha (1990, 292) defines as a split between "the continuist, accumulative temporality of the pedagogical and the repetitious, recursive strategy of the performative" in nationalist narratives. As teachers, they were asked to educate the future generations about the history and the accomplishments of the Turkish nation. At the same time, they were the first fruits of the Kemalist reforms, which promoted the introduction of women into the public sphere as a sign of modernity, as opposed to their seclusion, which Republicans portrayed as an Islamic custom (Göle 1996). As the first generation of trained teachers, their duties included both talking about the new nation and also publicly representing its latest body. For example, Pakize, one of the first female trained physical-education teachers and a devoted Kemalist, was conscious of her role as a model and representative of the success of Kemalist reforms.[10] During our interview in the fall of 1998 she told me,

As the first Turkish girl athlete, I participated in a race. People did not know, they said, could girls run? They were all closed-minded. We put our shorts on and with our German teachers ran one hundred meters, jumped over the pole, threw discs. We wanted the people to learn about this. It was our duty. We wanted the people to learn that women can do such things. We were conscious about being the first people doing this. If they write a book called *The Firsts*, they should write about us.[11]

First teachers of the Republic can be best defined as a cohort, not merely they were born around the same time but rather because they "developed a sense of identification in coming of age through particular political movements and state regimes," as Lisa Rofel has argued for other generations in China (1999, 22). The children of the republic not only lived through the same historical moment but also attended the same schools for training teachers. Most of the time, they were the daughters of well-educated or well-off men who showed their support for the regime by sending their daughters off to the new schools of the republic (Z. Arat 1998). The period during which the first generation of schoolteachers came of age and the education they received shaped their worldview.

In the post-1980s, as Turkey increasingly became part of the world economy, the previously privileged classes, including the vanguards of the republic such as the teachers described above, became relatively marginalized and experienced a loss. Uneducated entrepreneurs from nonurban backgrounds climbed up the social hierarchies and displaced the state-educated elite. The members of this cohort retired from their jobs in the 1970s. Their marginalization, however, increased as the new liberal state paid lower pensions. They saw the increasing economic liberalism, populist politics, and the growing power of political Islam as contributing to a loss of control over state power and, more important, as a departure from the state-led modernization Atatürk had outlined. In other words, during the seventy-fifth anniversary, this group was vanishing both in terms of demographics and in terms of their social and economic influence.

Although the first-generation teachers had retired long before the seventy-fifth anniversary, they still saw themselves and were treated as teachers. They considered the journalists, researchers, or neighbors who approached them as students who need to be taught about the Republican ideology. In Turkey, being a teacher usually is something that extends far beyond the school context. Neighbors and acquaintances call such people "my teacher" (hocam) and pay them respect regardless of the context of interaction.[12] The first-generation teachers consider themselves lifetime teachers even more than the following generation of educators since they see themselves as primarily responsible for passing on Republican values to future generations. The political scientist Zehra Arat (1998), who interviewed thirty such first-generation teachers, found that almost all her eighty- and ninety-year-old interviewees continued to consider themselves teachers, even if they practiced teaching only for a few years. "I am a child of the revolution," says Perihan Gökay, one of Arat's interviewees. "I cry when I see what counterrevolutionaries [i.e., Islamists] are doing on the television. That is why I will be a teacher until I die" (in Arat 1998, 157).[13] As a child and teacher of Republican values, Gökay has internalized the role of educating younger generations and of showing them what belongs to the past and what to the future. In the late 1990s, elderly Republicans such as Gökay found themselves sought after to reeducate the Turkish population. This time they were not asked to teach about Republican principles in abstract terms but to display them through their personal stories about how they internalized the public projects of the modernizing Turkish Republic as children.

VALORIZING THE PRIVATE NARRATIVES

When I tried to reach them, I found out that first-generation Republicans, especially those who appeared at public events, had a very hectic program during the seventy-fifth anniversary of the republic. They were repeatedly invited to award ceremonies, commemoration activities, talk shows on television, journalistic and academic interviews, and received visits from local activist secularists and neighbors. For example, eighty-three-year-old Refet Angın, one of the first history teachers of the republic who is still active at the Ministry of Education, was truly unable to spare time for me in her busy schedule of interviews. This was especially the case because she prioritized events that would give her greater publicity. Television programs or public gatherings to be recorded by television channels were the first on her list, followed by interviews by journalists and smaller award ceremonies. Whenever I made an appointment with her, a better opportunity came up that would enable her to tell a larger audience how she met

Atatürk at age fifteen and promised him to be a history teacher. She had already given me a photocopy of the story about this event after I had asked her permission to copy the same narrative hanging framed on the wall. With her short height, snow-white hair stacked in a bun on top of her head, and her smiling face clear of makeup, she became an increasingly famous celebrity, an indispensable part of commemorative activities. Because her schedule was overbooked, she ended up giving me a list with the names of about thirty other first-generation Republicans who she thought would be good for me to talk to. This, she told me, was also the list of people she gave to other journalists and activist organizations when she found herself too busy or if they wanted to contact people other than herself. When I looked at the list, I quickly recognized many of the names that appeared in newspapers and books for interviews or received awards for their contributions to the Turkish Republic. Not surprisingly, most of the people on the list consisted of teachers.

Although narratives of these few valorized first-generation Republicans were in rapid circulation, I wanted to meet these people personally and ask them the very same question they had to answer over and over again: "Could you please tell me what it was like to live during the early years of the republic?" Or as it is phrased more frequently: "Could you tell me some of your memories?" This way I hoped to personally witness the way in which these popular narratives were produced. I also aimed to see whether certain aspects of their stories were selected over others by the mass mediators. With these aims in mind, I interviewed twenty committed and already valorized first-generation Republicans.

When I contacted those already publicized, it was not difficult to persuade them to an interview. I explained my project briefly by saying, "I am writing a dissertation for a university in the United States on the life stories of people who lived through the early days of the Turkish Republic." Other than a couple of teachers who said that they did not feel healthy enough to tell their history or were too busy, most of the educators were very happy to talk to a researcher. None of them appeared surprised that I would be interested in their life stories because they all believed that their having witnessed such an important point in history made them worthy of attention. Besides, they were both willing and used to passing their story along to younger generations.

Many of my interviewees made an effort to express experiences as narrators who had told of their stories of the foundational years numerous times. When I entered their living rooms, I often found newspaper and magazine clippings of previous interviews carefully displayed on a table. If the earlier interviews had been conducted by television channels, elderly Republicans made a special effort to tell me about them. Shortly after we started chatting in her formal living room, Yegane, for example, pointed out the ordinary nature of the interview for her. "Yesterday I had ten visitors. They also came just like you, to listen to the old memories, anecdotes. People want to know about the days they have not lived through. Especially young people get curious about such things, and I answer them. When I talked to Star [a commercial television channel], I told them the same stories as well."

Because of the frequent media attention they received, my interviewees consistently mistook me for a journalist, although I had explicitly told them that I would like to interview them for my doctoral research in our initial phone conversation. When I rang the doorbell, time and again I heard the grandchildren yell, "The journalist has arrived!" I did indeed look like a journalist or a researcher wanting to promote Republican nostalgia. My bare head and plain urbanite apparel could be read as signs of a dedication to Republican values. The teachers probably assumed that I was there to share their nostalgia for the early days of the republic and rage about the current fallback from Republican reforms. I chose not to disappoint these elderly people with my critical position toward some of the policies of the early Republican regime and respectfully listened to their yearnings for the old days.

INSCRIBING THE PRIVATE SELF IN THE PUBLIC HISTORY OF THE REPUBLIC

In her seminal work on the topic, Charlotte Linde explains that life stories enable people to "express their sense of self," "negotiate group membership" and "make presuppositions about what can be taken as expected" (1993, 1). In their life-history narratives, the elderly Republicans did all three at once. They portrayed a self that had completely internalized a Republican modernization project that created and celebrated the public. By putting their personal narratives in mass circulation at this particular moment in time, the elderly citizens helped fortify the Republican myths of a unified and transformed nation in which individual citizens became one with the public cause. Finally, as their life stories became personal testimonies to the personal and private embrace of the Republican project by individual citizens, it became possible to expect that the new Turkish citizen could remain immune to private experiences in possible conflict with Republican goals.

The first-generation Republicans kept a strict separation between the public and the private in their life-story narratives. Most often, they minimized the description of any phenomenon they would consider private. During the interviews they insistently hid a more private self made of desires, experiences, and frustrations independent of national history. When I visited them in their homes, I found the female Republicans like Perihan Gökay dressed up in elegant two-piece knit sweaters, knee-length skirts, and house shoes, their hair freshly dyed and made up, and wearing makeup, while the men had put on two- or three-piece dark suits with colorful ties. Clearly these outfits were more fitting for public events than for receiving a guest at home. Accordingly, they greeted me in the formal living rooms reserved for guests who are not part of the family. More often than not they did not show me the interior parts of the home, where family members and intimate guests would spend most of their time. In other words, speakers placed a discreet distance between me and the private details of their home and their domestic clothing. Such a separation between the public and the private in their homes and dress paralleled the separation between a public version of their life stories told in the interview context and the private and personal details of their lives. I was able to glimpse pieces of their personal lives only during breaks in their testimony or in slips that occurred during the interview.

In the following section I give an account and analysis of the life-history interview I conducted with Meliha, a retired octogenarian teacher and the proud widow of an influential bureaucrat in the single-party regime. Meliha's story offers a typical but also a somewhat exaggerated example of the way many first-generation Republicans carefully undermined any details that may be considered private (özel) or personal (kişisel).

I met Meliha through a friend of mine who was her neighbor in the same apartment building. When I contacted her, Meliha expressed no surprise at all that I was interested in hearing her life story and possibly using it in my dissertation. She told me that she had been interviewed by several other doctoral students. The experienced teacher met me in the formal room of her apartment in Moda with a panoramic view of the Marmara Sea. Because it was a hot summer day, Meliha wore a simple but elegant sleeveless cotton dress with small green flowers. After she brought out some store-bought cookies, she apologized for her simple dress, one of the few clothes she said she could bear in the hot weather. As I was sipping my peach nectar, I realized that she seemed eager to get started with the interview so that we could finish quickly. Before I turned my tape recorder on, Meliha wanted to give me a sample narrative in order to make sure that it was the kind of narrative I was interested in. When I told her that I would like to listen to her life history, especially what was it like to live in the early years of the republic, she answered: "I do not remember what grade I was in; maybe second or third. But I was attending school when they declared the republic. I had four older sisters and a younger brother. Two of my sisters were teachers. At our home we discussed the topics of teacher-student relations and what the republic is. That was the atmosphere I grew up in. Atatürk's love was radiating. Do you want me to tell such things?" I assured her that I was interested in her life story in the way she wanted to tell it, and she continued without hesitation. She knew exactly what she wanted to say.

Since you are interested in Atatürk's era, I will tell you about those days. I was born and raised in Istanbul. I am a graduate of the geography department of Istanbul University. I graduated from high school in 1933. I will start from my childhood. I do not remember the very first years of the republic, but because I had two sisters who were elementary school teachers, they always talked about school at home. My parents were enlightened, smart people. . . . Now I realize that they raised us very well. We used to be afraid of them. I do not remember my father kissing or hugging me once. I was told that he would kiss me when I was asleep. Our family life was quite formal [Bir resmiyet vardı aile hayatında].

Meliha began her narrative by introducing herself through her education and family roots. She strongly emphasized being born into an "enlightened family" and being raised appropriately and formally. While describing how her father never hugged or kissed her as a child, Meliha did not express discontent. To the contrary, she was proud and interpreted it as a sign of good child-rearing practices. Intimacy among family members was limited to such an extent that she never personally experienced it, but only heard about it. Being raised in a family in which she internalized publicly appropriate behavior, she was well prepared to be a good citizen of the young Turkish Republic.

> When two of my sisters were teachers, and two still students, an important change happened in Turkey. The Turkish Republic was established replacing the Ottoman Empire. In the first few years following the republic, we studied in the Ottoman script. I graduated from elementary school in Ottoman. In 1928, the Latin script was accepted, and we learned it. The songs, games, marches they taught us in school in those years were made to remind us of war, stir our feelings against the enemies. We would sing marches against the Greeks and the Italians as if they were still invading our land. I remember we would go out with flags in our hands singing these marches, and all store owners would walk outside and applaud us. There was such excitement in the country. Now we had our freedom, and the enemies had left when the Turks won the War of Liberation.
>
> We fought the Battles of First İnönü and Second İnönü led by İsmet İnönü, the Battle of Sakarya led by Mustafa Kemal, and finally the Battle of Dumlupınar in Afyon Karahisar against the Greeks. Previously there were wars in Şanlı Urfa. In southeastern Anatolia, local people fought with the Turkish army against the French, and the enemies left the country. Where is their country, and where is our country? A handful of enemies dared to step on our land, and the Turkish army strangled them and threw them out. As these places were being liberated, Istanbul was still under siege. The British navy was anchored in Istanbul. Previously, during the Battle of Gallipoli, Atatürk declared that the foreign armies would go away just the way they came. So they went away. After they departed, a holiday was declared in Istanbul. This was the kind of climate we grew up in. Over time, love for Atatürk and his reforms such as the script reform, hat reform, political party reform, calendar reform took root. And there were further changes in the Turkish law. Tremendous efforts were spent on the justice system, for the establishment of democracy.

After giving a brief introduction to her official family life, Meliha quickly shifted from telling her life story to telling the history of the Turkish Republic. Undoubtedly Meliha's life was affected and transformed by the radical changes taking place in the country. However, as she tells the story, these changes stand at the center of her narrative. Meliha remains in the background as a witness legitimating the truth value of national history. At this point, it seemed as though she was giving me a lecture on Republican history starting from the War of Liberation and continuing with the Republican reforms. She never personally experienced many of the events she narrated and most likely did not even hear about them until much later, when the national history was written and these events were brought together. Although Meliha was not a history teacher, she probably lectured about the history of the Turkish Republic to students many times. In other words, she was providing me with a premade lecture previously performed in other settings, slightly changing the form and the content in accordance with the context.

Evidence of Meliha's personal distance from the Republican history became apparent in the way she named the wars and locations. The wars of First İnönü, Second İnönü, or Dumlupınar did not have these names when they were fought during her childhood. They received those names when the official history of the republic was written and made available to teachers. Moreover, the names of locations such as Şanlı Urfa (Glorified Urfa) or Afyon Karahisar were given to these cities years after the liberation war in order to Turkify place names of Greek or Armenian origin. Although textbooks and weather reports use these now official names, in daily life, people refer to these places by their old names. By using the official names, Meliha gives her narrative an official character distanced from her personal experience.

Right after this brief lecture on the history of the foundation of the Turkish Republic, Meliha told me about a personal memory from that time.

I have a memory from my childhood. It is a very important one for today. Radical Islamists say that Mustafa Kemal abolished religion. No, he did not. I am still alive, older than eighty years old. But, thank God, I have my mind still with me. When I was a child, I had a strong voice. . . . When I was in elementary school, a cart with one horse would come to our house. It belonged to a Greek doctor who lived in our neighborhood. They [the state officials] would take me to mosques every night during Ramadan. I remember going to four or five mosques a night. We would go to the mosques after the prayer, and this shows that religion was not abolished.

As you know, in Ramadan, they have an additional prayer [*Teravi Namaı*] at night. In the mosque they would put me into the place where the sultan would sit in the old days. Next to me a young man would hold the Turkish flag. I would lift my little arm up and recite our national anthem from beginning to end. They were using this as a propaganda opportunity to introduce the national anthem and the freedom we gained with the republic. After the prayer, people would turn and listen to me. At the end of the night the same cart would take me back home. Probably they asked my sisters [who were teachers at the time] whether they knew any little girl with a strong voice and good memory. I remember very well doing this in the Hırka-i Şerif Mosque, in Edirne Kapı Mosque, in little mosques. This proves that mosques were not closed down.

Even when Meliha tells a story that centralizes her experience, her primary goal is to illustrate an aspect of Republican history. She thinks contemporary Islamists unjustly attack Atatürk by saying that he eradicated religion. Through her lived experience she proves that religion was not abolished and that people kept praying in the mosques. Her story ironically reveals a little-known aspect of Republican history: that is, the way officials used mosques to spread the new ideology. However, Meliha's point is not to attract attention to this aspect of the Republican regime. Rather, she wants to oppose attacks on Atatürk and through her experience prove that people were openly fulfilling their religious duties. During the interview she was willing to introduce her personal experiences as long as they would further glorify or protect the early Republican regime and its public policies.

In middle school we used to have gymnastic holidays. In other words, there was a movement from the veiling days of the Ottoman era, when the women were in prison at home, toward emancipation and modernization. In those days, my eldest sister, Cemile, learned the new alphabet at the nation's schools and taught it to my mother at night. My mother was old. My sister was among the first who wore a hat [i.e., went unveiled] and taught people the new letters.

As we moved on to her early youth, Meliha launched into a discussion of how successful the early Republican reforms proved in liberating women. It is important that she framed this section of her narrative by saying,

"There was a movement from the veiling . . . to emancipation and modernization." In this part of her narrative, too, she uses her experience of the gymnastic demonstrations and her sister's role in teaching people the new letters to prove the widespread nature of these reforms: people were so enlightened that young women like Meliha were able to participate in gymnastic demonstrations and show their bodies in public.

> I finished high school in 1933 and started teaching. Nineteen thirty-three was the tenth anniversary of our republic. They had great celebrations for the republic, which was founded in 1923. . . . That year there was a competition for making the best Atatürk corner in every school. They asked my opinion in the school where I started teaching. I suggested that we make columns from plywood and put his picture behind them, so it looks like a temple. The art teacher, Kenan Bey, made the columns. He gilded the columns and made them look like marble. They put a table in the middle to give the effect of climbing up to a temple. And on top of it they put Atatürk's picture. We decorated the whole room with Atatürk's pictures taken during the war. Our school won the competition. As an award they took a picture of me in the exhibit. This event boosted my self-confidence.

Meliha started to tell about her career as a teacher by educating me about the foundation of the Turkish Republic. Then she connected her own story to the glorified tenth anniversary of the republic. Significantly, the only self-centered memory Meliha had regarding her experience as a young teacher concerned the way she organized an Atatürk corner in her school. This memory marked her interaction with the public history of the Turkish Republic at its tenth anniversary. At this moment, her hands literally touched and shaped a glorious moment in nationalist history. This story demonstrates her devotion as a citizen and shows how widespread nationalism was during the 1930s.

Only after she had given me this full lecture about early Republican history and her role in it as an educator did Meliha tell me about a very personal, private aspect of her life: the way she met her husband.

> This is how we studied at university. During those years my parents got me engaged to a man who really wanted to marry me. But I told him that I would continue my education. My fiancée said that he would wait for me

even if it took eighty years. In those days there was no such thing as going out. Couples would see each other only during holidays and in the presence of their parents. I got sick of him and broke the engagement off. I never thought about marriage again until I finished school. I was a good student, I was honest, and I never flirted [flört] with anyone as they call it now. I am not sorry either. Some say you did not take advantage of your youth, but I am not sorry. I respect myself. One day, İsmail Hakkı Uzunçarşılı [a well-known historian] came up to me. He said, "I know you. You regularly attend, you are hard-working, and have good manners." This gave me such strength and self-confidence. He was an old professor and a parliamentarian. In those days there was a lot of love and respect for parliamentarians. I was so proud that he recognized me.

Even when Meliha mentioned a personal aspect of her life, a broken engagement, and spoke of herself as a woman, at first she emphasized that she did not have any relations with men. She even told of her engagement as something that had happened to her and that she had nothing to do with. She was pleased to have broken off the engagement because she wanted to focus on her studies and was too busy to think about such things. It is significant that she immediately told a story about how a well-known university professor recognized her right after she spoke of her failed engagement and her disinterest in men. In other words, although she was not showing interest in or flirting with men, old and famous public figures recognized her in an asexualized manner as an exemplary student. As a good Republican young woman, she was more interested in such public interactions with men than in personal ones with potential mates. For Meliha, this period was marked by desexualization and the preparation for public service.[14]

After she had proven that her main interest lay with serving the public, Meliha gave a long narrative of how she met her husband Kenan at the Ministry of Education. First, they briefly met at his office, where he solved her housing problem in Ankara, a city to which she had come for higher education, by finding her another school dormitory downtown. To Meliha's surprise, a year later Kenan came to Istanbul to see her at her graduation ceremony and meet her family. Later he wrote a letter to her and her family asking for her hand. Meliha's family asked around about him and heard only good things. The pair got married and had two children. At the end of her narrative, Meliha evaluated their marriage in the following terms: "As a Kemalist couple, we both worked for our country. He worked hard to discover our folklore. . . . All his life he supported Atatürk, the republic, freedom, and modernization. . . . I also was known as a Kemalist in my teaching career."

Meliha's account of her relationship with her husband was by far the most personal testimony she offered. Even in this context, however, she still used the story of her relationship to prove the virtues of the period. For example, the way she and her husband never had a moment alone before they were married and the way he researched her background before asking for her hand all served as examples of how relations were different and better in the past because they did not involve sexuality unbound by domestic conjugality. More important, Meliha underlined the fact that hers was a well-calculated, rational, and thus modern marriage, rather than an irrational and lustful one that people not inculcated with Kemalist ideology would engage in.[15] When Meliha evaluated her marriage with her deceased husband, the most important thing for her was that they both worked hard to serve their country. She did not mention, for example, how happy they had been together, that they loved each other, and or raised children together.

As the end of our meeting approached, Meliha shifted from the linear narrative of her life history to the history of the Turkish Republic and gave me a detailed account of her approach to religion.

I am one of the women who are raised by the republic. I am proud of that. But I am also a religious person. Every time I take a bath I read the Yasin chapter from the Qur'an. I pray for God. But I cannot pray five times a day because I work. I pray only after I bathe. For me being Muslim is to be clean inside and out. I am clean inside. I like doing favors for people. I only think good of them. I do not harm people. I do not like wasting money. Aren't these the principles of Islam? I am not a selfish person. I like to go between people who do not talk to each other. This is being a Muslim, it is not shaking your head from side to side and saying, "Allah, Allah" [like a Sufi]. I am religious. But I have a modern lifestyle. I do not like being too free [açık saik]. Let me tell you why I do not like it. It gives an opportunity to religious people. They show girls in their bikinis on television. Such images have a bad effect on girls in the villages. The ignorant girls run away from home and come to Istanbul. I do not like such things. But when I bathe in the sea, I wear a bathing suit. I do not like going around in a bikini. This is not being a reactionary. As you see, I am not a reactionary person by any means. I lived in the United States and in Paris.

It might appear as if Meliha had shifted from telling me about the establishment of the Turkish Republic and her role in it to explaining her personal take on religion. However, what she shared with me was her interpretation of the early republic's approach to religion. This section ran parallel to her previous accounts of how the early Republican regime had not abolished religion. What the early Republican regime did instead was to place religion under the control of the state and impose a version that did not clash with the new modern life.[16] Moreover, Republican officials tried to limit religious symbols, identities, and discourses to the private sphere. Thus, in this final part of her narrative, Meliha reproduced the Republican ideology on Islam and defined religious experience such that attitude was more important than practice. She argued that it was acceptable not to pray five times a day if people were too busy. It was even permissible for women to wear a bathing suit as long as they were doing it only to engage in a Western practice. In order to be civilized, women had to publicly display their bodies. At the same time, they needed to avoid sexualization. Most important, Meliha regarded her approach to and practice of Islam as an ideal other religious people should emulate. She opposed other practices of Islam, especially Sufi ones, and claimed that what they practice is not Islam. Combining her identities as a model student, zealous teacher, and desexualized yet publicly visible woman, Meliha posed herself as an ideal citizen who had internalized the Republican cause and made it one with her private self.

Meliha told her life story in a nostalgic tone, one marked by desire for the lost days. She was proud that she came of age in a unique period in history and as a result became an exceptional citizen. At the same time, she was aware that her beliefs, ideals, ways of doing things did not belong to the present. Much like Mina Urgan, Meliha also considered herself a dinosaur. She wanted to tell her story to younger generations so that they could recognize how extraordinary and successful the Kemalist single-party regime was. But the very same story also attested to the fact that those exceptional features of the Kemalist regime no longer held.

The most common theme in the life-history narratives of the elderly Republicans was a strong nostalgia for the now lost values, commitments, and lifestyles of the early Turkish Republic. Central to these depictions was the idea that private citizens were in total congruence with the modernizing Turkish state and its goals. The elderly Republicans described the early days of the republic as a past utopia in which people were too innocent (*saf* or *masum*) to look after their private interests, which could conflict with the collective goal. In conversation, a Turkish friend ironically named this period "the time of happiness" (*asr-ı saadet*), as the Prophet Muhammad's time is called. Both of the nostalgias, Islamist or secularist, are constructed in relation to their present context. The elderly Republicans and others who circulate narratives about the early republic use a particular depiction of the past as a license to criticize the present and suggest it as a model to inspire change. More important, such narratives stand against the recent critiques by Islamists and liberal intellectuals of the foundational years as undemocratic and oppressive.

Such consciousness clearly appears in the words of Fethi, an eighty-three–year-old retired physical-education teacher. "Atatürk's era was like a heaven on earth. None of us should forget about that period. Others may try to make people forget about it. But we will make live this period together. [The memory] of this period will pass from generation to generation for eternity." Fethi makes this declaration, as he told me, to anyone who asks him about the early republic. Fethi believed that in order for the principles and teachings of Atatürk to live, people like himself should tell about the foundational days and help the memory of them circulate "eternally." He feared that there were people who wanted to forget this period. According to Fethi, this posed a major threat that might return Turkey to the days when Atatürk's reforms had not yet been realized.

The first-generation Republicans were fully conscious of the political function of their narratives. So were the listeners. Even though many of the stories told by first-generation Republicans had a premade character to be repeated to different kinds of audiences, the nostalgic interpretation of these narratives was constructed jointly and in relation to the larger framework of the contemporary critiques of Republican values.[17] Researchers who approached the elderly collected and edited parts that underlined the nostalgic elements. And the elderly selected only certain aspects of this period to speak about, highlighting features that contradicted the reality of contemporary Turkey. For example, Perihan Ergun, a devoted Republican People's Party member, published a book consisting of the life histories of thirty-eight vanguard women of the Turkish Republic. In *Our Women Vanguards in the Republican Enlightenment* she declares her aim in compiling the book as follows: "In the last few years I have been working with the civil society organizations in order to prevent those who try to darken the Republican enlightenment [i.e., Islamists]. At the time I felt the urge to study the lives of the first-generation women and the light they generated in order to go through the difficult times we were in" (1997, 8). The following four themes appeared frequently in the nostalgic narratives of the elderly Republicans collected by Ergun and others.

Love and Support for Atatürk and His Reforms "During Atatürk's time, there were no dissenting voices. Everyone used to follow him." What Mustafa, a retired literature teacher originally from Greece, told me is a typical statement made over and over again by committed elderly Republicans. Many argued that all Turkish citizens had supported Atatürk wholeheartedly and that he had no adversaries. When asked if there had existed any opposition toward him, or suppression of dissent, they forcefully lifted their heads up to say no. According to İlhan, a retired civil servant from a public bank in Bursa, "everyone did whatever Atatürk wanted them to do" simply because "they all loved him." Similarly, in her published interview, Bedia Akarsu, a retired university professor claimed, "Some say Atatürk was a dictator. There was no need for him to be. . . . Everyone was so happy in those days. They gave him full support" (qtd. in Gümüşoğlu 2001, 192).

In order to prove their point, the elderly often told anecdotes revealing the popular support around the leader. Neriman, a retired mathematics teacher, disapprovingly contrasted the earlier days with today: "During the tenth anniversary celebrations we were in Ankara. It was very crowded. Everyone was enthusiastic. Now some bigots appeared. Then there was no such thing." To Neriman, the emergence of the present-day bigots appeared as unexplainable and anachronistic; totally alien to the enthusiasm she perceived as shared by everyone.

Another commonly used form of evidence for the unopposed support Atatürk received was to tell how he had constantly been around people without ever needing protection. As Hatice was telling me about one of the times where she had seen Atatürk, she said: "He was driving in Ankara in a convertible. There were only two motorcycles in front of his car and two behind it. He did not have any of the protection politicians have today. It means he was not afraid of anyone."

The idea that citizens and leaders were united in love was not a spontaneous perception by citizens. Atatürk had taken an active role in defining the relationship between him and the nation as one of love, rather than force. In a well-known conversation he had with a journalist, he answered the question of why he did not like to be called a dictator in the following words: "I am not a dictator. They say that I have power, this is true. There is nothing I will not be able to do if I want to because I do not know how to act cruelly and forcefully. According to me, a dictator is one who forces others' wills. I like to command by winning hearts, not breaking them" (qtd. in Parla 1991, 91). By emphasizing a collective love toward him, Atatürk presented himself as a natural representation of the whole nation.

Love toward the leader constituted an emergent emotive symbol that legitimated the single-party regime and set it apart as different from the sultanate, which supposedly ruled by force (Sirman 2002, 240). Elderly Republicans revitalized this early Republican myth and affective affiliation toward the leader in order to reject the present criticisms of Atatürk's authoritarian leadership.

Secularity   A related point that elderly Republicans made over and over again was that in the 1930s there were no religious people around and women did not veil. Every single elderly female teacher I interviewed referred nostalgically to the fact that fewer women veiled during the early Republican days and that they would even wear shorts during gymnastic demonstrations. The same theme is repeated in almost every other life-history interview published by committed female Republicans.[18]

Vedia, a retired history teacher from Izmir, especially emphasized how women did not veil during the early days of the republic.[19] One of her most distinctive memories about childhood was the lack of veiling in her home city and her family: "Veils were very few then. I do not remember either my mother or grandmother veiling. They wore a scarf, but they would put it in different styles, embellish it. They did not believe that you should not show even one piece of hair, as women think today. . . . In those days in Izmir, if women went out in veils, young men would grab their veils and rip them off. Or these women would have to pay a fine of sixty or seventy liras for veiling. After several months, veiling totally disappeared."

During our interview, when we talked about her childhood and her experiences at school and as a teacher, Vedia wanted to return to the issue of veiling several times. She told me how in her family even older women would not veil, that they did not have sex segregation, and thus in the past had a much more progressive life than religious people call for today. Even when asked questions about other issues, she persistently said: "I will answer this question later. Let me finish what I was telling you," and continued to talk about the lack of veiling. The importance she attributes to the fact that women, especially the women in her family, did not veil tells us that this is a key phenomenon puzzling her positivistic and secularist understanding of temporality. Even as I was getting ready to leave, she again turned to me and said, "Women were so ready to unveil then. I do not understand how they like to veil today."

Vedia was educated in the first university of the early republic. As a modernist historian and a devoted Westernist, she expressed surprise at how things had become more conservative in Turkey over the years. It was important for her to tell me, someone in the younger generation who would potentially circulate her story, that in the early years of the republic, and even prior to it, women did not veil. First-generation teachers like Vedia were upset about what they saw as a recent backward transformation toward increasing religiosity and veiling. They argued that even provincial cities such as Bursa, Afyon, Konya, and Kars were not conservative. Or, as Nephan Sarran, the first anthropology professor of the young republic, claimed in her published interview: "Then, there was not a single conservative town" (qtd. in Gümüşoğlu 2001, 148). It was only now, they argued, that people in Anatolia were becoming conservative. They made an effort to prove that in the past, and even in provincial towns, things were different. Such a claim would discredit contemporary Islamic practices and the naming of them as the traditional and true practices of the Anatolian people. Through their narratives these women thus tried to demonstrate that Islamists did not have historical roots in Turkish society and that they made alien and meaningless demands.[20]

In the newly religious political situation, the fact that these women choose to go around unveiled despite their old age is a political statement in itself. For example, Ayşe, who worked as a teacher in Konya, a very religious town, stated her personal discomfort with the increasing religiosity of her hometown and told how she reacted to it as a defining event in her life history: "We used to go around in short sleeves in Konya, even though it was a conservative place. We would act decently and no one would put pressure on us. After a long time I went to Konya. My son was having a heart operation. In the minibus no one told me to cover my hair because they knew that I was the daughter of so-and-so. But I felt the pressure on me to cover my hair. I fought with myself and did not cover my hair."

Hikmet, an eighty-year-old retired nurse, also told me about similar pressures she recently started to feel from young religious men as she went around bareheaded. They called out to her that she would die soon and should be afraid of the day of judgment. She told me that in such instances she reminded them that they all lived in Atatürk's Turkey. While Ayşe called for the shelter of the local kinship lineages she is a part of, Hikmet sought the protection of the founding father. Seeking protection and legitimacy from two different sets of paternalistic authority, neither Ayşe nor Hikmet really challenged the patriarchal order of gender circulation. Rather, they suggested, the familial unity of the nation should make it unnecessary for women to veil even in public.

Peace and Unity   According to the first-generation Republicans, peace and unity, experienced with a feeling of bliss, were the defining features of the early republic. They claimed that the fractured state of politics in contemporary Turkey and the resulting conflicts were nonexistent in the "heavenly" days of the early republic. When I asked Ayşe what it was like in the early days of the republic, she replied:

AYŞE: We were very peaceful, very comfortable, and very free in our ideas. We loved talking to our friends. We used to talk as much as we could. There was peace and unity. Then there was no difference between men and women. We were friends with all of them. In my five-year-long education [after elementary school], I do not remember a single person with bad intentions. We were all helping each other out, and we were like an amalgam.

ESRA: What do you mean by peaceful?

AYŞE: No one had bad intentions. No one was another's enemy across the country. But now everyone is fighting with each other. The children and the families used to be tied to each other. The main reason for our peace was the close family ties. We were together with our friends and family. My mother was friends with my friends. We were comfortable. We used to do gymnastics during ceremonies. When I think about it now, I do not understand. How can they not allow girls to wear short skirts? In those days, we used to wear shorts while doing gymnastics. Now I get surprised, I do not understand how they prevent them. They say Konya is reactionary. Why is it reactionary? We used to wear shorts there. May 19 was sports day; we would participate in the ceremonies, and be active.

In her narrative, Ayşe mentioned three levels of unity that she thought brought peace to the early days of the republic. The first level is the unity of the nation, akin to that of a family. This unity was possible with absolute harmony between the sexes, the generations, and the classes. Only in the desexualized atmosphere of the early Republican capital, where youth acted as if "there was no difference between men and women," was it acceptable for men and women to get together and talk to each other in public. The duty of providing this gender harmony often fell on women's shoulders. Scholars of this period in Turkey emphasize how women had given up their sexuality in order to appear in public (Durakbaşa 1988; Kandiyoti 1987). The shorts young women wore in those days served as a symbol of the desexualization of their barelegged bodies displayed in public. Despite the encouragement they received for being out in public, they felt the pressure to deter potential sexualized interest in them.[21] Only in complete desexualization could they feel peace and comfort outside the domestic sphere.

The second level of unity Ayşe mentioned existed across generations. In those days her mother used to be friends with Ayşe's friends, and thus people in the family across generations were tied to each other. Although she did not mention them, the other levels of unity during the Republican era transected lines of class and ethnicity. What Ayşe defines as an "amalgam" where no one had "bad intentions" is close to what Taha Parla (1985) defines as corporatism for the dominant ideology of the early republic. Parla argues that the early Republican leaders aimed to achieve a society that was neither socialist nor capitalist and in which people from different occupations cooperated with each other under a single-party rule. This understanding aimed to avoid a conflict of interests and social classes.

Other interviewees attributed the feeling of safety to the success of the new government at separating the different classes from each other, rather than uniting them. Nazmiye, who had lived in Ankara since the very early years of the republic, believed that the capital used to be very safe because of its elite nature. She said: "We used to go to bed without locking our door. Ankara was such a safe place. It was a different city then. It had a very high-quality parliament. For example, the members of the Republican People's Party were appointed [as opposed to being elected]. The people they chose for such offices were all educated, successful people. They brought in governors, judges, and the best known people." In her nostalgia, Nazmiye remembered the whole city as a home or an intimate space writ large, a place where no one needed to lock doors. In contrast to Ayşe's testimony about complete harmony, Nazmiye's narration proves more perceptive of the power inequalities that defined the early Republican era. She recognized that the elite residents of the city like her felt safe because they were surrounded by people of similar backgrounds. She knew that the nonelite people not inculcated with the Republican ideology would corrode the sense of unity established among the elite citizens of Ankara. Some other interviewees mentioned that in the first years of the republic, the police would walk around the center of Ankara and make sure that there were no peasants or poor people wandering around in the streets.[22] The "amalgam" Ayşe mentioned was maintained by clearing Ankara of those who would not mix well with the new elite.

İsmail, on the other hand, attributed feelings of safety to a high level of discipline and to efforts of the authorities to instigate fear. He and his friend were coming home late one night after chatting with each other when a police officer stopped them to ask what they were doing out at such a late hour. They told the officer they were busy planning a sports activity for the summer. After advising them not to be out late at night again, he let them go. But as they were talking to the police officer, a drunken man also appeared. The policeman stopped him and asked if he was married, telling him not to go out at night leaving his wife and children at home alone.[23]

"Both to us and him, the policemen said, 'we do not want to see you like this again.' This is how attentive they were in the old days. Everything was more disciplined; people had fear, and had respect as a result of the fear. All of these feelings were present. Some of them might still be around, but some of them are lost."

For İsmail, such direct involvement with individual lives showed how ← much the state cared for its citizens and kept them under discipline. Moreover, instead of provoking anger, this kind of behavior gave him a feeling of safety and of being taken care of and lovingly protected by the paternalist state and the founding father.

The End of the Golden Age with the Democrat Party   The first-generation Republicans agreed that the golden age came to an end with the first fair general elections of 1950, when the Democrat Party replaced the Republican People's Party. Everything apparently got worse afterwards. In Yegane's words:

YEGANE: I had a wonderful childhood. During our youth, Turkey had its golden age. Everything was cheap and people lived in peace. My father was a teacher, and six of us could live comfortably on his single income.

ESRA: When do you think things started to change?

YEGANE: In 1950, when the Democrat Party came to power. At first people lived comfortably. But soon things got out of order. People had trouble living economically. People could no longer establish dialogue with each other, and they became enemies. In those days, partisanship started. During the single-party era we were governed so well. Everyone was friends with each other.

The problem was not the electoral failure of a party they supported. To individuals like Yegane, regime change and the shift to a multiparty system indicated a weakening central government. Suddenly there was more than one party and people were divided along party lines, which meant that citizens were no longer in unison with each other or the state.

As individuals who became politically inculcated to the corporatist ideology of single-party Kemalism, they saw the multiparty system as a major threat to national unity. Children of the republic found themselves uncomfortable with the expansion in the number of political parties—and the emergence of multiple father figures. To them, this development pointed not to democracy but rather to the increasing selfishness of people pursuing their personal and conflicting interests rather than the public good. Many witnesses to the early republic argued that it was bad for the country to have many parties. As Ahmet, a retired banker said, "I do not understand why they have so many parties. They should come together and rule the country. It would be fine with me even if they had four or five parties, but now they have twenty of them. This feels really wrong to me."

According to Ahmet, the multiplication of parties erodes the national unity established under Atatürk during the single-party era. Through their narratives of universal support, Ahmet and other early Republicans discredited the current political parties, which define themselves as a voice for different groups in society. Instead, the old Republicans promoted the benefits of a system that gave priority to unity. For them, this was the path by which the Turkish Republic first achieved modernity. Early Republicans were able to do so by suppressing what they believed to be the nonmodernist demands of people, now given voice to by the multiple parties competing for votes.

In their narratives, the elderly Republicans emphasized a nonforced, emotional, and thus fully internalized devotion to the modernist state. Such personalized and emotionally loaded eyewitness narratives about loving commitment to the leader and his regime were suggested as proofs of voluntary and all-encompassing support for the early republic. They were posed against recent critiques of single-party rule as authoritarian and applying force toward its citizens.

THE PUBLIC TEMPORALITY OF PRIVATE LIFE

In the late 1990s, the elderly Republicans represented the past not only through the specific pieces of information they provided about the foundational days but also through the self they displayed and the narrative strategies they employed. A close analysis of their life-history narratives demonstrates that they carefully present a kind of self subsumed under the common cause of the republic. They do this by conflating their life history with that of the textbook version of Republican history and by deemphasizing the private concerns and interests of the individuals.

In his 1991 *The Death of Luigi Trastulli*, Alessandro Portelli tells us that it is common for individuals to imaginatively link life stories to bigger historical events in order to add meaning to their lives. He mentions the case of a steelworker in Turin killed during the struggle against Italy's participation in NATO. But years later, people remembered him as having been killed during their socialist struggle for jobs. According to Portelli, it is this shared "misremembering" that made the death of Luigi Trastulli more meaningful. He argues that one reason for such disassociations is the nature of the memory mechanism, which breaks down continuous time into a sequence of discrete events. In other words, Portelli considers such mistaken associations the result of a built-in dysfunction of the human memory mechanism.

The members of the early Republican generation, like the residents of Turin, connected many events that took place in their childhood to the milestones of political history. To them, the foundation of the Turkish Republic constituted the biggest event. Such associations between life narratives and the history of the republic, are not, I suggest, a result of disfunctioning memory, as Portelli argues. Rather, they reflect the individuals' conscious efforts to connect their own lives to bigger historical events. In this way, they not only become part of a shared history, or a myth, but also gain legitimacy as the witnesses of such important events. It should not be surprising to find that nationalist myths, the most powerful myths in the era of nation-states, pervade individual narratives and life histories. In my analysis of their life-history narratives, I found that elderly Republicans who were born at the beginning of the twentieth century were able to utilize two calendars available to them in order to associate, as well as disassociate, distinct parts of their own lives with Republican history.

Born in 1909, Semiha was one of my oldest interviewees, with a crystal-clear memory and unending energy to talk about her life. Having reached adolescence under Ottoman rule, she grew up with the Muslim calendar starting in 622 C.E. and measures the year eleven days shorter than the solar calendar. When Semiha was fourteen years old, in 1924, the newly established Turkish Republic adopted the solar Gregorian calendar. The Turkish Republic set itself in a new temporal plane and cut ties with the Ottoman past as the nationalist historians rewrote the history of the Turkish nation in creation. Coupled with the script reform that replaced the Arabic alphabet with Latin, the calendar change made the recent Ottoman past inaccessible. Due to a six-hundred-year difference in dates, even relatively recent events of the Ottoman Empire appeared centuries old if the nationalist historians did not translate them into the Gregorian calendar and included them into the new flow of time. Thus people like Semiha had lived the first part of their lives in the 1300s, while the second part took place in the 1900s. The eleven-day time difference between the lunar and solar calendars makes the translation between the two dating systems difficult, leaving the Ottoman and Republican temporalities flow parallel and at different speeds. Just like bilingual individuals who pick and choose between two languages, individuals like Semiha became bitemporals able to name events, especially those prior to 1924, in two different ways. Below I describe how Semiha utilized the Gregorian calendar in order to connect the significant dates of Republican history to her own life history, while disconnecting others.

I reached Semiha through Refet Angın at the Ministry of Education. When I called her on the phone and told her about my project, she expressed great enthusiasm about working with me. She told me that she had lived through very important times and wanted to leave a document of her life story to her children and grandchildren before passing away. When she was getting ready to write her memoirs a few years earlier, she had lost her eyesight and now did not enjoy the idea of speaking into a tape recorder by herself. She saw the interview as an opportunity to realize an important project of hers. Besides, she told me, she thought there might be other researchers interested in reading her life story.

When I visited Semiha in her apartment in Üsküdar, built in the 1930s after the old family mansion had been demolished on the same spot, she seemed well prepared for the event. She wore a pale pink, short-sleeved sweater and a brown skirt. At age ninety, she appeared a fragile and small old lady, but she was energetic enough to bend and put down patent leather guest slippers right next to my feet and climb up on a small wooden stool to reach her nicer tea cups to serve me. She also put out a folder consisting of interviews or news articles about her for my scrutiny. Three other journalists had already interviewed her about her life story. She had also appeared in the local Üsküdar newspaper numerous times for putting together Atatürk exhibits in the local schools for the national holidays.

Semiha greeted me in her formal living room, crowded with a usual four-piece set seating seven people, covered under white sheets; a dinner table for eight; and a large glass cabinet containing some antique glasses from her family, as well as souvenirs such as a bottle of ouzo she bought during her visit to Greece and coasters with pictures of the Eiffel Tower that a friend brought from Paris. On the walls there were several posters of Atatürk, as well as nature paintings done by her deceased brother who used to be a colonel in the Turkish army. After a short conversation, she suggested that we head to her office to start working on recording the oral history. I quickly took my tape out and followed her to a smaller room in the back. Her study was occupied by several bookcases mostly full of encyclopedias, a television set, two pictures of Atatürk, and family pictures including those of her deceased husband, parents, and siblings, as well as images of her grandchildren.

As soon as we sat across from each other, Semiha told me that she would like to tell her life story to me in three separate meetings since her life consisted of three parts. The dates that marked different phases of her life corresponded to the most important events in Republican history. Even though they took place before the calendar reform, she preferred to name these dates in the Gregorian calendar, much as they are recited in the public history of the nation. While talking about these events, she took the time to specifically point to the national significance of these dates. She started her narrative by making a connection between her birth and the first important duty of Mustafa Kemal in Istanbul as an Ottoman army officer: "Let's start with my birth. When the Action Army [Hareket Ordusu] came to Istanbul in 1909,[24] I was in my mother's belly. My mom used to say, 'When the Action Army arrived, I was one and a half months pregnant with you.' I do not know the exact date, but I was born in 1909." Two other turning points in her life include the departure of her family from Istanbul in 1919 (when Mustafa Kemal started a national uprising against the Greek army and the Ottoman rulers); and when she started teachers' school in 1923 (when the Turkish Republic was founded). To my surprise, Semiha did not mark any dates as turning points for the remaining seventy-six-year period of her life after 1923. Moreover, she was reluctant to talk about her life especially after 1950, when the glorious initial period of the republic came to an end by the election of the Democrat Party.

The feelings Semiha attached to the different sections of her life story show parallels with those associated with similar segments in national mythical history. Semiha describes her early childhood as a happy and bountiful period cut off from tragic transformations happening in the country, such as the invasion of Istanbul by foreign powers. Semiha grew up in a rich family in Istanbul with close ties to the dynasty. Her father was a colonel in the Ottoman army, and he took Semiha along to Ottoman palaces, where she had a chance to play house with some of the numerous grandchildren of the sultan. Her description of the way she played with expensive dolls and ate delicious pastries are reminiscent of the way nationalist narratives describe palace life as indulged in pleasure and blind to the tragic developments surrounding the palace.

Semiha started telling me about the second section of her life from 1919 to 1923 during my second visit. This section of her life consisted of a period during which Semiha had to grow up prematurely at age ten when Mustafa Kemal started a national uprising in 1919. Perihan's father decided to join Mustafa Kemal in Anatolia. Again, by naming it with a Gregorian date, Semiha sees 1919 as a new page not only in the life of the Turkish nation but in her individual life history as well. In opposition to the comforts and pleasures of her early childhood, the second section of Semiha's life was marked by difficulty, fear, and sorrow. Shortly after her father left home, Semiha's mother decided to join him, even though she was severely ill with tuberculosis. They left all their belongings behind, joined her father after a very difficult journey, and started a thorny life in Anatolia right behind the war front. Semiha took several hours to describe this section and portrayed numerous hurdles the family faced during this trip in detail. One of the most tragic moments involved her father and mother breaking all the glass negatives of their photographs when they realized that they could neither carry them along anymore nor wanted anyone else to find them. As the nationalist elite were asking the public to rid themselves of their memories about the Ottoman past, her family shattered its own memories of the bountiful life in Istanbul. This section of her life ended with her mother's death in 1922.

The third section of Semiha's life began in 1923, when she, her father, and siblings moved to Izmir after the defeat of the Greek army. This date also marks the foundation of the Turkish Republic. In Izmir, Semiha, her sister, and her brother spent a happy but brief time with their father. He eventually sent his kids away to live with their relatives in Istanbul and married another woman. After this point, Semiha continued to tell about the rest of her life in a relatively uninterested and unanimated manner, paying less attention to details. As opposed to the first two sections, for which she had well thought-of anecdotes, she had to think about what to tell next. When she listened to her narrative on tape, she told me that she really disliked this part because it looked so disorganized and uninteresting. Other events she told me about in this section of her life included her starting teachers' school in 1923 and her personal observations about the changes that followed the foundation of the republic.

Interestingly, Semiha did not divide the final seventy-six years of her life into sections. It could be marked by other dates that commonly define turning points in life such as finishing school, beginning work, getting married, having children, or retiring. Semiha did not consider such dates worthy of being recorded by a researcher and handed down to the next generation. The rest, she said, were merely personal (özel) details, some of which she even asked me to erase from the final tape we made for her family. Such a rupture happened as she was telling me the story about how in Izmir the family's landlord had asked them to leave the house they rented, and the family immediately moving out because they turned it into an issue of honor. She said: "I am telling you about this, but we can delete it afterwards." After finishing her story by telling me about how the family tried to find a new place and sell her piano to pay the rent, she said, "What I just told you is a private thing. I want them [to be recorded] for me, for my children. I don't think you will find such things interesting."[25] After this narrative, which she found too private and therefore insignificant for a researcher, she moved on to another story about the old hotels of Istanbul, which she thought would interest me more. After all, hotels are public versions of homes, things that could be discussed in a public narrative.

More interesting was the way Semiha shifted back and forth between the Muslim and Gregorian calendars in her narrative. Although she clearly named the most important dates in her life, as well as those of the Turkish Republic, in the Gregorian calendar, she used the Muslim calendar for some other personal dates. For example, when I asked for the exact date, she named the birth of her sister in the Muslim calendar. To my surprise, she did not know how to translate this date into the Gregorian calendar: "My sister was born in 1340. What year is that? We need to add 558 or 528 to it. You need to look it up in the book." Because this date did not exist in the prearranged narrative of her life story neatly tied to the public nationalist history, she had not thought about it. Another elderly person I interviewed named birthdates in the Muslim calendar as well and did not translate them to the Gregorian calendar for me either. For some interviewees, personal narratives ran on a different temporal plane than national history. For committed Republicans like Semiha, personal histories and Republican history intersected and became one at special turning points. In both cases, however, the Muslim calendar helped them, consciously or not, differentiate between the personal dates and the public national temporal order.

CONCLUSION

Some Turkish and American scholars with whom I shared the earlier drafts of this chapter challenged the value of my interviews and of the narratives I analyzed. They argued that as a good researcher, I should have challenged the first-generation Republicans more and not let them get away with reproducing nationalist history. Some wanted to see my transcripts and predicted that they would find some contradictory information in them. Others stated that because I did not represent the private lives of my interviewees, they appeared as cardboard images. I definitely agree that my interviewees' lives are not limited to what they have told me. I have no doubt that they have personal concerns and interests that either have nothing to do with Republican aims or even contradict them. Such details actually did come up during our conversations as well. For example, despite the glorifying Kemalist discourse about the emancipation of women through unveiling, women complained that they were still stuck with having to do all the housework. Or, although they told me that in those days everyone was ready to sacrifice for the nation, they gave me detailed accounts of bureaucratic tricks they employed in order not to be appointed to isolated places. I did not push my interviewees hard to squeeze more such claims out of them so that I could have access to a more "unbiased" or "nuanced" account of the early Turkish Republic because I was particularly interested in analyzing the framing of narratives they wanted to tell me. I assumed, and later was reassured, that these were the kind of narratives they were giving to other curious visitors, journalists, and television programmers.

The value of these narratives at the end of the 1990s lay not in the secrets they revealed about the past, but rather in their very specific depiction of the early Republican days as a joyous time in which individual citizens were ideologically and emotionally united with their state. The characteristics of this utopia are set up as a critique of contemporary Turkey, where citizens are divided along the lines of gender, class, ethnicity, and religion. Through their narratives, the elderly interviewees demonstrated that the first-generation Republicans had voluntarily accepted radical Kemalist reforms and were not forced to do so by the state. They thereby challenged recent critiques of the early Republican era as an authoritarian regime. Yet at the same time, their nostalgia for the past marked that period as irretrievably lost, similar to one's happy childhood during which all the family members loved each other under the protective authority of the father.

A content analysis of the narratives also demonstrates a crucial difference between the earlier and more contemporary conceptions of what constitutes a modern self. Initially, the younger Kemalists inspired by market symbolism had turned their attention to the first-generation Republicans in order to hear the private stories and experiences of the Kemalist modernization project. Although the first-generation Republicans personally embraced the goal of creating public virtue for the nation, they rarely valued their involvement as a personal choice. Rather, their self-esteem came from forming an integral part of the national, and thus, public narrative. Unlike market-inspired neo-Kemalists, who celebrate the private, the first-generation Republicans aimed to suppress what they considered the private aspects of their life. Nilüfer Göle (1996) shows that the central aspect of Turkish modernity has been the appearance of women in public. What she does not mention is that as the first-generation women left the domesticity of their homes and appeared in public, they also learned how to suppress any implications of the private in the public. The Republican regime clearly did not eliminate the private, but it did teach its vanguard elite to distinguish it from the new public. The elderly Republican women who divided their apartments into public and private zones, as many middle-class urban Turkish citizens do today, also divided their life stories into two narratives, a public and a private one.[26] They greeted me in their formal dresses and shoes appropriate for a public gathering outside the home, iconic of the public narrative they were going to tell me for a public audience through my tape recorder. At other times, they met with their family, neighbors, and friends in the private section of their apartments, in casual clothes and slippers, without makeup or hairdos, and talked about personal issues and concerns in addition to giving an evaluation of contemporary politics.

The contemporary interest in the supposedly private or personal lives of the first-generation Republicans was a very peculiar one. The nostalgic Kemalists who yearned for the early Republican commitment to modernity sought the elite vanguard of the Kemalist era. They glorified these people, especially women, for being able to suppress their private concerns and interests, for being able to participate and submerge themselves in public life. The Republican understanding of modernity, which prioritizes the public over the private, however, is also what made the elderly women not exactly fit into the present trend toward privatization. Individualized stories of the Republican history gained currency in the private markets of the publication industry. The same market that circulated personal narratives also turned them into objects that could be privately owned and thus transported outside the state-initiated public-history narrative circuits.

In the next chapter, I turn my attention from the individual narratives of vanguard Republicans to museum exhibits of the early Republican period. Such exhibits reflected a parallel interest in the private lives of the first generation of the Turkish Republic and aimed to rewrite the history of this period as one in which individuals took an active and voluntary role in modernizing their lifestyles according to the Kemalist state's wishes.

CHAPTER 2

Wedded to the Republic

Displaying Transformations in Private Lives

Like many visitors to Family Albums of the Republic, a public exhibit held at the Imperial Mint Building, in the courtyard of the Topkapı Palace, I was curious to see the official wedding ceremonies conducted as part of the display. During my third visit to the exhibit, a smiling, enthusiastic guard informed me at the gate, "Today at four o'clock we have a wedding. Be sure to be there." It was already close to four, so I rushed to the wedding room, which was decorated with life-size black-and-white wedding pictures of Turkish citizens from different periods and diverse ethnic and class backgrounds. The room was already filled with stylishly coiffed guests in three-piece suits and fine dresses. Journalists were also on hand, as were a small number of exhibit visitors, and guards who were peeking in. Soon, the bride and groom arrived in a car adorned with flowers and ribbons. The bride, in her early twenties, had her dyed blonde hair put up and wore heavy makeup and a low-cut, sleeveless white wedding gown. A red ribbon belt signaled her reproductive powers, and several gold coins attached to her dress were wedding gifts from the guests. The groom, ten years older, wore a dark suit and a colorful tie. They looked just like any other middle-class, urban, secular couple. What distinguished them was the not-so-small pictures of Mustafa Kemal Atatürk pinned to their chests.

The couple's Atatürk pictures delighted Ayfer Atay, the secularist mayor of Beşiktaş, who was to preside over the ceremony.[1] After the mayor put on the red coat symbolizing his office, he began the civil ceremony with a speech emphasizing the importance of the ritual:

> This is the seventy-fifth anniversary of the republic. It is an especially important anniversary because of the attacks against the republic. Along with the precautions taken against these attacks, the government wanted to have celebrations with great popular participation. Accordingly, the History Foundation organized the Family Albums of the Republic Exhibit. Today, we are adding a new family album to it. One of the most important gifts of the republic is the civil wedding ceremony. Due to the anniversary of the republic, these friends we have here will marry in a civil marriage. Instead of an Islamic marriage, which prioritizes man over woman and allows him to divorce his wife by saying "be divorced" [boş ol] three times, we will have a civil ceremony, which is based on equality and gives security to women. Thank you for allowing me to perform this historic wedding.

Atay's speech, which stressed the political nature of the wedding, received loud applause from the guests. Later he performed the brief official ceremony by asking the bride and groom whether they wanted to marry each other of their own free will. He then turned to the audience and made the customary wish: "May all the single people gathered here today also marry soon" (Darısı bekarların başına).

At first sight, the wedding ceremony I describe above looked typical. Unique was its location and the fact that the ceremony took place as part of Family Albums of the Republic, part of the "Three Generations of the Republic" exhibit organized by the History Foundation, a nongovernmental association. The larger exhibit, which commemorated the seventy-fifth anniversary of the republic in 1998, showed scenes of domestic intimacy drawn from three generations of Turkish family life. At the same time, the Yapı Kredi bank organized an exhibit entitled To Create a Citizen, which focused on the private lives of citizens during the 1930s. Throughout its seventy-five-year history, the Turkish state has taken the leading role in narrating and celebrating the republic (Öztürkmen 2001). Most often such narratives and performances have concentrated on the public achievements of the Turkish state. The private-sector investment in Republic Day celebrations is a recent trend in Turkey, and it is explicitly dedicated to a public redefinition of the ideal model of Turkish national intimacy. The new model is designed to suggest that from the earliest days of the republic, private citizens have voluntarily embraced secularism and modernity in their everyday lives.

This model departs markedly from an older symbolism of paternalistic, state-centered intimacy invoked by the first-generation Republicans I discussed in the previous chapter, which is epitomized by the veneration of Atatürk. Modernity and secularism, in the more established view, are gifts given by Atatürk to his children, who should be thankful and cherish these gifts because the father figure, who knew their value, instructed them to do so. Atatürk remained conspicuously absent from the exhibits I examine in this chapter, but many of the visitors (as well as the couples married as part of the "Three Generations of the Republic" display) invoked the older paternalistic notions of family and intimacy—which stress obedience and respect, not choice and desire—to express their relationship to Turkish modernity and the state. The new public interest in the intimate lives of Turkish citizens, supposedly the domain most distant from state intervention, is another manifestation of the privatization of state ideology, or the fact that the Republican ideology is carried to the domestic realm. These exhibits also made a reference to the changing emotional content of citizenship from paternalistic to conjugal love as political activists, intellectuals, and citizens attempted to conceptualize what form of government seemed the most appropriate for Turkey as it relocated itself in the changing power dynamics of the post–Cold War era. A simultaneous analysis of these popular exhibits and their reception reveals that the market-inspired model of governance builds on but does not totally replace the paternalistic model.

METAPHORS OF FAMILIAL INTIMACY
IN NATIONALISM AND NEOLIBERALISM

The effectiveness of kinship metaphors in defining state-citizen relations is well known. Throughout the nineteenth and twentieth centuries, nationalist ideologies typically conceptualized the relationship between the nation and the land, as well as the nation and the state, as a family relationship (Sommer 1991; Malkki 1995; McClintoc 1995; Shryock and Howell 2001). Nationhood is often based on the idea of fraternity among male citizens

(Mosse 1985; Pateman 1988; Hunt 1992), established through imagining the homeland as a woman (Najmabadi 1997). Such ideas legitimize the power of the nation-state over its population and turn the nation into a sphere in which men and women "naturally" play out their gender roles (Williams 1995; Nagel 1998). Turkish nationalism has not been an exception to this rule. The anthropologist Carol Delaney (1995a) argues that the foundation of Turkey was based on the metaphor of the rebirth of the nation through the union of the motherland (Anadolu) and the father leader (Atatürk). The single-party regime of the early Turkish Republic explicitly used the family metaphor in order to define ideal citizens as children of the state who are eternally indebted to the parent (Şerifsoy 2000).

New conceptualizations of nation and state typically go hand in hand with efforts to reorganize family and gender relations (Jayawerdena 1986; Phillips 1988; L. Abu-Lughod 1998). As Suzanne Brenner states regarding the policies of the new order regime in Indonesia, "the family often takes the foreground as the site on which the seeds of a 'modern,' 'orderly,' and 'developed' nation can be planted" (1998, 228). In the Turkish case, officials of the new nation-state worked hard to break up the extended family ties that challenged the authority of the state (Kandiyoti 1991). In her analysis of the relationship between gender and nationalism in Turkey, the anthropologist Nükhet Sirman argues that whereas "men needed to be pashas of the large households in order to have power in the old order; in the new order all husbands would be pashas. The classless society ideal would be realized in the fraternal community based on the assumption that men [who all own a family] would be equal" (2002, 238). When the Turkish Republic was founded in 1923, the first policies of the new regime involved regulating family and gender relations. Turkish officials adopted the Swiss Civil Code, which replaced Islamic marriage with civil marriage, abolished polygamy, gave women the right to initiate a divorce, and allowed them to keep children after divorce.[2] They also actively encouraged women to take part in public life through education, working outside the home, or simply by unveiling (Göle 1996). In this way, the state became involved in the regulation of one of the most intimate spheres of life, one formerly handled by religious communities or by male heads of household.

At the turn of the twenty-first century, as centralized states are losing ground in their control over the redistribution of power and wealth, the intimate metaphor of the family is gaining new currency in international and Turkish political discourse. The conjugal family represents the epitome of the private sphere, in which individuals voluntarily enter into truly binding relationships without the involvement of the state. The museum exhibits on family, marriage, and the private life of Turkish citizens I analyze in this chapter emphasized both the voluntary and contractual nature of European bourgeois concepts of conjugal intimacy, highlighting their separation from the state. Organizers utilized displays of a modern and secular domestic life to symbolize the free and willing relationship citizens have fostered with the state and its modernization project since the early years of the republic. The wedding ceremonies featured in the Family Albums exhibit underlined the voluntary nature of the marriage contract and the mutual desire of bride and groom. In the civil ceremony, which Turkish authorities adapted from Western counterparts, one of the few questions wedding officials are required to ask is whether both partners decided to marry of their own free will. In the Turkish case, a civil ceremony involves an additional level of choice. Although it is illegal to be married only through Islamic rites, it is still a widely practiced alternative.[3] Thus when Turkish couples choose to make their contract through civil marriage, they also agree to have the most intimate aspects of their lives shaped by the laws of a conspicuously Westernizing state.[4]

FAMILY ALBUMS OF THE REPUBLIC AND
MULTICULTURAL CITIZENSHIP

Three Generations of the Republic, one of the major activities organized to celebrate the seventy-fifth anniversary, exhibited the holistic changes that have taken place in the daily lives of citizens since the foundation of the republic. The most popular section of the exhibit, entitled "Family Albums of the Republic," concentrated on family life rather than the public accomplishments of the Turkish state. This section consisted of a display of family albums constructed by the organizers based on pictures collected from seventeen real families. Each album was accompanied by personalized stories of the changes three generations of family members had experienced since the foundation of the republic.

Family pictures and family albums are popular media used around the world to produce domestic intimacy and display it to others. Families actively manipulate the way they appear in these pictures and select only particular images to be included in albums. As Susan Sontag put it eloquently, "each family constructs a portrait chronicle of itself—a portable kit of images that bear witness to its connectedness" (1977, 8). Most often, family pictures and albums represent the family as if it were part of a unit larger than itself. At the same time, they exclude many personal relationships from the record. Given all the emotional and arduous work that goes into defining who make up the significant members of a family, it is interesting to explore how exhibit organizers narrated and represented the families of the Republic.

Even though the republic's modernity aimed to suppress different ethnic identities, the exhibit organizers showcased the diversity of Turkish citizens. Each of the seventeen families displayed in the exhibit represents a different ethnic, religious, or class background in Turkish society. The exhibit included Jewish, Greek, Armenian, Kurdish, Alevi (Alawite), Bektashi, Circassian, and Sunni Turkish families. The organizers also characterized class diversity, displaying two poor working-class families side by side with one of the richest families of Turkey: the Eczacıbaşıs. They also complemented families from metropolitan Istanbul with those from Anatolian cities and villages. In this respect, the exhibit made a statement about the multicultural nature of the Turkish Republic and the intimate connections of such diverse citizens to each other, as if they formed one family.

This novel mosaic approach to the Turkish nation/family has been shaped by, and constitutes a reaction to, Islamist, Kurdish, and liberal critiques of the homogenization policies of the Turkish state. According to the Treaty of Lausanne in 1924, only Christians and Jews were considered minorities. The Turkish state resisted accepting any other groups, such as Kurds, as minorities, or as non-Turk, for that matter. Despite this official position, in the 1990s a group of Islamist and liberal intellectuals engaged in a vibrant discussion of multiculturalism in Turkey. The most important factors that led to the development of this discussion were the increasing demands of Kurds and of religious people to be recognized by the state as distinct groups with cultural rights. A group of Islamic intellectuals led by Ali Bulaç (1992, 1993) suggested that Islamic law was multicultural because it allowed different groups to have their own laws and regulations.[5] Supporters of this argument, including the now banned Welfare Party, emphasized that the Ottomans had allowed different religious groups to have their own courts of law and were tolerant of religious differences. Especially in their party propaganda during the 1994 elections, the Welfare Party leaders repeatedly emphasized that their social model for Turkish society allowed for multicultural practices, rather than suppressing cultural differences as the current Turkish government does.

In reaction to such critiques, Family Albums of the Republic depicted the family of the Turkish Republic as one in which diverse cultures co-existed and intimately related to one another. The exhibit suggested that if different groups have assimilated over time, they have done so by their own choice. Between the lines, the Family Albums exhibit also recognized the hardships religious minorities such as Greeks, Jews, and Armenians had faced. For instance, the exhibit made reference to the infamous September 1955 anti-Greek riots in Istanbul, the 1942 so-called Wealth Tax for non-Muslims, which caused thousands of citizens to end up in work camps, and even the 1915 massacres of Armenians.

Despite the fact that exhibit organizers exerted great efforts to mention different identities present in Turkey, in the main text accompanying the exhibit, they emphasized similarities and commonalities among Turkish citizens. The text reads:

Different regions, different classes, different occupations, different beliefs, different languages . . . . Despite the differences, similar joys, similar sorrows. Babies, whether they are baptized or circumcised, bring happiness. Wedding pictures are full of hope. Brides and grooms smile at the cameras. In pictures student wear black uniforms and white collars or private school uniforms. Facial lines are formed as a result of the weight of the years, and those who are lost. . . . Joys and sorrow, which would not change much, even if we chose different families.

The exhibit organizer Oya Baydar told me that one of the main goals of the exhibit was to show how a diverse range of citizens throughout the country participated in Turkish modernization. Likewise, the co-organizer, Feride Çiçekoğlu, explained how curators chose to display pictures that were "typical" and would help visitors remember parallel transformations that had occurred in their own families. The official wedding ceremonies that accompanied the exhibit emphasized the continuous, contractual, and commonplace nature of Republican modernity.

Similarly, through photographs and narratives exhibit panels showed families becoming homogenous, secular, and Westernized. For example, over three generations the women of the Edhemağalar family unveil and even start wearing bathing suits; members of the Alevi Tanrıverdi family lose their positions of religious leadership in their community; the Turkoman Hacimirzaoğlu family cease being nomads and settle down in a village, and as the first generation builds a mosque, the following generations build a school; the second and third generation members of the Kurdish Kalkan family stop polygamy and wife beating; the extended Bektashi family of the Ulusoys divides into nuclear families.

As the family stories on display emphasized certain kinds of transformations, they silenced others that would have pointed to the failure of Republican ideals. Although over the past two decades more families have become religious and started to live according to Islamic principles, no second- or third-generation woman in the exhibit was veiled. This stood in contrast to the exhibit's tendency to accept the ethnic differences of family members. According to organizers, the ideal family of the Turkish Republic is one in which members choose to assimilate and follow the modernist teachings of the republic despite their differences. In other words, the exhibit celebrated the voluntarily and intimately internalized effects of Turkish state policy toward homogenization, secularization, and modernization. The official wedding ceremonies that took place as part of the exhibit emphasized the continuity of this process. They also stressed that through each wedding, individuals participated in the modernist policies of the Turkish state willingly and contractually, rather than being forced to do so.

TO CREATE A CITIZEN

A private bank, Yapı Kredi, organized To Create a Citizen: Introduction to Warfare for Creating a Modern Civilization, the second major exhibit commemorating the seventy-fifth anniversary of the republic.[6] Despite its militaristic title, reminiscent of the language of the initial years of the republic, this exhibit also concentrated on mundane transformations in the daily lives of citizens in the 1930s. More important, it emphasized how people readily internalized modernist transformations even in the most intimate aspects of their lives.

Located on İstiklal Caddesi, the busiest avenue of Taksim in Istanbul, the exhibit was easily noticeable despite the competing advertisements and signs on the hectic pedestrian-only boulevard. The nationalist songs and marches from the 1930s that radiated from the exhibit made it the center of attention. Passersby could not help but see the newly constructed six bright red walls covered with black-and-white pictures of ordinary citizens from the 1930s and 1940s. The walls were built in the shape of the six arrows of Atatürk's Republican People's Party. Their bright red color was reminiscent of both the Turkish flag and the official emblem of the RPP.

In the corridors formed between the six walls, four of the six Kemalist principles were emphasized: nationalism, populism, statism, and republicanism. The pictures on the walls showed changes in public life that resulted from the application of these principles by the single-party regime. For example, in the corridor representing statism, there were pictures of workers in state-owned factories; the corridor devoted to populism displayed pictures of peasant children in Republican schools; pictures of Turkish politicians and political meetings were displayed in the corridor of republicanism; and finally, pictures of small producers supported by heavy taxes on imported goods appeared in the nationalism corridor. Along with the pictures there were quotes of the two presidents of the period, Mustafa Kemal Atatürk and İsmet İnönü, as well as some popular songs and sayings. Both the idea of setting up exhibits on the street and the graphic designs used were suggestive of the propaganda methods favored by the single-party regime. Because there was no guiding text that situated the exhibit in the framework of 1998, viewers could feel that they had (re)entered the world of the single-party regime. Life-size images of citizens from the 1930s merged with pedestrians walking beside them in the street.

The corridors between the arrow walls led visitors to the second part of the exhibit, located inside the building. The internal space of the exhibit represented the two remaining Kemalist principles: laicism and revolutionarism. Unlike the first part of the exhibit, which concentrated on public transformations, the second part focused on changes in the private sphere. It displayed pictures of women, children, and youth, each of them a social category the single-party regime had emphatically worked to transform and make part of public life. The location of the second part of the exhibit and the material displayed there referred to a separation of public and private spheres yet at the same time demonstrated the continuity between them.

1. Exterior of the To Create a Citizen exhibit.

The last two principles of the Kemalist regime were represented by images of the private sphere adopting well to the new public life and represented by women and the domestic sphere. In this section women appeared in nightclubs in 1920s European evening gowns, Girl Scouts were seen forming orderly lines, and young women were portrayed doing gymnastic demonstrations in stadiums. In addition to these pictures, there were also personal items belonging to Atatürk, İnönü, and Vehbi Koç, a Turkish Muslim businessman who became rich during the early years of the republic. Their tuxedos, rather than Atatürk and İnönü's military uniforms, were on display. These three men probably wore these outfits during balls organized in the 1930s and 1940s in order to Westernize Turkish people. Along with the display of women's ballroom dancing clothes, this section featured a privately enjoyed (yet publicly oriented) European bourgeois lifestyle during the single-party era.

The new private sphere of the young republic that was in tune with the European public seemed best characterized in this exhibit by a "modern" living room from the 1930s, fitted with European furniture such as armchairs, a coffee table, and a radio. Aided by pictures of women dressed in European clothes, this room symbolized the integration of public developments toward creating modern bourgeois citizens into the private lives of the people, transforming their lifestyles and habits.[7] The small size of the room and the presence of only two armchairs suggested that some early Republican Turks were already living in nuclear monogamous families,[8] which Jürgen Habermas (1989) saw as the basis of the European public sphere.[9] The furniture also implied that the new Republican Turkish family who lived in this room sat on armchairs instead of cushions; ate at the table rather than on the floor; and listened to the radio to feel part of the new "imagined community" (Anderson 1991) of the Turkish nation instead of reading the Qur'an and thus being part of the Muslim world. The exhibit declared that ordinary people have long transformed their habits and lifestyles according to European standards in the domesticity of their homes, outside the direct authority of the state but in line with its teachings.

The architecture of a museum space and the way it is organized for visitors to walk through is at least as important as the material exhibited (Benett 1995). The architectural design of To Create a Citizen was especially important in the absence of guiding texts that told the visitor what or how to think. The act of entering the exhibit from the public sphere of the

2. Interior of the To Create a Citizen exhibit.

street and progressing toward a representation of a domestic living room was possibly the only thread the visitor could follow as a link to the different parts of the exhibit.

Visitors to the exhibit came from İstiklal Avenue, along which hundreds of thousands of people pass every day. İstiklal Avenue was built in the nineteenth century as one of the first Westernizing efforts. As such, it houses all the institutions commonly associated with the European bourgeois public sphere, from cafés and salons to theaters. Based on the model of a wide Parisian boulevard, it cuts across districts and connects them (Çelik 1986). This new boulevard obviously differs from the spiraling culs-de-sac of Istanbul and other Middle Eastern cities, into which people not part of the local neighborhood are not expected to wander freely (Eickelman 1974; J. Abu-Lughod 1987; Messick 1993). Target visitors for the exhibit were passersby who already formed part of the nonhierarchical public space of the avenue. When they encountered the exhibit, the visitors started walking through one of the corridors created by the six two-meter-high red walls.

Although creating a sense of freedom similar to that of the avenue, all corridors in the exhibit led visitors toward a particular point. They merged at the entrance to the second part of the exhibit, which depicted how earlier citizens of the republic freely transformed their private lives. Moreover, the corridors directed visitors from the east westward, iconically representing the way Kemalist principles directed citizens from their Eastern roots toward Western "civilization" as they transformed even the most intimate spheres of their lives. The organizers carefully planned such architectural details. According to Ahmet Özgüner, one of the exhibit organizers, "The structure has its own language. People can enter from any point and wander around. They can reconstruct the Republican ideology in the way they perceive it. After wandering freely, they merge in one point" (*Cumhuriyet*, October 31, 1998). Since the exhibit represented the Kemalist single-party era, the unforced guidance built into its architecture could be interpreted as a statement against contemporary critics of the early Republican regime, who define it as authoritarian and Turkish citizens as victims of state oppression. The exhibit architecture suggested that Turkish people acted with a sense of freedom as they incorporated Kemalist principles into their daily lives and became citizens through this process. Though not forced to do so, early Turkish citizens still chose to move in the direction the Republican regime advocated.

A guided or self-disciplining sense of freedom is at the same time iconic of the way Yapı Kredi bank exhibit organizers saw their role in relation to Republican ideology. This became clear to me during my interview with Münevver Eminoğlu, the coordinator of the Yapı Kredi exhibit space. When I asked her why a private bank like Yapı Kredi went to the trouble of organizing an exhibit for the seventy-fifth anniversary, she said there was nothing special about it because the bank always tried to put up exhibits in line with public discussions. For example, shortly after To Create a Citizen, the bank sponsored a display of arts and crafts celebrating the seven hundredth anniversary of the founding of the Ottoman Empire. In reply to a question about the absence of any explanatory or guiding texts in the exhibit, however, Eminoğlu stated the role of her institution more explicitly: "We want everyone to read the exhibit in the way they want to. We want them to understand what they can. We are not the state. We are not going to say things by hitting them over the head."

For Eminoğlu, it would be inappropriate for a private bank to assume the manner of the state and say things forcefully. Rather, Yapı Kredi should create choices and discreetly guide customer-citizens toward the product it promotes. In other words, even when engaged in political affairs, the bank should act in accordance with market principles. As Yapı Kredi chooses freely to support the secular principles of the republic, it takes on the qualities of the ideal citizen, as supposedly did early Republican citizens, who voluntarily followed the official ideology and embraced the common interests determined by the state. According to this model, the bank, the early Republican citizen, and the contemporary exhibit visitor freely and willingly submit to the state's broader project and equate their private interests with those of the state.

THE PUBLIC AUDIENCE OF REPUBLICAN INTIMACY

In *The Structural Transformation of the Public Sphere: An Inquiry into a Category of Bourgeois Society* (1989), Habermas defines the audience of bourgeois intimacy as an undifferentiated public, one consisting of private individuals who can imagine this public because they personally experience a domestic familiarity set apart from and defined by publicness. In *Cultural Intimacy: Social Poetics in the Nation-State* (1997), Michael Herzfeld argues that cultural intimacy creates a sense of familiarity among the nation's insiders. Intimacy of this kind needs to be expressed apart from the foreign gaze if it is to facilitate a sense of exclusive connection. At the same time, however, cultural intimacy is shaped by the knowledge that outsiders might be watching; hence it constantly reminds its performers and spectators of the possibility of embarrassment should intimate things become visible beyond contexts of national containment. If the intended audience of intimacy is crucial in defining its form, meaning, and modes of performance, then who is the imagined viewer of the domesticity displayed in exhibits like Family Albums of the Republic and To Create a Citizen? What influence do the exhibit organizers hope to have on this viewership?

Both Republic Day exhibits addressed a primarily Turkish-speaking audience by limiting the exhibit language to Turkish. The organizers of the Yapi Kredi bank exhibit also took into account the foreign—yet familiarized—gaze of Europe. Much like the cultural intimacy Herzfeld describes, the Turkish privacy on display in To Create a Citizen was explicitly constructed to avoid embarrassment, as if imaginary European Union officials would be scrutinizing the exhibit to determine whether Turks are truly modern and European. In my interview with Zafer Toprak, a professor of history at Boğaziçi University in Istanbul and the main curator of the Yapı Kredi exhibit and the original organizer of Three Generations of the Republic, he pointed out that his main goal in putting up these exhibits was to prepare the Turkish public to become part of the European Union. Two years after the show was set up, he defined the primary emphasis of the exhibit as the universal (read European), rather than the Turkish, character of Kemalist reforms. One of the effective tools he utilized was to choose pictures that did not give clues about their Middle Eastern context: "We chose pictures of people who do not carry any national characteristics. You can take these pictures to any country and no one can tell that the people in the pictures are Turks. We were not in search of the Turkish identity."

At a time when Turkey's full integration into the European Union was being earnestly discussed, deemphasizing the nationalist character of the Turkish Republic's foundational principles made for a noteworthy political statement. It asserted both to Turks and to the imaginary European viewer that Turkey had been part of Europe since its foundation as a modern state. Another strategy Toprak followed in order to establish a historical connection between Turkey and Europe was to highlight aspects of the early Republican regime that mimicked Europe, rather than demonstrating how the same regime also defined itself through the wars it fought with Western powers: "In these exhibits, we started with the national struggle and ended with the republic. We chose a very peaceful discourse and emphasized commonalities [with Europe]. We could have celebrated the national values as well. . . . For example, when I chose pictures of İsmet İnönü and Celal Bayar, I only used their pictures with Western clothes instead of uniforms. I wanted to show that now Turkish society is ready to be part of the European Union."

According to Toprak, a nonmilitaristic representation of the Turkish Republic, in which Turkish citizens have transformed both public and personal aspects of their lives, would move contemporary Turks beyond their nationalist feelings and toward integration with the European Union. The militaristic and patriarchal feelings associated with the early Republican era no longer match the contemporary ideals of European modernism, which promotes voluntarism and free will in state-citizen relations.

Toprak stated that one of the most important functions of the exhibit was to help Turks evaluate the early Republican period as a completed stage in history that allowed them now to move to the next stage. Namely, it aimed to equip citizens to move beyond the nation-state into a global era as part of the European Union: "We need to evaluate our past. The European Union is beyond the nation-state stage. We do not need to go out to the streets and yell 'fully independent Turkey.' We need to provide an easy transition [to the European Union]. That is our duty."

Toprak's emphasis on the European Union at first sight appears different from the Kemalist nationalist perspective that stresses public support for the Turkish Republic's secularist and unitarian principles. In fact, Toprak calls attention to how citizens willingly accept the modernist principles of the Kemalist republic without state pressure. He concentrates on transformations in the lives of ordinary citizens and makes a statement about the deep effects of Turkish modernization on private lives. The exhibit presented ideal citizens as those who willingly abandoned non-Kemalist practices in order to make themselves part of the larger project of national progress. Turkish citizens appear as both privately and publicly committed to Turkish modernity, just like the officially wedded spouses in a love marriage.

NOT LOVE BUT ARRANGED MARRIAGE—BY ATATÜRK

Despite the organizers' intentions, however, my interviews with exhibit visitors and the notes they wrote in exhibit guest books made clear that most visitors did not interpret the Republican privacy on display as a symbol of voluntary and loving engagement with Turkish modernity.[10] Instead of seeing the exhibits as places in which private individuals could come together to witness transformations that occurred in the lives of older fellow citizens, visitors perceived the exhibits as contact zones between themselves as citizens and a powerful state that had shaped them. Although neither exhibit included a picture of the founding father of the Turkish state—at least not in a central location—visitors found ways to venerate Atatürk and even tried to communicate with him. In other words, the exhibits reminded them not of a voluntary love affair between equals, but of their obligation to the founding father who arranged a fitting marriage for them. This sentiment was especially clear in the exhibit notebooks for To Create a Citizen.

Yapı Kredi always provides visitor books at its exhibits, but never had they been so popular. During To Create a Citizen, thousands of visitors filled 1,600 pages in eight volumes. Many pages contained multiple messages, and most notes were written collectively by groups of students, families, siblings, or couples. Remarkably, almost all the notes were written to Atatürk. The majority consisted of short formulaic messages referring to the Turkish state as Atatürk's trust (emanet) and describing the right way of acting as the path provided by him: "My Father [Atam], I am responsible for your trust"; or, "We are on your path, Atam." Contrary to the exhibit's statement about how Turkish citizens found their own path toward Turkish modernization, Republican visitors claimed that they were merely walking on the path Atatürk had shown them. Many visitors utilized the notebooks to express their love and commitment to the leader, rather than to the modernization project itself:

If you lived, I would spend my whole life kissing your hands.
[name]

We never did or will forget you. You are an immortal treasure. If we live independently and freely today, we owe it to you. I am sure that you see us and realize the condition in which the country is. I will always love you.
Respectfully,
[name]

Atam,
Since you founded the republic in 1923, we never made concessions and we never will. If you lived you would see how proud your own children are. I swear that I will always follow your revolutions, I will never forget you, and I will always be with you.
[name]

Most exalted of the exalted, Atam,
As youth we promise to protect what you have left us. We will live only for you. We will receive strength when we look at your pictures and we will keep walking faster and stronger.
I love you.
We did not forget the reason of our existence [i.e., Atatürk].
Bakırköy Lycee
[name]

In the same notebooks many visitors promised Atatürk that they would fulfill his goals by being good citizens, protecting the republic, and educating new generations in Republican ideology:

> Atam, I promise that I will protect this republic, which you founded by putting your life in danger. I also promise that I will raise new Republican generations. Sleep comfortably.
> [name]

> Great Leader [Ulu Önder] Atatürk;[11]
> I fought and fought all over Anatolia, hungry, thirsty, in cold or hot, in order to protect the republic to which you entrusted us and to raise new generations who believe in the homeland, the flag, and you. I did great amounts of work for your children because I am a teacher of your children. You told me that "the new generations will be your work of art." Following this principle, I dedicated my life to them. I have been working and working for thirty years. I will work more. May your soul be pleased [ruhun şad olsun].
> May the seventy-fifth anniversary of the republic be celebrated by the whole nation.
> Atam, the republic is entrusted to us. Sleep well. With my endless love.
> We are with your principles.
> [name]

Although many visitors told Atatürk they were following in his path, some confessed that they or fellow citizens could not do it to the full extent and asked for forgiveness.

> My Exalted Ancestor [Yüce Atam];
> As I write these words to you my head is bowed [with embarrassment] because we could not take responsibility for [sahip çıkamadık] the republic you left us. You did everything in order to elevate the Turkish youth. Your aim was to have the Turkish youth carry the Turkish nation to a better place. I hope you will forgive me for this: but maybe you were wrong for the first time in trusting in the Turkish youth. Probably you do not hear or see your followers, but I am sure you feel them at a far-away place.

My Father, do not forget that, even if it is not everyone, the Turkish children who love their country are always on your path. We are the guardians of this nation.

Dear Atam,

If I can breathe, I owe it to you. Unfortunately, there are still a number of people who dare to call you traitor. They are lower than human beings and have serious brain damage. I ask for forgiveness for a thousand times in their name.

They should know that the Turkish youth is here . . .

[name]

Dear Atatürk,

As of the year 1998, we accomplished a lot in the path you set toward reaching contemporary civilization. But there are people who try to divide the nation by acting as if they are Atatürkist or Republican. As a real Atatürkist, I really regret this situation. We love you and miss you.

[name]

In addition to feeling embarrassed about contemporary critics of Atatürk, many visitors wanted to reflect on what they perceived as the now lost accomplishments of the leader.[12] Young and old visitors alike complained to the leader about current officials and sometimes asked him to come back to put things back in order, sometimes seriously and at other times playfully:

Dear Atam;

I sometimes wonder whether this nation deserves the gift of the republic. Tomorrow we will celebrate the seventy-fifth anniversary of the republic. I hope there will be many other seventy-five years. But I observe many unbalanced situations. What we have is only the name of the republic. They always told us that the republic is self-government of the people. Do these people govern themselves in the best possible way? Which of the rulers think about the people? Which of the ruled seek their rights? Will we ever be able to be a world-class state or a state of law? I wish you could be here to get rid of all the wrongs. I wish we could get together to suppress all of these things. Anyway, I thank you a thousand times. What if you never existed? Today we would either be a colony or like Iran. I am so glad that you were born. I am so glad that you are still alive. You will be alive as long as people like me are around.

[name]

Atam;

We are three Turkish fourteen-year-old girls. We are working hard to lead this country forward and make it stronger than you left it for us. We are the Atatürks of the future. Atam, who did you leave this country to? Our rulers keep going backwards rather than forward. Atam, please get up from the soil you are lying in and save this republic, country, and the youth. Atam, we would rather have you sleep peacefully under the earth, but we are loosing the country. The adults you left the country to are destroying the youth. . . . Atam, we are following you. Atam, we really love you and miss you.

[Three names]

I love you,

I am thankful that you taught me and others how to think and how to be a human. But there are some people who misunderstand your principles and ideas. I am sure your bones are aching in your grave. I am a second-year student in dental school. I cannot receive a student ID if I do not cut my hair short. This is ridiculous. I wish you lived, so that we would not have to deal with such stupid people. I am sure that you will reincarnate [reenkerne olursun] one day. I am waiting for that day. It will be a lot of fun. Atam, please cut off your peace and do something. You can do it. I am really sick of these people. These are all nutcases who hide behind your principles. I want you back.

Trying to be a student.

[name]

Of the visitors and guides at Family Albums of the Turkish Republic I was able to interview none who saw voluntarism or individual choice as a fundamental aspect of the Republican regime. Most often the exhibits made visitors nostalgic for Atatürk's presidency, a time when the Turkish Republic rigidly forced its principles on people. My friend Hatice was among the devoted Republicans who spared at least half her day to visit the exhibit.[13] Hatice and I met at the entrance of Family Albums of the Republic on a Sunday afternoon. She told me that she "felt awful" after visiting the exhibit. I was eager to learn what stirred such strong emotions. She started talking without waiting for our tea to be served: "When you look at those old pictures, you see that people were more decent, their faces were glowing [yüzleri aydınlıktı], they had a sense of responsibility. We do not have that any more."

As for many other visitors, for Hatice the exhibit represented the golden era of the early republic. She believed that in the early days, when citizens could not choose their government, people glowed with Republican enlightenment and felt responsible for the nation rather than for themselves. Unlike exhibit organizers who emphasized free-willed engagement with the state, Hatice—similarly to the first-generation Republicans I discussed in the previous chapter—saw as the best part of the Republican project its success at achieving total submission. "In the old days," she said, "even the stupid ones followed orders [of the state]; they wanted to do what they were doing well. But now it is not like that. People have no belief, no hope, no aim. No one believes in either the nation or order."

As a devoted Republican, Hatice believed that the end of the single-party regime and the transition to democracy formed the starting point of selfishness in Turkey. "Things started to change in the 1950s. In the exhibit they tell about the transition to the multiparty system, but they do not tell about the compromises [verilen tavizler, yavşaklıklar]." Her argument ran similarly to that of many Republicans who claim that the transition to democracy, which brought the rule of the people rather than of the state, inhibited the Turkish nation from reaching the highest Republican goals. This position presupposes that an authoritarian, elitist state is better prepared than a democratic one to bring its citizens to the level of Western civilization.

Many visitors to the exhibit, as well as the guides, shared Hatice's impression that the Republican project deteriorated following Atatürk's death in 1938, and more so after the 1950 elections. When I followed people visiting the exhibit, I was surprised to see how many visitors interpreted the display as a representation of a past utopia. Comments about how people were happy in the old days, looked clean, and had glowing faces came up repeatedly. A middle-aged male visitor shouted, "The disaster [rezalet] started here!" when he saw a famous political campaign ad used by the Democrat Party during the 1950 elections. In his mind, the first free elections diminished the authority of the state, while populist politicians prioritized the immediate interests of their voters rather than the public good. The same visitor became nostalgic when he and his wife looked at the old stadium demonstrations and saw a nationally shared ecstasy in them: "Look at these pictures! People have a smile on their faces. There are no strange, nonsensical [abuk sabuk] people around. If you were to take this picture now, it would be full of men with beards or long hair. This picture is taken without their noticing it, and everyone looks happy."

Beards and long hair on men are symbols of opposition in Turkey. The latter is commonly associated with either Islamic mystics or, more likely, with rockers, rebellious youth, whereas the term *beards* codes religious conservatives. Uncontrolled hair for both men and women means not being controlled by an authority figure, such as a father, a husband, or the state (Delaney 1994).[14] Thus the visitor's comment about hair is very telling. What he meant is that people in the past used to be obedient to the paternalistic state, which made them embrace Turkish modernization. Today, by comparison, individuals are free to develop oppositional political ideologies of their own, and this clearly upset the visitor. Such freedom, he no doubt believed, leads to chaos and unhappiness by breaking up the homogeneity of the nation and diluting the complete obedience of citizens to the Turkish (father) state.

GUIDING THE YOUTH, GUARDING THE REPUBLIC

My last source of information about the interpretation of the exhibits comes from the guides for the Three Generations of the Republic exhibit. They were enthusiastic, college-aged men and women, whose duties included giving information to the visitors, making sure that the multimedia functions of the exhibit were running smoothly, and guiding groups of students through the exhibit. During my interviews with nine guides I found out that these young men and women—selected from middle-class, urban, and secular university students—felt very proud of their jobs. When Özlem, a second-year student of chemistry at Istanbul University, said, "I really like what I am doing; I would do it even if they did not pay me," other guides nodded enthusiastically.

The guides in the exhibit received no specific training. When they first started, they toured the exhibit on their own and then told the students whatever they considered important. In that sense their views did not necessarily correspond to the organizers' intentions, but were very much their own. Although hired primarily to watch over groups of student visitors, the guides took their responsibilities seriously and saw it as an important Republican duty to create good citizens who appreciated the Republican project. Serving as guides transformed them from university students who worked for pocket money to good citizens devoted to a public cause. Most important, the guides had internalized the didactic function of the public intellectual as a teacher in Turkey and embraced the mission of educating young visitors about the virtues of the republic.

During their break, I asked a group of guides what kinds of things they told students. Özlem replied first: "I want all the children to be Republicans. I place the most emphasis on elementary school children because they are young and I can mold them." At this point, Selda added, "I personally really enjoy giving consciousness to students because they are very ignorant. I think 80 percent of the exhibit should be geared toward children. I want them to know that Suna Kan [a famous violinist] is also a woman of the republic." Taner also joined in by saying, "I try to teach them that they should know the value of the Republican regime that we have, so they can protect it when they grow up." To these college students, being a guide to this exhibit became a political mission of educating the youth about Republican values. By teaching them about classical music performers and other modernist products of the Republican regime, they hoped to turn young students into passionate Republican citizens rather than its aloof critics.

Sometimes the guides were direct in teaching the students about how they should be protecting the republic. For example, when I followed Özlem guiding a group of middle school students in front of a panel about national celebrations, she gave them advice: "In the old days, people commemorated the national days with much enthusiasm. Today, we should do the same as well." At other times the guides were subtle about their messages. They worked hard to fulfill their mission of inculcating the youth with Republican ideology and came up with creative ways to have their teachings better heard by students. Özgür, who at the time was a third-year engineering student at Yıldız Technical University, told me about the methods he used to influence students: "The couple of hours they spend in the exhibit may change these students. So I do my best to influence them. I talk about Atatürk like a human being. I tell about his human side, his loneliness. I call him 'that guy' [o herif], for example. Then they really listen to me and understand that this exhibit is something different from their history books. And my messages hit the target."

Özgür's approach was indeed innovative. Having recently been a high school student himself, he was aware that students were tired of studying the virtues of the republic over and over again. To hold the attention of students adept at closing their ears to propaganda, Özgür related his message in ways that echoed those favored by the Yapı Kredi bank and the History Foundation. This newly intimate style, whether conveyed in a casual way of talking about Atatürk or in the carefully considered text and physical layouts of museum exhibitions, has slanted the Republican message toward more voluntaristic models of citizenship. For Özgür, however, and perhaps for most of his student listeners, another set of messages still came through, and it would seem that these messages were more easily felt and understood.

Guides who took up the mission of guarding the republic seemed happy with most of the exhibit. They, however, unanimously hated the section labeled "Economic Awakening" ("Ekonomik Uyanış") in the Three Generations of the Republic exhibit. This section formed the third and final part of the controversial series called "National Sovereignty."[15] By consecutively lining up panels devoted to the transition from the constitution to the republic ("Meşrutiyetten Cumhuriyete"), from authoritarianism to democracy ("Yeter! Söz Milletin"), and the development of economic liberalism, Hakan Yılmaz, one of the exhibit organizers, gave a particular interpretation of the Republican history. In the book that accompanies the exhibit, he defines these three incidents as developments that turned "the society into an autonomous being, which could understand and govern itself and maintain itself economically" (Tanyeli 1998, 31). In other words, he defined the development of the liberal economy in the post-1980 era as the final stage of the development of independent Turkish citizens who could govern and maintain themselves independent of the state. The final section of the series consisted of a small room with three white walls. On the walls were printed inscriptions of quotes from Turgut Özal, the prime minister who implemented the economic liberalization in the 1980s, and major Turkish businessmen's declarations about their market-oriented philosophies.

Özgür told me that he hated this section so much that he did not even take students to it. He made them walk around it and go to the next panel. When I asked why, he answered, "Because it has nothing to do with the republic." Almost annoyed by the way I did not understand how and thus kept asking what exactly bothered him about the section, he explained: "It is wrong to associate the post-1980 period with the republic. It is not appropriate to discuss the businessmen, who take risks to make more money. There is no place for Sakıp Sabancı in this exhibit. This thing they call 'economic awakening' damages the independence of the republic. Since it started, everything is becoming worse and worse for the republic."

Özgür could not stand the Turkish businessmen who looked after their own interests and became rich in the past two decades. He even found it inappropriate to spell out their names in an exhibit about the republic. Interestingly enough, he singled out Sakıp Sabancı, the head of one of the two largest family corporations in the country, but did not mention Vehbi Koç and his family. Although both families became rich in the 1930s under the tutelage of the Turkish state and thanks to the Turkification of the economy, they have different relations to Republican ideology.[16] The Koç family owned a small business in Ankara when the town was chosen to be the capital. The family always had close connections with the leaders of the RPP and actively supported the party.

The Sabancı family, on the other hand, came from a rural background and could not establish close ties with party officials. It was only in 1950, when the Democrat Party came to power, that they established an alliance with the government and flourished. In addition to their original distance from the Republican elite, the Sabancı family later had closer relations with Turgut Özal, who worked with them just before he became the prime minister in 1983 and started the economic liberalization program. Moreover, unlike the Koç family, the Sabancı family never became public spokespersons for the Republican ideology. Thus, for Özgür, it is not the accumulation of wealth, but the way a company relates itself to the state that can make it close to or distant from the Republican ideology.

In addition to being angry at businessmen who created independent economic spheres for themselves, Özgür much resented international capital. At the end of the 1990s, global trends were posing heavy challenges to Republican independence. Özgür thought that international companies had a place neither in the country nor in the exhibit. In his tours, he specifically warned the students against these developments. He chose a relevant example for high school students, reminding them of the way American fast food was replacing a famous Istanbul meatball restaurant. He said he told them that "Atatürk did not found the Republic so that Sultanahmet Köftecisi [a historical meatball restaurant] would be replaced by McDonalds."

CONCLUSION

The way the Family Albums of the Republic and Creating a Citizen exhibits frame the Republican past and its domestic intimacy is closely related to both the particular historical process in which citizenship developed in Turkey and contemporary debates about this issue. Since its beginning in the nineteenth century, Turkish modernization has developed as a top-down project in which a modernizing elite defines the collective interests of Turkish citizens (Mardin 1962; Bozdoğan and Kasaba 1997; Keyman 1997). Hence Turkish citizenship has corresponded more to a classical model than a liberal one, according to a popular way of categorization wherein citizens are defined through their duties toward the state rather than their rights (Kadıoğlu 1998). The modernist Turkish state frequently interfered in, manipulated, and defined the boundaries of domestic lives and made sure that citizens engaged in the necessary practices of modernity in private so that they could, as an aggregate of individuals, constitute a modern and secular public sphere. Changing marriage rules, taking control of religious practices, and engaging in clothing reform were some of the ways in which this intervention took place. Thus both exhibits, which focus on the personal lives of new Turkish citizens, reflect the Republican state's long-standing preoccupation with family, domesticity, and intimacy as tools for creating a modern, secular public in Turkey.

In this chapter I have tried to show that ideas about privacy and domesticity are deeply intermeshed with Turkish perceptions of the public sphere. The single-party officials and contemporary public intellectuals resemble each other in the sense that they both perceive private lives as sites of direct control and manipulation. Unlike their predecessors who openly manipulated the private sphere, however, contemporary Republican intellectuals conceptualize the domestic and the affective realms as outside the authority of the state. In that sense, they embrace the Habermasian understanding that sees the intimate private sphere as a prerequisite of a truly modern public sphere. Yet in contrast to Habermas's concept of other-oriented intimacy, in which the subjective experiences of the new bourgeois family flowed naturally into the rational-critical public sphere that expanded and completed them, the secularist public intellectuals fabricated intimacy-oriented publics. They took an active, calculated role in displaying images of secular and modern family life as proofs of the willing, collectively shared, and intimately internalized relationship of citizens to Turkish modernity. By doing so, Republic Day exhibits asserted a close historical connection with the West and included Turkey in a post–Cold War European cultural and political intimacy in the past, present, and, hopefully, in the future.

Most visitors to the Republican exhibits were receptive to the polyvalent symbols of family and intimacy as interpretive tools to appreciate their own history and connection to the state. However, they tended to understand the relationship between Turkish modernity and familial intimacy not in the neoliberal framework of freedom and voluntarism, but in the nationalist model of paternalism and obligation. In both exhibits the images of early Turkish citizens reminded visitors of the founding father who modernized the nation. They repeatedly referred to their desire and need to follow Atatürk's path in order to be modern. They also voiced nostalgia for the happy days when the founding father was alive and the paternalistic state made the best decisions for its citizens. If organizers hoped to depict the relationship between the modernizing Turkish state and its citizens as a love marriage wherein partners freely choose each other, for many of the Republican visitors the intimacy on display brought to mind a protective parent-child relationship. The couple married as part of Family Albums of the Republic, with Atatürk pictures on their chest, transformed a personal relationship into a performative symbol of their commitment to the secular and modernist principles of the Turkish Republic. As Republicans were challenged by oppositional groups in Turkey, they acted out their belief that ideal citizens of Turkey should be wedded to the republic because this union was arranged by the founding father who knew what was best for his citizen children.

During my interviews with exhibit organizers, I noticed that they remained unaware of the contradictions between their aims and visitors' interpretations. Instead, the organizers embraced the traditional role of the cultural elite in Turkey by introducing the newest European conceptions of modernity into Turkish political life. In the new models of citizenship and governmentality they now endorsed, the authoritarian aspects of Turkish political identity were coded as embarrassing in relation to neoliberal ideology and the political culture of the European Union. Earlier codes had merely required that nonmodern aspects of life, such as the veiling of women, be hidden from view or confined to the private sphere, and these moves were understood as obligatory acts of submission to the state. The newer conventions, by contrast, aimed to conceal the paternalistic inclinations of the Turkish state (and its supporters) by delegating much of the state's representational agenda to nongovernmental organizations and commercial interests, such as private banks, which speak a market-oriented language of autonomy and choice. These organizations could now teach ordinary Turkish citizens to love the modernist state freely and passionately.

CHAPTER 3

Miniaturizing Atatürk

The Commodification of State Iconography

Visitors to Turkey are immediately greeted with images and reminders of Mustafa Kemal Atatürk. When travelers land at the Atatürk Airport in Istanbul, two gigantic pictures of the leader welcome them. The shuttle from the airport drops them in Taksim Square, across from the Atatürk library and the monument to the struggle for independence led by Atatürk. When they tour the city, visitors pass by the Atatürk Bridge, only then to encounter the numerous statues, portraits, and sayings of the leader that encumber every available public space.

Not only newcomers notice this proliferation of Atatürk images. Since the late 1990s Turkish natives have also observed an exponential increase in the already ubiquitous images of Atatürk. Although I grew up under the penetrating gaze of the founding father, I was astonished by the omnipresence of Atatürk images on my return to the country after several years' absence. What startled me most was not the multiplication of his image, but his appearance in strange, new places and in novel poses—the very commodification of the leader. Kemalist entrepreneurs and consumers had creatively adopted the founding father into their personal lives and ventures. Suddenly, it seemed, there was an appropriate picture of Atatürk for every trade: Atatürk at a table for restaurants and bars; several poses of Atatürk drinking coffee for coffee shops; a dancing Atatürk for nightclubs;

and even Atatürk with cats and dogs for veterinarians. Unique posters of Atatürk or inscriptions of his image in previously unusual contexts such as T-shirts, mugs, and crystal spheres have become popular as birthday gifts and wedding favors. Most surprisingly in the newly popular images, Atatürk appeared smiling, much in contrast to his fierce looks in pictures that decorate state offices.

In the 1990s Kemalist politicians and intellectuals frequently reflected on the meaning of this new Atatürk imagery. They contrasted the interest in the leader with the hatred people elsewhere were displaying toward other state leaders at the time and took the difference as a sign of the strength of Atatürk's principles. Several years ago, for example, the then ex- and future prime minister Bülent Ecevit said proudly, "[Hitler, Mussolini, and Stalin] have been buried in the dark pages of history. But Atatürk is still alive in our hearts sixty years after his death" (qtd. in Sarıdoğan 1998, 15). Many politicians and intellectuals describe the recent interest in Atatürk as a kind of resurrection (yeniden diriliş) or an awakening (uyanış). While there is something new about this interest in Atatürk, the man never really died in the Turkish imagination. Kemalism has been the official ideology of the Turkish Republic since the 1930s, and the leader has been venerated by large segments of the population since his death in 1938. I argue, rather, that what is new is the privatization of the production, circulation, and consumption of Atatürk's image, as well as the personalization of the form and content of the representations of him.

The newly popular images of the leader do not radiate the usual somber and even fearful expression familiar to three generations of Turkish citizens of all ages—especially to my generation, who grew up under the extensive Atatürk campaign of the 1980 military junta.[1] Instead, the commodified pictures of Atatürk that decorate homes and businesses today depict the leader not as a stern soldier or a state leader, but as a jovial bourgeois who enjoyed simple but highly marked pleasures such as wearing European outfits, eating food at a table rather than on the floor, drinking alcohol, bathing in the sea, and being in the company of unveiled and stylish women. Consumers are willing to pay up to hundreds of dollars for such pictures representing the leader enjoying Western bourgeois pleasures, even though his likeness is the most common item in the Turkish visual repertoire.

In this chapter I aim to integrate a discussion of personalized consumption into the production of the state effect as it is discussed by recent scholars of the state (Abrams 1977; Taussig 1993; Gupta 1995; Coronil 1997; Mitchell 1999). A focus on the consumption of the material symbols of the state is crucial for understanding the recent privatization of state ideology in an era in which the market has become "a political icon or a formal economic abstraction" (Carrier 1997, 1). Just like the state that "arises from techniques that enable mundane material practices to take on the appearance of an abstract, non-material form" (Mitchell 1999, 77), daily consumer activity in the market and the concept of the consumer now appear as abstract realities with political significance.

In studying the privatization of Turkish state symbols through their consumption I utilize Arjun Appadurai's insight that consumption constitutes a means to both send and receive messages (1986, 31) and argue that the recent hegemony of market symbolism made these messages doubly influential. As I compare the recent images of Atatürk in the market with those distributed by the state throughout the history of the republic, I demonstrate that citizen-consumers prefer physically and metaphorically miniaturized images of the founding father that they can incorporate into their private lives and engage with in a less hierarchical relationship. Acquiring such imagery allows citizens to send the message to the critics of the Turkish state that there is a public that voluntarily and personally embraces the founding principles of the Turkish Republic. Yet at the same time, by bringing the image of Atatürk into their businesses and homes, these citizens also receive messages about the ubiquitous authority of the Turkish state, although this authority transforms in this very process.

THE ESTABLISHMENT AND SPREAD OF ATATÜRK IMAGERY

Shortly after the Turkish Republic was founded in 1923, the ruling cadre mobilized the limited resources of the new state to create and disseminate the Atatürk cult as the new symbol to unify the nation. As early as 1927, Atatürk himself defined his role as a charismatic and authoritarian leader of the new regime and nation in his famous marathon speech, delivered in thirty-six hours over six days to the National Assembly (Parla 1991). Early representations of the leader depict him as the sole victor of the Greco-Turkish war and the creator of a new nation (Ünder 2001). Such portrayals aimed to legitimate the new leader by locating him at a higher position than the sultans of the Ottoman Empire he had replaced. The cult of Atatürk gained further importance following the leader's death in 1938, turning the founder's body into an immortal symbol of the nation (Ökten 2001).

The visual symbolism of the new leadership has formed an indispensable part of the Atatürk cult. Personal photographers regularly accompanied the leader to take carefully choreographed pictures depicting the founding father in his rich collection of Western clothes such as tuxedos, golf pants, capes, and walking sticks and engaged in supposedly modern social activities such as dancing the waltz, drinking alcohol, or socializing with women. Well-known European sculptors, such as Henrich Krippel and Peter Canonica, were invited to make statues of Atatürk while he was alive (Elibal 1973; Bozdoğan 2001). They portrayed the leader in Western civilian clothes, in military outfits, or sometimes even naked, but always looking very solemn.[2] Thus Atatürk came to represent and embody the new nation and the "new man" that the republic aimed to create (Gür 2001).

Since the early days of Atatürk's rule, statues of the leader and their countless replications started to decorate every city and town center in the country. Laws and regulations were set up to maintain that Atatürk was represented in every public office, classroom, courthouse, prison, and police station. State-funded artists, the State Supplies Office, and privately owned businesses satisfied the great demand from state institutions. The few styles of Atatürk imagery in the market fit the serious aura of such institutions. As Mehmet İnci, the owner of one of the oldest production houses of Atatürk statues sold in Istanbul, told me, there are basically three kinds of Atatürk statues: those depicting him as a soldier, as a statesman, or as a man of the people. When I asked him about the possibility of sculpting new kinds of Atatürk statues to add to this stock of molds, he told me that there was no need since these three kinds sufficed to meet any kind of demand from governors and mayors with diverse political positions.

Even though the sculpture market still served public needs, the late 1990s witnessed the emergence of a private market for Atatürk pictures and posters that demanded different kinds of images than the ones used to decorate state offices. This demand was supplied by private printing companies and photography studios searching for new photographs of Atatürk previously hidden from the popular gaze. As a result, the same companies that printed posters of the most popular pop stars, of cute babies wrapped in towels, or of dramatic sunsets began to print posters of Atatürk laughing on a swing set or bathing in a swimsuit. Some photographers and graphic artists utilized new computer technologies to color the old black-and-white pictures. The owner of one of the oldest and most established photography studios in Turkey, who I will call Haşim, told me in his office that he was coloring Atatürk's pictures "in order to make Atatürk contemporary and renew his imagery," so that "the new generations also love the leader." Haşim told me that he was constantly in search of new pictures of Atatürk showing him among the people because "when people realize that Atatürk was mixed with the people, they love him much more." During our conversation he repeatedly emphasized that he was not doing this to make money, but "to spread love and respect for Atatürk" at a time when "a few ignorant people dare to smear his name."

COMPETING WITH ISLAMIC PARAPHERNALIA IN THE MARKET

An important factor that led to the commercialization and privatization of Atatürk imagery in the 1990s was the emergence of Islamic symbols in the public political market. Veiled female university students crowding the secularist institutions of the modern republic were the first signs of the public visibility of Islam (Göle 1996). This trend reached its climax when the İslamist Welfare Party won local elections and painted the road signs the Islamic color of green, planned a huge mosque complex at the heart of Istanbul's hotel and bar district, and opened Islamic tea gardens in the city (Bartu 1999; Çınar 2001; Gülalp 2001; Houston 2001a). Islam increasingly became "an issue, something that [had] to be addressed and confronted" (Öncü 1995, 53).

The public appearance of Islam became possible partly through the commodification of Islamic symbols. The consumer culture of the 1980s and 1990s created a commodity-based identity politics and lifestyle. Islamists began to enjoy their own five-star hotels where they could swim in sex-segregated pools (Bilici 2000), frequent restaurants that did not serve alcohol (Houston 2001a), listen to Islamic radio stations (Azak 2000), and attend fashion shows in order to be in tune with the new designs in head scarves and overcoats (Navaro-Yashin 2002; White 2002). These Islamic symbols or paraphernalia were not the first to exist in the market. *Bismillahirahmanirrahim* (in the name of God, the compassionate, the merciful) stickers have long existed as popular car decorations that protect the automobile or remind the drivers to recite God's name before they turn on the engine.[3] The new stickers of the 1990s, which read "Peace is in Islam" ("Huzur İslamdadır"), were located in the rear window rather than on the front panel, and thus directed toward people outside the car, rather than those inside.

Kemalists reacted to the public appearance of Islam in two ways. First, the secular state officials and military officers actively added considerable numbers to the tens of thousands of public statues, busts, and portraits of Atatürk already displayed in public spaces. The military made an effort to erect statues of the founding leader, particularly in newly developing shantytown neighborhoods, which predominantly voted for the Islamist party in the 1995 elections. The attempt to suppress Islamic symbolism with the official secular representation constitutes an old strategy that has been practiced since the founding years of the republic. A new strategy involved the commodification of Kemalist symbolism to compete with the Islamic symbols. In the 1990s, the veil and the portrait of Atatürk became symbols of cultural identity through which the two sides of the debate competed with one another in the marketplace (Hart 1999; Türkmen 2000; Navaro-Yashin 2002). I argue that competition over potent symbols had significant consequences for political positions and cultural identities. As Kemalist consumers moved the official state imagery out of the traditional realm of the state and into the market and their homes, they privatized state symbolism. Atatürk's images, which used to mark the spaces owned and controlled by the state, were now carried to nonstate spheres through the free-willed and consumerist acts of citizens. More important, for the first time in the history of the Turkish Republic citizens perceived the official state ideology as in need of their protection and took personal responsibility for promoting it.

In Istanbul I asked several store owners why they displayed Atatürk pictures in their shops; they told me they wanted to show their love for Atatürk to those who smeared his name. An office-supplies shop owner in Beyoğlu, who displayed several Atatürk posters and a *Bismillahirahmanirrahim* sign in his store, said:

These idiots [Islamists] do not realize that they would not be here if Atatürk had not saved this country. Their names would be Elena or Kostas, and they would be crossing themselves in churches. If they can hear the call to prayer five times a day and if they can pray in mosques, it is because Atatürk saved this country from the Greeks and the Westerners. And now, they dare to bash the name of this beautiful man. These pictures show them that the people of this country love Atatürk. They always did and they always will.

The middle-aged store owner's view is in line with official Kemalism in the sense that he utilizes the post-1980 military coup official discourse on the compatibility of Islam with Kemalism in order to counter Islamist critiques of the leader and his ideology. Furthermore, he accuses religious Muslims for being unfaithful to their true savior who saved the country from being divided and possibly Christianized by the Allies during World War I. What is unique in his position is that he takes personal responsibility for disseminating this particular version of the official position through conflating Atatürk pictures with Islamic paraphernalia. He clearly does not find the state efforts sufficient or powerful enough to give a strong message to Islamists. He has made a special effort to teach Islamists a lesson by showing that Atatürk is not an imposition of the state, but that private citizens like him love the leader.

My own mother, a staunch Kemalist activist living in the predominantly secular and upscale Istanbul neighborhood of Erenköy, told me that she started wearing an Atatürk pin after Islamists gained power in the 1994 local elections. She said, "When I am walking on the street, I want to show that there are people who are dedicated to Atatürk's principles. Look, now there are veiled women walking around even in this neighborhood. I push my chest forward to show them my pin as I pass by them. I have my Atatürk against their veils." My mother utilizes her own body to display pictures of Atatürk in a neighborhood in which there is no scarcity of Atatürk statues or busts erected by government funds. As she encounters symbols of the Islamic lifestyle, she feels a personal responsibility to display state symbols as her individualized political position.

Not only do individual Kemalist citizens and consumers use symbols to challenge the Islamist movement, but companies have also dutifully joined the war of symbols between Islamists and Kemalists. An accountant friend told me one such story in his office:

After the [1994] elections, the Islamist municipality banned posting bathing suit advertisements with women models on billboards. One of the
companies, Zeki Triko, put up a picture of Atatürk in his bathing suit on
the billboards all over the city. Underneath they wrote: "We miss the sun."
It was such a great idea because it was winter time, so the sun referred
both to the real sun and to Atatürk. Everyone loved it. Zeki Triko sent this
ad to everyone; people put it on their desks. It was a great war of symbols.

This advertisement was the first in an extensive series of other examples in
which companies utilized Atatürk pictures to market their products and
mark their companies as Kemalist. In the 1990s, having Atatürk monuments in city centers was not enough for Kemalist citizens and groups to
express popular support for the founding father. Companies showed their
dedication to the leader by using him in their advertisements and emphasizing personalized emotions for him. Similarly, ordinary citizens put his
picture on their desks and jackets and verbalized their feelings of "love" for
the leader. To counter the appearance of Islamic symbols in the public
sphere, and the acceptability of Islamic identity indicated by the consumption of such symbols, Kemalists carried their icons from the conventional
realm of the state into the private realm of civil society, the market, and the
home. Some of these spheres did seek a public audience, but they were all
marked by a deliberate engagement of private citizens in embracing Atatürk's symbolism, rather than being under the direct control of the state.

FORCED VERSUS VOLUNTARY KEMALISM:
BOTH UNDER THE HEELS OF THE ARMY

Kemalist citizens I talked to frequently contrasted the recent voluntarism
in commitment to Kemalism to the forced Atatürk campaign of the three-
year military rule between 1980 and 1983. In drawing the distinction, they
often referred to the consumer interest in Atatürk paraphernalia and thus
to Kemalist ideology as having been initiated by independent individuals
without the imposition of the state. They defined the new interest as genuine, voluntary, and sincere, as opposed to the previously forced and artificial interest in the leader. Even the most devoted Kemalists agreed that the
earlier Atatürk campaign of the post-1980 military regime was "overdone"
and had alienated most citizens from his ideology.

The 1980 coup Kemalists referred to was preceded by a decade of political deadlock in parliament, social violence, and economic crisis. On September 12, 1980, the Turkish army interfered in politics and abolished the parliament, which had been unable to control the country's political situation. The military applied strict measures of depoliticization and economic restructuring. The junta used Atatürk as its main symbol in order to bring the divided nation together and reinstate the authority of the state. For the people I talked to, the most obvious contrast between Atatürk campaigns of the early 1980s and the late 1990s, almost twenty years apart, was that the first one was imposed by the state whereas the second one was initiated by citizens and consumers. A thirty-five-year-old administrator in a private school in Istanbul, whom I will call Sinan, compared the two campaigns when I asked him his opinion about the recent interest in Atatürk: "After the 1980 military coup, they forced Atatürk on everyone. I remember soldiers used to bring dozens of Atatürk pictures to my father's electrical-supplies store. All store owners in the mall put them up because they had to, but they didn't care. My father put one up on the side of his desk. He did not even frame it; just attached it with Scotch tape. Other posters yellowed in a corner somewhere." He continued: "In 1980, the army worked very hard but could not accomplish what is happening now by the free will of people. Now people are rushing to buy Atatürk pictures and Turkish flags as if they have been starving for them. And they are doing it completely of their own will."

Sinan later said that his father currently has an Atatürk poster in his store, but it differs from the one the military junta delivered to him. He had purchased a commercial poster and had it framed, rather than attaching it to the wall with Scotch tape. According to my friend, and many other Kemalists in Turkey, the interest in Atatürk in the late 1990s was distinguished by such acts of purchasing Atatürk paraphernalia. The existence of a market for Atatürk's images, in other words, served as a sign of a freewill affection and commitment for the leader, one previously nonexistent when the army had forced the leader on its citizens.

Another comparison between the two Atatürk campaigns comes from Zülfü Livaneli, a social democrat politician, singer, and journalist. Livaneli was one of numerous leftist intellectuals who sought political asylum in Europe in order to escape the brutal oppression of the 1980 military junta. In the late 1990s, he was more of a hard-core Kemalist and anti-Islamist than a leftist interested in the redistribution of wealth. For Republic Day in 1998, he wrote the following piece in the daily *Sabah*:

> Our friends and enemies see that the seventy-fifth anniversary is being celebrated with extraordinary splendor. Millions of people are marching, and the love of Atatürk is growing like a snowball rolling down a hill. And all of this is happening with the will of the people. There is no enforcement as some claim. We need to go back seventeen years [to 1981] in order to understand the contemporary situation better. You remember, [during the 1980 military coup] Kenan Evren wanted to deepen the love of Atatürk with the "Atatürk is one hundred years old" campaign. But because it was a top-down effort, people did not embrace it. Celebrations were limited to the official level. Now, it is the opposite." (Sabah, October 26, 1998)

Livaneli emphasized the voluntary nature of interest in Atatürk in order to stand against the Islamists' complaints about the pressures they faced as a result of the 1997 military intervention. Just as Islamists defined themselves as the genuine voice of the real people who are pressured by the state, the Kemalists stressed that their interest in Atatürk was completely voluntary. The commodification of Atatürk symbolism constituted a new form of showing the kind of support that emphasized citizens' contractual commitment to Kemalist state ideology. The changing content of this symbolism in its commodified form, I argue below, also proved integral to the new message Kemalist consumers sent about the novel ways in which they venerated the state and conceptualized their relationship to it.

THE MINIATURIZATION OF ATATÜRK

The clearest transformation that took place in Atatürk representations during the late 1990s was not only their commercialization but also a decrease in their size. Susan Stewart's (1993) meditations on objects of desire in Western culture provide us with insights into the symbolic importance of size for subject formation. Stewart observes that especially in the West during the eighteenth century, objects of desire commonly took either "gigantic" or "miniature" forms. She argues that the gigantic form, which constitutes an exaggeration of the exterior, is a "metaphor for the abstract authority of the state, and the collective, public life" (xxii). The miniature form, on the other hand, "is a metaphor for the interior space and time of the bourgeois subject" (xii). Although Ottoman political aesthetics differed quite markedly from those of their Western counterparts, Stewart's discussion still proves helpful for studying the recent transformation of Turkish images of the state.[4]

Early representations of Atatürk's imagery were reminiscent of the fascist political aesthetics of 1930s Europe, which emphasized the omnipotent authority of the state through colossal representations of leaders visible in public spaces (Falasca-Zamponi 1997). Even today, traditional representations of Atatürk produced and distributed by the state depict him in massive sizes whenever possible. All city and town centers in Turkey are marked with towering statues of him, the height determined by local budget. During national holidays, state-funded artists paint building-sized portraits of Atatürk on cloth to hang on the largest state buildings.

The 1980 military junta was very successful at covering national time-space with giant representations of Atatürk. In addition to naming all major physical projects for Atatürk, including the largest dams, bridges, and airports, it also covered the mountain slopes with his picture. In 1982, the junta made a mountain portrait of Atatürk in Erzincan, which covered a 7.5-square-kilometer area. The choice of a mountain slope as a canvas for Atatürk's portrait is symbolically meaningful; it establishes an iconical relationship between the leader and the mountains, implying that the leader and the state he founded are as old and as stable as the mountains. Moreover, through his location on mountaintops, Atatürk is seen as above and beyond ordinary human beings. Even today the Turkish army covers mountain slopes with giant pictures and phrases of Atatürk such as "Happy is the one who says I am a Turk." The production of such paintings increases at times of political crisis, and the images especially abound in the Kurdish regions of the country.

A particularly interesting practice of naturalizing Atatürk was invented several years ago in the Yukarı Gündeş village in the Damal region of Ardahan. Every year between June 25 and July 5, thousands of people gather in this isolated Alevi village to watch Atatürk's silhouette appear on a mountain slope just before sunset. The silhouette is formed naturally in a valley where the shadow of one side reflects on the other. The people of Yukarı Gündeş claim they have various reasons to celebrate the Damal Festival in Atatürk's Path and Shadow (Atatürk'ün İzinde ve Gölgesinde

3. An Atatürk portrait hung on a building in Istanbul. The caption reads: "Happy is the one who says I am a Turk."

Damal Şenlikleri) including the traditional Alevi dedication to Atatürk and the hope that the festival will bring some wealth to the poverty-stricken village.[5] The Turkish army and the national media take the event quite seriously and send representatives every year. Photographs of the event testify to a Kemalist miracle and decorate newspapers as well as calendars.[6]

Associating nationalist or state imagery with nature is a common strategy used to cover relations of power (Yanagisako and Delaney 1995). Both Israelis and Palestinians associate their nation and land with trees and forests (Bardenstein 1999). For Venezuelans, oil stands for the power of the state (Coronil 1997). Since the 1930s Atatürk has been associated with the sun that brought the country from darkness to light. The imagery of the sun naturalizes the abstract authority of Atatürk's Westernizing state and its enlightenment discourse, which define the religious Ottoman past as darkness and the secularist Republican future as illumination.

The newly popular and commercialized Atatürk paraphernalia differ significantly from the gigantic and naturalized representations discussed above. Most often, they take miniature forms such as pins, crystal ornaments, or small pictures. As opposed to traditional representations, which

4. Atatürk's shadow in Damal.

occupy public places owned by no one (and, thus, owned only by the state), the miniature representations are displayed in private businesses, homes, and, more important, on the bodies of private citizens, all outside the direct authority of the state. In such miniature forms, Atatürk's representations, although still icons of the state, become a part of the bourgeois subject's domestic sphere. Significantly, these images are privatized through the act of purchase on the market by individual citizens. Possessing and displaying a miniaturized and commercialized Atatürk image in private indicates as personal relationship with the state that an individual citizen chooses to activate through the market mechanisms of consumer choice. Figure 5 shows an example of how Kemalist families willingly include Atatürk's image among their family photographs, turning him, through their own deliberate choice, from a national and stately ancestor imposed on them into a familial one embraced voluntarily.

In examining transformations in Turkish state imagery I follow Bruce Grant's take on the meaning of state monuments that he developed while analyzing the new monuments of Moscow inspired by Russian fairy tales. "The point, then," he claims, "is to see monuments and their mythical

5. A picture of Atatürk placed among family pictures.

properties as a form of political practice itself, rather than as a meta-language derived from the hidden realities. They create new subject effects, new cognitions, and new forms of political legitimacy" (2001, 340). I argue that the new images of Atatürk, too, point to and produce a different state ideal, as well as a subject position for the citizen. The new images reduce the (at least mental) effects of an all-powerful state that forces itself on its citizens and suggest a less controlling one to which citizens can relate less hierarchically through their own choice. Yet despite its seemingly diminished power, state symbolism still proliferates in private places considered outside the state realm.

THE GIANT AND THE MINIATURE AS METAPHORS

The contrast between the gigantic and miniature representations of Ata-türk in the late 1990s was not limited to their physical size but emerged in the metaphorical realm as well. Representations of Atatürk as a super-natural human, and more specifically, a progenitor of the whole nation and the country, were created during the early years of the Republican regime. Such portrayals were created to inspire the masses to unquestioningly admire and valorize the leader, and they coexisted with more humane ones that circulated among the limited circles of the Kemalist elite. It is very likely that the image of Atatürk as a parent made it possible for citizens to perceive him both as a stately giant and a humane family member. The gigantic portrayals were especially promoted by the military officials of the 1980 coup, who wanted to invoke a strong and unified image of the state. In the 1990s, although the metaphorically gigantic portrayals have not disappeared, other images that depict him as an ordinary human with a social life and desires have been exceptionally popular.

The political scientist Claude Lefort (1986) claims that the idea of creation lies at the center of totalitarian politics. Totalitarian leaders who derive their legitimacy from creating a new world out of an older one usually come to be depicted as creators themselves. Mussolini (Falasca-Zamponi 1997), Lenin (Tumarkin 1983), and Mao (Yang 1994) were fetishized as semigodly leaders who created a new world for their nations. As a totalitarian leader, a contemporary to others, Atatürk has also frequently been depicted as a progenitor and, sometimes, as a creator. Atatürk as progenitor is reflected best in his last name, literally Father Turk or Ancestor Turk, which he adopted in 1934 following the law of last names (Delaney 1995).[7]

The concept of Atatürk progenitor was used most recently as a theme for an advertisement entitled "The Unending Dance" ("Bitmeyen Dans"), funded by the Turkish government for the seventy-fifth anniversary of the republic in 1998 and broadcast on CNN in the United States and on Turkish televison.[8] The commercial was based on a famous photograph of Atatürk dancing with one of his adopted daughters during her wedding. In the ad, actors recreate the moment when Atatürk and the bride dance a waltz. Later, other couples join them on the dance floor. The commercial continues with images of the industrial and technological developments that followed the foundation of the republic in 1923. At the end, a male voice says, "The Turkish Republic is rooted and strong as if a thousand years old, and is young and dynamic as if one year old. This dance will never end."

Although the original picture depicts Atatürk's adopted daughter's wedding, Atatürk appears in the ad as the groom, dressed in a black tuxedo and dancing with a bride in white. In this commercial, Atatürk, the father of Turks, metaphorically marries Turkey, which takes the form of a bride. Atatürk's marriage with Turkey gives birth to the Turkish nation represented first by the other couples joining in the dance and then by the industrial and technological developments depicted following the wedding scene.

In their psychological biography of Atatürk, Namık Volkan and Norman Itzkowitz (1984) argue that the leader stands both as a mother and a father to the Turks, bearing characteristics of both. These authors are correct in the sense that Atatürk is usually represented as the sole progenitor of Turkey. The ad described above, which includes a woman, is not typical. One elderly Kemalist woman whom I interviewed succinctly voiced the common perspective on Atatürk as the gender-neutral parent when she said, "Atatürk is my mother, my father, the water I drink, and the earth I step on. I am thankful [minnettarim] to Atatürk, the father of fathers, for everything I have." In keeping with her perspective on the leader, this woman had decorated her apartment in Istanbul only with pictures of her mother, father, and Atatürk; both of the latter, she told me, have the same death anniversary.

A more classic representation of Atatürk's generative powers was depicted again on the cover of the October 29 issue of Milliyet for the seventy-fifth anniversary of the republic. The newspaper section carries a colored drawing of Atatürk's eyes, the bushy eyebrows and distinctive blue irises familiar to Turkish readers as his. Underneath the drawing of his eyes are eleven photographs showing technological and military developments and the activities of modern youth. These pictures include children playing computer games and the guitar; girls with short skirts in gymnastic demonstrations; major construction projects such as the Keban water dam, the Bosporus Bridge, Istanbul metro, and skyscrapers; the first Turkish satellite; and finally, military equipment including F-16 planes and tanks. The only writing on the page, found at the bottom in red, reads, "Your creation" (senin eserin). In the image, Atatürk'e eyes appear otherworldly, as if he were watching his creations like a god. All of these images of youth and children engaged in Western activities and technological developments are meant to be seen as his creations or children.

The way Kemalist citizens feel indebted to Atatürk and attribute everything they have to him can be understood best when we think about his role as a parent. The anthropologist Nükhet Sirman (1990) writes about how elderly men in Turkish villages struggle to keep their role as providers of land for the younger generations, since it is one of the major sources of their authority. When parents are the only providers, children are always considered indebted to them. The parenthood right (*ana-babalık hakkı*) and the milk right (*süt hakkı*) stand for all the gifts impossible to reciprocate parents have given their offspring. In turn, the offspring provide the parents with a right to expect respect and care in old age. Even then, the offspring cannot repay their debt. According to the nationalist discourse, Atatürk is another parent, particularly a father, to whom citizens should feel indefinitely indebted.

HUMANIZED ATATÜRK

Although metaphorically gigantic representations of Atatürk were still produced and distributed in the late 1990s, representations that reduced him to an ordinary human being, simply a man rather than a semigod or even a father, also became widespread. Atatürk's private life, especially his relationships with women, became an increasingly popular subject for depiction. *Mustafa Kemal'le 1000 gün* (*One Thousand Days with Atatürk*), a 1993 book by Nezihe Araz that concentrates on Atatürk's relationship with his wife, set the tone. Araz, a devoted Kemalist and the daughter of a parliamentarian who served in Atatürk's single-party government in the 1930s, states in her acknowledgments that she wrote the book in order to present Atatürk as a mere person to new generations. This approach, she believes, would help to defend the leader against recent criticism from Islamists and liberal intellectuals: "For the first generation of the republic, Atatürk was not a human but almost a god from Olympus. He was an abstract concept, a godly power that could make the impossible possible and perform miracles. Even if people saw him on the roads of Ankara, in his car, in the National Assembly, and sometimes in schools, sport arenas, horse races, they actually could not perceive him" (2–3). Araz believes that godly representations of Atatürk, even if done with good intentions, are wrong, because they lead people to question his legacy. If she can show the human side of Atatürk as a person with weaknesses, she hopes people will feel closer to him. The trend Araz started by discussing the leader's human qualities reached its climax when the state-sponsored movie *Cumhuriyet* (*The Republic*), directed by Ziya Öztan, concentrated in 1998 on Atatürk's personal life.[9] The central story of the movie revolves around Atatürk's relationship with two women—his common-law wife, Fikriye, and his wife, Latife, from whom he was later divorced.[10] Dolunay Sert, who portrayed Latife, said in a newspaper interview, "The movie is similar to a documentary. We wanted to break some taboos and shed light on some things. Atatürk is a great leader, but he is also a human. There is a very human side in his relations to Latife and Fikriye" (Radikal, October 29, 1998). The unprecedented nature of the movie becomes clear when one considers a previous movie sponsored by the official television channel that deals with the Greco-Turkish war. Even though that movie, shot ten years earlier, had the same director, scriptwriter, and lead actor as The Republic, it never made mention of Atatürk's personal life.

The Republic had a record number of viewers across the country. Its audience was swelled by students taken to watch the film by their teachers. I viewed it in a theater filled with middle and high school students who were so moved by the film that they booed for Atatürk's wife, whom they did not like, and clapped for the leader when he divorced her. Most of the students learned about personal aspects of Atatürk's life for the first time through this film. After the movie was released, I heard and participated in many conversations about Atatürk's personal life. Atatürk's life, which had been confined to classrooms and political speeches, entered new spheres such as the gossip circles of family, friends, and neighbors.

The fact that artists could portray Atatürk in such diverse settings as movies, fashion shows, and other events also points to the trend to depict him as an ordinary human. Until the 1980s, actors were not able to portray Atatürk in movies and plays. Although Atatürk himself appeared in many documentaries, his portrayal by another actor was a taboo that lasted for more than forty years after his death.[11] During his lifetime Atatürk wanted Russian directors experienced in making propagandistic documentaries to make a movie about his life. Significantly, rather than having a professional actor depict him, Atatürk suggested that he portray himself, that he wear his old clothes and act out what he had done in previous years. Such a film, however, was never made (Dorsay 1990). The anthropologists Richard and Nancy Tapper note that the taboo of portraying Atatürk much resembles that of the Prophet Muhammad. In the Saudi Arabian–funded 1976 movie about the life of Muhammad, Al risalah (The Message), directed by Moustapha Akkad, the prophet never appears on the screen. When the anthropologist couple asked residents of Eğridir, Turkey, why they thought no actor had ever played Muhammad or Atatürk, they pointed to the impossibility of such an idea: "What men could possibly play such parts?" (1991, 70).

The taboo of portraying Atatürk was first broken in 1981, when a movie about his life was released for his one hundredth birth anniversary. It is significant that the first actor to portray Atatürk was not Turkish but Belgian. As a European actor, Marc Mopty did not challenge the belief that it was impossible to cast a local actor as the leader. A few years after this biopic, filmed at the end of the 1980s, Turkish actors started to play Atatürk in movies, and by the late 1990s, there were almost no limits on who might perform as Atatürk. Along with The Republic, numerous plays depicted Atatürk like any other historical figure.

The trend toward depicting the human, rather than the almighty authoritarian, side of Atatürk also began to be reflected in his statues. The great majority of Atatürk sculptures that stand today are replicas of the original statues made by European artists and commissioned during the leader's lifetime. In the late 1990s several artists made innovative paintings and sculptures of Atatürk showing his human side. The first such painting that received public attention was made by the well-known Kemalist artist Bedri Baykam, who depicted Atatürk playing backgammon. During our conversation about his painting, Baykam declared that he had wanted "to show the leader as a bon vivant, who loves good conversation, pretty women, alcohol, and playing backgammon. You know," he added with a smile on his face, "he was a real human being." This piece by Baykam, which was never sold or displayed in public other than in an avant-garde gallery, did not raise controversy. A public sculpture depicting Atatürk smiling, however, caused heated public debate. This piece was made in 1998 in Sincan, a religious town that had witnessed a controversial pro-Palestinian Jerusalem Night meeting in 1997, organized by the Islamist Welfare Party. The day after this meeting, the secular Turkish army rolled their tanks through the streets of the town as a warning to Islamists who had made a call for implementing Islamic law during the gathering. The appointed governor of the town and the Atatürkist Thought Association ordered the sculptor Burhan Alkar to make a statue for the town square for the seventy-fifth anniversary of the republic. The sculptor depicted Atatürk as smiling and opening his arms wide to young girls presenting a bunch of tulips to him. After the statue was erected, the governor Ali Gün expressed concern that it was inappropriate to represent Atatürk smiling; rather, he felt the leader should be portrayed as a serious person. Gün even appealed to the Association of Artists and Owners of Fine Arts, asking it to report on the appropriateness of this Atatürk depiction. He told journalists that if the report was not in favor of the sculpture, he would go to court and make sure that it was removed. According to newspapers reports, the vice president of the association had declared that his organization would not interfere with the freedom of the artist and that it approved the statue. In the end, the statue was unveiled for the seventy-fifth anniversary, revealing the first publicly smiling Atatürk.

FROM HEAD TO BODY

Another contrast between the stately and commercial representations of Atatürk concerns a new representation that transforms the leader from an authoritative head to a full-bodied human being. The traditional images of Atatürk, especially those displayed by law in government offices, are limited to his upper body. These portraits, reproductions of photographs or paintings, usually include his neck and shoulders and reveal either a military or a civilian outfit. In addition to portraits, state offices frequently display sculpted busts, which often depict Atatürk's head, but not his shoulders or neck. The statues of Atatürk decorating all city and town centers in the country do display his body. Most of the time, however, the body is clearly sculpted with much less care than the head and often violates even the most basic anatomical rules. It appears as if the body functions as an elevated stand on which to carry the head, the part that receives the most care and attention.

Such a focus on the leader's head borrows from both contemporary Western political aesthetics and Turkish physical anthropological inquiry. In contrast to Western political imagery, sultans in Ottoman miniatures were almost always depicted in full figure (Necipoğlu 2000). At the same time that commissioned European sculptors were working hard to create the most impressive representation of Atatürk's head, a few Turkish anthropologists, including Atatürk's surrogate wife Afet İnan, traveled in Anatolia taking skull measurements in order to prove that the Turkish "race" was the ancestor of all civilizations. Following Atatürk's orders in 1937, İnan conducted the most extensive anthropometric survey to date and took skull measurements of 64,000 people in Anatolia and Trace (Aydın

2001). Her aim was to contest the allegations that Turks belonged to the "secondary yellow race" and show that instead they formed part of the white European homo alpinus race, and also that Turks consisted of a homogenous race.[12] In her research, she defined the characteristics of the Turkish race with fair skin, a straight nose, and blue or green eyes (see Aydın 2001, 362). A small percentage of Turkish citizens, including Atatürk, have features that fit the characteristics listed, but such a physiognomic description leaves most of the population out of the "Turkish race." İnan's selective definition of the Turk idealized Atatürk's, or the ancestor Turk's, head as representative of the perfect (read European) race that the Turkish nation was now aiming to be a part of.

Atatürk's head, on display, not only represented the perfect cranium of the Turkish nation but also indexed the nature of power in the new state. Placing Atatürk's head in a state office turned everything and everyone in the surrounding space into an extension of his head—in other words, into his body. This became possible only after turning the masses into the body of a nation, a process that Claude Lefort (1986) describes as making "People-as-One" in fascist politics. What Mayfair Mei-hui Yang (1994) argues for the Mao cult holds true for the cult of Atatürk as well. The flattening of differences and a general homogenization creates the body of society and places every individual at an equal distance from the head. Yang defines this process as "a unified body and a single head" (264).

As opposed to the solemn and solitary portraits limited to his head, Atatürk's newly popular photos in the 1990s depict him in full body and in social contexts. Moreover, in most of these pictures, Atatürk is laughing, dancing, and enjoying simple pleasures such as eating or playing with his youngest adopted daughter, Ülkü. When I asked a street peddler in Istanbul, who mainly sold Atatürk pictures, to identify the most popular pictures in his stand, he pointed to one of Atatürk drinking coffee on a white wicker chair. He then pointed to a solemn bust portrait in military outfit as the least popular one. He said, "No one buys this kind of picture anymore." The civilians who want an approachable, egalitarian image of Atatürk were repelled by his pictures reminiscent of the official portraits, especially those in military outfits.

Some consumers told me that what drew them to a certain picture was Atatürk's smiling, unofficial expression, which was something they had never seen before. Consider the following narrative of a forty-year-old

6. A popular picture of Atatürk sold in the market.

bank employee, discussing his excitement when he saw such a picture on sale, leading him to purchase an Atatürk portrayal for the first time in his life:

> Three years ago, I saw an amazing picture in the window of a photo store. They had colored it, enlarged it, and put it in the window. I heard about it through a friend and went there to check it out. It was so different from the ones we are used to. He was lying down on the grass, singing with the villagers. Clearly he was drunk, and he looked so happy. I loved this picture; I immediately bought the picture for myself. Then my father-in-law saw it, and then I gave it to him and bought another one for myself.

The sight of Atatürk in social contexts and engaged in pleasurable activities has created excitement among Kemalist citizens. A picture of Atatürk drinking, lying on the ground, and singing with villagers differs dramatically from those that hang in government offices. Such pictures, which include the whole body of the leader and show him engaged in mundane activities, also help to desacralize him. His smile reminds the viewers of the joy and happiness experienced in the 1930s. Furthermore, the photographs allow the viewer to establish a more equal relationship with him. By giving more contextual clues about the state he was in, such pictures refer to him as a part of the past rather than of the present. The less hierarchical position of the leader located in the past creates the emotional space needed for consumer-citizens to admire the leader and then to purchase his representation.

Because of the way they reflect Atatürk's daily life, these pictures also serve as icons of a Westernized, secular, and bourgeois lifestyle. Photographs of Atatürk in which he poses at rakı tables (rakı is the national alcoholic beverage flavored with anise) have proven especially popular among secular Turks, who started to see their lifestyle threatened after the victory of political Islam in the 1990s. Thereafter, Kemalism represented not only the state ideology but also a secular and bourgeois lifestyle particular to Turkey, which involved wearing European clothes, having mixed-gender social gatherings, and drinking alcohol. The newly popular pictures of the leader associated certain commodities and expenditure contexts with his teachings and encouraged Kemalist citizens to practice a consumption-based political identity.

CHANGING RELATIONS OF THE GAZE

The traditional and commercial representations of Atatürk also differ in the quality of the gaze displayed in each type of image. The former representations and narratives of Atatürk tended to focus on his eyes, familiar to Turkish citizens. Occasionally, traditional Atatürk representations are even limited to his eyes, as in a relief or painting in which he metaphorically watches his citizens. There are many rumors about the special quality of Atatürk's eyes, including about his supposed ability to look right into the eye of every single person in a crowd. His contemporaries also reported that it was impossible for people to look directly into his eyes (Volkan and Itzkowitz 1984; Urgan 1998). Sixty or even seventy years later, elderly teachers I interviewed still trembled with fear, joy, and pride as they recounted the moment they made eye contact with the founding leader during parades.

In his discussion of the Ottoman imperial order, Michael Meeker (2002) suggests valuable clues to the roots in Turkish-Ottoman political culture of this fascination with and fear of Atatürk's gaze. Based on an analysis of the ceremonial architecture of the Topkapi Palace in Istanbul, Meeker argues that the sultan's gaze was so central to his rule that it was inscribed in the structural design: the elevated pierced windows and the overlooks represent "the sight of the sovereign" (1119). Meeker contends that "each instance of the relationship [of gaze and rule] symbolizes the sovereign situated within an interior space overlooking an external space occupied by subjects" (119). Although such overlooks may make the palace appear like a Benthamian panopticon, Meeker maintains that the place is essentially different from a modern prison because the one who is looking out of these windows is the sultan himself, rather than some other ward.

It is clear that Atatürk inherited the authority associated with the personal gaze of the ruler from his Ottoman predecessors and utilized it effectively to symbolize the new kind of powers the Republican regime aimed for in engaging with its citizens. Unlike the sultan who observed his subjects only from the pierced windows and without being seen, Atatürk presented his citizens with a direct and thus reciprocal gaze available to any individual willing to greet him in public. This new practice was not only shocking to contemporary citizens but also proved representative of the new and direct gaze of the Republican regime. Atatürk's frequent tours around the country during his presidency, and the fact that all students in the area were made to parade in front of him, have proven important to the creation of citizenship as a new sense of subjectivity. In his study of the nineteenth-century Meiji era, Takashi Fujitani argues that similar instances of imperial pageantry "coerced people into becoming objects of the emperor's gaze" (1996, 24). This created an interiorized sense of surveillance, hence turning the populace into citizenry. Turkish subjects already found themselves under the ruler's surveillance long before the new regime was established. Yet the newly widespread availability of the ruler's gaze and the direct relationship with it citizens could engage in symbolized a new and symbolically unmediated relationship between the state and the citizen.

Unlike the situation under Ottoman sultans who, on death, smoothly passed on the duty of gazing at the imperial subjects to their sons, Republican rule is still closely linked with Atatürk's gaze. More than seventy years after his death, Atatürk still keeps his citizens under surveillance through the millions of painted and sculpted busts that decorate public spaces throughout the country. Elementary school students memorize poems about the power of Atatürk's gaze as if he were personally looking at them through pictures. Although not linked to any technology with surveillance capabilities, Atatürk's pictures in the state's modernized institutions—schools, hospitals, prisons, factories—are reminiscent of the undifferentiatingly disciplining gaze of the modern state (Foucault 1979). Ironically, attaching a person's face to such a gaze helps to depersonalize the real officials who carry out the regulations.

The following poem entitled "The Picture" ("Resim"), authored by the nationalist poet Behçet Necatigil and commonly learned in elementary school, teaches students how to feel about Atatürk's pictures, which face them in every classroom:

We work hard	Çalışkanız çünkü
Because when we work	Çalışınca
We see Atatürk smiles	Bakarız Atatürk güldü
When we make a mistake	Bir yanlışlık yapsak
His eyes get cloudy	Bulutlanır gözleri
We understand	Anlarız
Atatürk became sad	Atatürk üzüldü
If we go right next to the wall	Gelsek kürsünün dibine
He still sees us	Görür bizi
As he looks down	Eğilince
If we go all the way back	Kalksak gitsek gerilere
If we sit at the back	Otursak arkalarda
We feel without lifting our head up	Başımızı kaldırmadan duyarız
Atatürk is there	Atatürk orada
. . .	
Atatürk, through my life	Atatürk artık ömrüm oldukça
You are in front of me with this picture	Bu resminle karşımdasın
. . .	
Just like in the classroom	Tıpkı sınıftaki gibi
In everything I do	Yapacağım bir işte
This picture is my guide	Bu resimdir rehberim
If I reach toward something bad	Kötülüğe uzanırsam
Frown your eyes	Çat kaşlarını

Let my hands freeze	*Tutulsun ellerim*
Just like in the classroom	*Tıpkı sınıftaki gibi*
Through my whole life	*Bütün ömrüm boyunca*
In everything I do	*Yaptığım her işte*
If I am right and good	*İyi doğru oldumsa*
Show me your happiness	*Sevincini belli et*
Smile	*Gülümse*

Many of his followers believe that Atatürk's eyes had other special abilities such as seeing the future in a way that ordinary people could not. In 1998, Ali Bektan published *Prophecies of Atatürk (Atatürk'ün kehanetleri)*. Despite being printed on cheap paper, the book's red cover is striking, emphasizing Atatürk's radiant blue eyes. Prepared by Bektan, a journalist, after eighteen years of research, the book argues that Atatürk had a supernatural power to predict the future: "Why did Mustafa Kemal have access to this skill? Because he had a mission. . . . He was going to save the country. . . . He was going to found a brand-new modern state on top of the crumbling Ottoman Empire. . . . Atatürk used his ability to predict the future while encountering difficulties during this process. We can accept that he received this power from God" (31).

Bektan's book contains a list of cases in which Atatürk predicted the future. These events range from simple facts relating to his own life to military attacks and international developments that would take place after his death. The author notes, for example, that Atatürk predicted that World War II would take place, and he noted that it would be begun by Germany and ended by the United States. He also predicted that the USSR would split at the end of the century. The Turkish general Çevik Bir, at a May 1998 NATO meeting, also mentioned how Atatürk predicted these international developments. The forecasting ability of the modernizing leader and the state promised to propel the nation toward a utopian future.

Although pictures of Atatürk keep looking at students and all other citizens, the newly popular pictures offer a different kind of gaze between leader and citizen. In most of these pictures, Atatürk does not look back at the camera, and thus at the viewer. His attention is often concentrated on the activity in which he is engaged, such as rowing, dancing, or watching military games. In the most popular picture on the street peddler's stand, Atatürk is sipping coffee and holding a cigarette. His eyes are either closed, or he is looking into the coffee cup. As one looks at the picture, one can tell how much Atatürk is enjoying the coffee. In other words, the founding father is indulging in pleasure rather than screening the people around him.

Looking at a picture in which Atatürk does not gaze back gives pleasure to the viewer rather than instilling fear. In the widespread exhibition of Atatürk's photographs in social contexts for the seventy-fifth anniversary of the republic in 1998, I frequently observed that visitors approached the pictures closely, enjoying the rare pleasure of looking closely at Atatürk without him looking back at them. Many times I heard cheerful exclamations such as, "He is such a handsome man!" Only in pictures in which Atatürk does not look back could visitors see in him a fellow individual and comment on his looks. In November 1998, for the sixtieth anniversary of his death, numerous daily newspapers published photo spreads of Atatürk, emphasizing that these were "very special" or "never before seen" pictures. They showed him not as a leader but as an individual engaged in mundane activities, like any other human being. Although not a secret, these photographs had not been widely circulated or popularly consumed. The phrase "never before seen" alluded to a sense of lifting the veil and looking at Atatürk in a way never before possible.

SELLING WITH ATATÜRK

In the late 1990s, Atatürk was not only a popular commercial image. He also became a common figure in commercial advertisements used to sell other products. Especially during the seventy-fifth anniversary of the Turkish Republic and the sixtieth anniversary of Atatürk's death in 1998, the pages of mainstream newspapers were covered with advertisements using Atatürk as the main image. In Turkey, it is an established practice for companies to take out advertisements wishing happy holidays to their customers for religious and national holidays. However, until the late 1990s, these advertisements were small and consisted of a few words in a frame, such as "Pelin cologne wishes you a happy holiday."

Between late October and early November 1998, I counted fifty-one different companies that displayed ads in newspapers either using the image of Atatürk and/or his words. Depending on their budget, some companies displayed full-page color ads; others took out smaller black-and-white ones. On October 29, for example, *Sabah*, a mass-circulated daily newspaper, had a total of 96 pictures of Atatürk in advertisements, in addition to 225 other pictures of Atatürk the newspaper published that day.[13] Despite the abundance of Atatürk images, companies used his image to bring visibility to their own companies and products.[14] Such advertisements and events depicted Atatürk as a bourgeois leader educating citizens to become elite consumers.

Textile companies, a booming industry after Turkey's integration with the global market in the 1980s, used Atatürk's taste for elegant dress in their advertisements and made references to his elite taste as a consumer. Sarar, for example, advertised their company with the following sentence under a picture of Atatürk in a nice coat: "He taught us how to dress." A fashion show organized for the sixtieth anniversary of Atatürk's death also emphasized how he led the Turkish nation toward being good consumers, at least in style. On November 10, Faruk Saraç, a fashion designer, displayed over forty of Atatürk's outfits that he had replicated to a select audience. Famous models displayed his clothes as Atatürk's original pictures were reflected on a screen. In a newspaper interview about the event, the designer said: "Atatürk used to wear the long tuxedo jackets that became fashionable in Europe and in Turkey in the past two years, and he did this in the year 1919. Through preparing this show, I came to realize that Atatürk was a leader in fashion as well" (Milliyet, October 19, 1998).

Although still referring to his role as the teacher, envisioner, and leader, such advertisements emphasize the bourgeois nature of his wisdom. Such a representation for Atatürk was a novel construct that appeared in the late 1990s. It differed radically from the traditional view of the early Republican years under Atatürk's leadership, which emphasized state controlled production and undermined consumption, as a period of hardship. The view of Atatürk as an elite consumer reflects more of a desired model for the contemporary state than a historical argument about the founding state.

Interestingly enough, a great number of companies that used Atatürk's images were of foreign origin, including Mitsubishi, Nokia, Phillips, and Panasonic. Such companies made special efforts to emphasize their loyalty to the founding father and his principles by using Atatürk's images. For example, an advertisement for Mitsubishi air conditioners included a well-known picture of Atatürk sleeping on snow during the national liberation war.[15] Under the picture, it says: "We wanted to remind you of the difficul-

7. The Dufy shirt advertisement using Atatürk.

ties involved during the founding of the republic." Panasonic fax machine sellers used a common portrait of Atatürk and wrote only, "He is totally different." Nokia had a picture of Turkey's map, turned around by ninety degrees, creating an erect rather than flat rectangle. Inserted in the map was a picture of Atatürk in civilian clothes and the caption: "We are standing upright thanks to you." None of these advertisements have any direct reference to the products the companies are selling. Rather than being about the product, advertisements were actually about the company, declaring their allegiance to the Turkish Republic, its founding father, and his principles. Using pictures of Atatürk became a way to localize the global companies in the context of a new market-based Turkish nationalism.

Turkish companies' advertisements similarly emphasized dedication to Atatürk rather than focusing on products. The firms used the ads as an opportunity to show their success in fulfilling the foundational goals of Atatürk. For example, the shirt company Dufy's advertisement included a picture of Atatürk in a tuxedo shirt and a picture of a folded tuxedo. Underneath his picture, Atatürk says: "We do not need anything, other than hard work!" Next to it, Dufy replies: "We worked hard! At the seventy-fifth anniversary of the republic, we are selling Dufy shirts to the world." The main slogan of the advertisement was, "We are proud of our Father [Atamızla] and our collar [yakamızla]."

A popular weekly magazine, Aktüel, published a news article about this advertisement. The article says:

> There is a shirt that reminds us of Atatürk no matter where we see it: Ata collar shirts. Today Ata collar shirts are a symbol of modernity, just like they were in the 1920s. In 1923 Atatürk said, "No matter how big political and military victories are, they will not be continuous if they are not crowned by economic victories. They will deflate in a short period." To-day, Dufy's high-tech factories produce chic shirts with care. Millions of men around the world wear Turkish shirts. By exporting shirts, Dufy helps the economic victory Atatürk had defined. (Korkut 1998, 212–13)

As the weekly interpreted the ad, Dufy was making two statements. First, the company successfully managed to associate their product with the image of Atatürk. Even though at the turn of the twentieth century the entire Ottoman elite wore tuxedos and tuxedo shirts, this practice came to be associated with Atatürk, the modernizing father of the country, to such an extent that the shirts are named Ata collar shirts. As the article states, these shirts symbolize a modern and elite lifestyle as much as does the leader. Thus wearing Dufy shirts involves a political statement about the kind of lifestyle people prefer and associate with the founding father. Second, as a company, Dufy demonstrated that it has been successful in achieving one of Atatürk's goals. In the advertisement, it proudly replies to a statement Atatürk made over sixty years ago.

A private bank, Bankexpress, also used the popular tool of using one of the leader's phrases and then answering back to him. The ad first displays Atatürk's phrase: "What the Republic wants from you is generations with a free mind, a free conscience." Like Dufy, Bankexpress replies proudly: "The smart, hardworking, cultured new generations that were dreamt of seventy-five years ago for the future of the Turkish Republic are now work-ing for you at Bankexpress." The picture in the ad shows the collar of a jacket adorned with two pins: one of Atatürk and one of Bankexpress.

Other companies, too, have bragged about how they have been instru-mental in fulfilling Atatürk's goals. In its ad the consulting company SAP states: "His purpose was to bring Turkey to the level of developed na-tions. Our aim is to help Turkish corporations compete at the international level. . . . We commemorate the seventy-fifth year of all Republicans who aim to carry our country to the future." Such positive statements about reaching Atatürk's goals contradict the negative evaluation of politicians' achievements in this direction. It appears that once again, private business, outside the authority of the state, is taking the initiative and doing better in achieving his aims. In other words, SAP redefines Atatürk's claim about making Turkey rise to stand "at the level of developed nations" in terms of being an international business partner, although the early republic was more of a closed economy. According to this new definition, SAP declares its business as an important step toward fulfilling Atatürk's goals.

In many of these advertisements Turkish as well as international companies depict themselves as the ones who best fulfill the original intentions of Atatürk and best serve the interests of the Turkish state. The uniqueness of this approach becomes more apparent when we consider that in Turkey, private interest has commonly been seen to contradict good citizenship's prioritizing of common goals (Kadıoğlu 1998). The increasing popularity of the market-based model of citizenship based on voluntarism and independence from the state, however, made it possible for private companies working for profit to represent themselves as ideal citizens. In these advertisements, private companies propagated the idea that only they, not state officials, could fulfill the Kemalist goals of the Turkish Republic through their private engagement in the market.

CONCLUSION

In the late 1990s, and especially during the seventy-fifth anniversary of the Turkish Republic in 1998, radical transformations took place in the content and circulation of Atatürk's imagery. In opposition to his old images—depicting him as serious, solemn, and superhuman—the newly popular pictures portrayed him as a smiling human happily engaged in social activities and mundane pleasures. What I call the new and privatized images were not, in fact, new discoveries or creations, but old photographs of Atatürk dusted from the archives of private collectors. The novelty was the popular attention these pictures received, as well as their commodifiction. In the meantime, the old or traditional images kept being reproduced by and for state offices in great numbers in the 1990s.

The commodification of the Turkish state's most potent symbol indicates a transformation of the kind of state ideal at least some citizens aspire to and promote. The gigantic depictions of Atatürk promoted and distributed by the government produced and pointed to an omnipotent and omnipresent view of the state. Such depictions naturalized Atatürk and turned everyone around him into his natural extensions, into his body as the head of all. In the late 1990s, large groups of Turkish citizens preferred to purchase miniaturized representations of Atatürk that they could carry to their private domains and of which they could claim personal ownership. The mere act of personally choosing and purchasing what has traditionally been an icon of the Turkish state created a new kind of relationship with the idea of the state, one based on the free will and voluntary choice of the private citizen. The more "human" images of Atatürk, wherein viewers could see his whole body and establish a reciprocal gaze, pointed toward a more equal and personalized relationship between the state and its citizens. Furthermore, it allowed subjects to conceptualize their relationship as a market exchange based on the freedom of private consumer choice.

The recent conflation of consumerism and politics is far from unique to Turkey (Crouch, Eder, and Tambini 2001). In the Turkish case, the market-based relationship with the state gave a new kind of legitimacy to the Turkish state in the neoliberal era. The act of purchasing and privatizing a state icon proved that citizens supported the state and its official ideology by their own free will. Furthermore, in this model, private companies could conceptualize themselves as ideal citizens who contributed to the economy and at the same time financed the privatized publicity of Atatürk and his ideology. These acts of consumer choice celebrated the ideology of the market yet at the same time allowed the most potent symbol of the state to enter into nonstate and intimate domains such as homes and businesses. This melding of market symbolism and etatism transformed the very nature of the political field and created a new understanding of governmentality in Turkey.

In the next chapter, I will turn my attention to the privatization of another momentous symbol of the Turkish state: the celebration of the republic on its seventy-fifth anniversary.

CHAPTER 4

Hand in Hand with the Republic

Civilian Celebrations of the Turkish State

Over the past several decades, Republic Day celebrations, which commemorate the declaration of the Turkish Republic on October 29, 1923, have been limited to poorly attended military and student parades in stadiums or town centers and badly acted and outmoded nationalist skits in schools. In the mid-1990s, however, civil society organizations—supported and funded by Turkish state officials—organized participatory celebrations as a way to oppose Islamists and Kurdish separatists and demonstrate popular support for the nationalist and secularist ideals of the Turkish Republic. Nongovernmental organizations coordinated an impressive and festive celebration for the seventy-fifth anniversary in 1998 involving masses of citizens. The citizen-organized celebrations looked quite different from previous ones as hundreds of thousands of people filled major town and city squares (rather than stadiums), danced to popular music (rather than watching parades of students marching), and shouted slogans about how they would protect the Turkish Republic and its secularist principles (rather than remaining quietly observant).

The seventy-fifth anniversary was modeled on the nostalgic memory of the mythologized tenth-anniversary celebration of 1933. Organizers and participants recalled the earlier celebration as a truly popular event that captured the unifying and transformative spirit of the early republic. Many of the celebratory activities in 1998, such as the Creating a Citizen exhibit I discussed in a previous chapter, emulated the organizational forms of the tenth anniversary. Although a new march was composed for the seventy-fifth anniversary, all events were marked by the repeated singings of the tenth anniversary march—sometimes pumped up by a pop star's new recording—giving participants the enthusiastic spirit of the earlier anniversary during which the state and its citizens seemed to be united in the nationalist cause.

This chapter compares the official descriptions of the tenth-anniversary celebrations organized by the single-party regime in 1933 with the first civil society–organized celebration of 1998. It suggests that the seventy-fifth anniversary utilized market-inspired symbols such as civilian participation, voluntarism, and spontaneity to carry the celebration out of the symbolic field of the state into the realms of civil society and the market. The celebrations also became a way to display and orchestrate a shared passion for the Turkish Republic and the feeling of a unified public against its critics. Yet many of these emotions and symbols introduced as brand-new and nonstate actually had their roots in the corporatist nationalism of early Republican ideology and its celebratory symbolism. Thus I argue that the nongovernmental organizers of the seventy-fifth anniversary celebration were able to successfully blend the key symbols of 1930s state-led modernity with those of the market-led modernity of the 1990s, creating something simultaneously new and old.

THE POPULAR CELEBRATION OF THE NEW REGIME

The 1933 tenth-anniversary celebration of the young republic constitutes one of the benchmark events almost any Kemalist elderly citizen I interviewed recollected fondly and as one of the most significant events of her or his childhood. Even those not old enough to have participated in the event shared the nationalist nostalgia toward it. During my or other researchers' interviews, the elderly frequently complained that the contemporary holidays did not compare with the older ones. Consider the retired movie director Turgut Özakman's comparison of the Republic Day celebrations in the 1930s with those of today:[1]

Let me tell you about holidays during my childhood. They were not artifi- 𝐴
cial like they are today. People were sincere and very passionate. I don't
even remember if the state had an influence on the holidays. We didn't feel
anything like that. In those days my father used to be a worker, and we
lived in a very modest house. But during Republic Day my father would
decorate the house with bay branches, and he would put up electric bulbs
in the shape of a crescent and a moon. Was it only my father doing such
things? No! Everyone was like that. Everyone tried to match their house to
the holiday spirit. You cannot accomplish this with force or by a decree
from the municipality. It has to be voluntary. . . . Now holidays are cold.
They are official, distant, and detached from the people. Or maybe the
people do not have the necessary consciousness to participate.

Similar to Özakman's account, contemporary publications of the single-
party regime repeatedly emphasized enthusiasm as the key aspect of the
tenth-anniversary celebration. The original celebration program, for example, prescribed the event to be celebrated "enthusiastically, sincerely, and
collectively for three days and nights" (Behnan 1934, 6). Whether the 1933
celebration was truly collective and sincere or not, this is how the event is
inscribed into Kemalist collective memory.

The authoritarian single-party regime put together an impressive tenth-
anniversary celebration, especially when one considers the dire economic
conditions the country found itself in. At the time, the young republic
had declared its independence, delineated its national territory, completed
most of its Westernizing reforms, and solidified the authority of the single-
party regime. The tenth anniversary celebrated these accomplishments. At
the same time, it displayed popular support for the authoritarian Kemalist
regime that had suppressed all possible oppositional groups.[2] More important, the anniversary aimed to create a new historical continuity, and
thus subjectivity, for the new nation-state, as well as cut off its ties from its
Ottoman past. Scholars of nationalism (Bhabha 1990; Duara 1995; Gills
1994) have indicated the split tendency of nationalist history to narrate the
nation both as an eternal and a novel subject. In her discussion of Turkish
national time, Alev Çınar states that "one of the vital mechanisms through
which the effect of newness is produced involves the creation of a temporal
rupture, a break from the immediate past which serves to mark the onset of

the nation-state in a new beginning or a 'founding moment'" (2001, 368). She further argues that "this intervention in time gives time a form, by creating a turning-point which marks the end of the old and the beginning of the new. It is at this moment of historical rupture that the nation-state inserts itself into being" (368).

The original Republic Day constituted the historical rupture creating the Turkish nation as a new subject in time that Çınar mentions. Yet it was the tenth anniversary of Republic Day that established the Turkish Republic as continuous, as an agent that moved along its national flow of time. It is significant that graphics prepared for the event commonly used symbols including the number ten and the symbol of infinity, two circles connected to each other. A banner prepared for the anniversary stated the dual narrative of time most clearly: "Gazi is the youngest command of the strongest history" (Behnan 1934, 4).[3]

The tenth-anniversary celebrations reflected the desire to reorganize not only the time but also the space and bodies of the new nation. The celebrations took place in Ankara, the new capital of the Turkish Republic, instead of in Istanbul, the Ottoman capital and site of imperial ceremonial power. The celebration committee worked for four months to prepare widely participatory parades and bleachers around Republic Square for eighty thousand people. A great majority of the population in Ankara (then sixty thousand people), as well as visitors from other cities, participated in the event. At the time, Turkey had survived World War I with great losses and had a meager population of 13 million, mostly consisting of women and the elderly. The new regime celebrated and nationalized the recovered bodies both in terms of individual health and quantity of the masses.

Deliberately organized parades, as well as the controlled masses in the stadium-style seating, displayed the disciplined bodies of the population to the founding father and to the people themselves. Just like nationalist history, which creates the nation as its subject and object at the same time, the nationalist displays of bodies also created what Michel Foucault refers to as the "empirico-transcendental doublet of man" that "appears in his ambiguous position as an object of knowledge and as a subject that knows; enslaved sovereign, observed spectator" (1979, 312). In the case of the stadium, both the paraders and the spectators were there to observe and be observed, to know and be known at the same time. Through this double process they created the national body as a knowable and display-able object.

Such orderly parades and choreographed demonstrations also celebrated the power of the Turkish state in centrally planning and coordinating the bodies of the nation. "The rendering of movement in grandiose and rigid patterns," Susan Sontag claims, is common to both fascist and communist regimes, "for such choreography rehearses the very unity of polity" (qtd. in Hoberman 1984, 11). Parades demonstrated the ability of the centralized Turkish state to turn individual citizens into parts of a political machine that acted in perfect harmony and reached higher goals if they follow the authority of the state.[4] The celebratory activities were in line with the corporatist-solidarist ideology of the early Republican regime which emphasized central coordination, the division of labor, and harmony in society (Parla 1989).

The physical setup of the bodies in the celebration also made it possible for the citizens to see and be seen by the leader. In the Ottoman Empire's classical age, the sultans would hide from the public gaze and be visible only to their immediate circle in the palace. Sultans would not even directly talk to many people in the palace, but use intermediaries or a sign language mediating the communication instead. Atatürk, following new technologies of governmentality, established a direct relationship of rule and gaze between the modern state and its citizens (see chapter 3). Thus his appearance in Republic Square for the tenth anniversary and his public speech constituted the center piece of the celebration, establishing a direct connection between the authoritarian leader and the people turned into the unified body of the nation.

A party publication of the time describes well how the tenth anniversary constructed a nationalized and unified time/space/body with the leader:

> It is a sunny day. . . . It is 10 o'clock. . . . Everyone is waiting for the Gazi, and all hearts are filled with excitement. Guests are curious, and spectators are anxious. . . . All hearts are beating for him in unison. It is ten past ten. Suddenly eighty thousand people start to tremble as if electrified. The sound of a horn. . . . Two cars pass by the tenth-anniversary arch. . . . His excellency, the president, passes behind the tribunes and toward the sol-

diers lined up. At this moment the people surge up, and their slogans and applause shake the earth and the sky. This is a very new experience for everyone. Those who have the honor of witnessing the young excitement of a nation who established a new state can brag by saying, "I experienced the highest pleasure of my time."

Thousands of people gathered in the square start to run after the president's car like a snowfall from a mountain, like a wave from the sea. Peddlers with trays on their head, peasant girls with purple head scarves, women with sandals, and village youth are pushing each other to see Gazi. People were screaming madly: "Live!" "Long live Gazi!" . . . He got off his car and climbs up to the presidential tribune. In front of Gazi, his Excellency, was a mass of eighty thousand people. Eighty thousand eyes were looking at the depth of a pair of blue eyes.

Following his last sentence, Republic Square groaned with applause for minutes. It was such a rare honor for a big mass of people to stand in such an orderly manner. People were trembling with happiness and excitement. Thousands of people did not say a word to each other. They directed their eyes to Gazi's mouth, listening to his high words in a spiritual calmness. (Behnan 1934, 11–15)

So that the rest of the nation, who could not be physically present for this passionate moment, would feel able to unify with Atatürk's words, the speech was broadcast around the country through loudspeakers placed in city and town squares. In this way, "the whole nation had an opportunity to listen to this historical speech at the same moment" (15) and be aware of other members' simultaneous presence in the Andersonian homogenous empty time of the new nation (Anderson 1991).

Following this audiovisual connection with the leader, representative symbols and accomplishments of the young republic started to parade in front of the leader and the nation's body mass. The orderly soldiers "represent the power of the nation to persevere and be independent" (Behnan 1934, 17). They also reflected the health of the nation's body. "They look so lively that their faces are red like bronze. In the squadron there is no single weak or faint soldier. All soldiers are the living witnesses of the Turkish race" (17). The parade of soldiers was followed by armory, war planes, and tanks. After that, the educated and disciplined youth representing the future of the country passed along. The republic was "watching the healthy fruits of the past ten years, and it was making its power evident" (18).

The second day of the celebration involved a ceremony that unified the newly delineated homeland by presenting Atatürk with small amounts of soil from different parts of the country. These soil samples represented people's "unmatched feelings of gratefulness" (29). The soil was considered a precious gift because "this soil, which is kneaded with our ancestors' blood, was wrapped in a red flag as a bouquet of our collective heart" (29). Soil gathered from various regions occupied by different ethnic groups—such as Kurds in southeastern Turkey, Laz in the Black Sea region, or Alevis in central Anatolia—symbolically unified them. The reference to blood mixed in with the soil also underlined this symbolic fusion.[5] Moreover, the mixing of blood and soil also rooted the present population in Anatolia, despite the fact that what is now Turkey has served as a homeland to multiple non-Turkish populations. It is significant that this event took place after Atatürk ended his speech with his famous saying, "How happy is the person who says I am a Turk." This phrase and the mixed soil wrapped in the Turkish flag Turkified the new citizens, as well as the territories of the young republic.

As the soil was being picked up from Republic Square in Ankara, party officials made emotional speeches about the event and highlighted the connection between land, blood, and the unifying role of the leader. Mümtaz Bey, a member of the Republican People's Party Ankara administration council said:

> Today we gathered here for two purposes. On the one hand, we want to show our nation's gratefulness to our savior, our Great Leader. On the other hand, we want to demonstrate Turkey's unity, indivisibility, and collectivity in the path toward Gazi's ideal. If he accepted, we would take our hearts out and give them to him. . . . We are giving him a piece of soil from Republic Square, which was beating like a heart with us yesterday. We give this soil as the heart of the whole nation. And we want to declare to the whole world that our homeland is indivisible. (quoted in Behnan 1934, 29–34)

The tenth-anniversary celebration proved such a significant event that the following anniversary celebrations have commemorated not only the declaration of the republic but also the tenth-anniversary celebrations. Many of the practices in later years replicated the activities invented for the tenth anniversary. Even today the school celebrations of Republic Day begin by playing Atatürk's creaky recordings of his tenth-anniversary speech. Reminding listeners of the low-tech quality of recording and broadcasting at the time, these records bring the historical moment to the present. Today, similar kinds of parades display the disciplined bodies of the young soldiers and students to orderly citizens on ascending stadium seats. Heroic nationalist speeches repeat similar themes of liberation, the indivisible unity of the nation, and commitment to Atatürk's path. They were revised in 1994 for the civilian celebrations but continue to be performed in schools.

Participation in and enthusiasm for the celebrations dramatically decreased after the Republican People's Party lost the first free elections in 1950. Nonetheless, the celebrations continued in a routine manner. Throughout my childhood and early youth—from the 1970s to the early 1990s—each October 29 Republic Day celebration looked almost exactly the same to me. When I was in primary and secondary school in Ankara, we were obliged every year to come to school just to have a ceremony (tören) in which we would line up in the cement school yard and listen to poetry, sing marches, and occasionally watch skits prepared by teachers and presented by students. As they lined us up according to our height, teachers would make sure that everyone wore their black uniforms, black shoes, and white socks; girls had their hair in tight ponytails and boys had short hair. Usually teachers' pet students with the loudest voices would be selected to dramatically recite nationalist poems. My schoolmates and I would join the nationalist marches as the music teacher gave the rhythm: "Atatüüüüüürk didn't dieeeee, [he] lives iiiiin my heaaaaart / He carriies the flaaaag in the civilization waaaar / He overcoooomes all difficultiiieees" (Atatüüüüüürk ölmediiiiii yüreğimdeeee yaşıyoooor / Uygaaaarlık savaşında bayrağıı oooooo taşıyoooor / Her gücü ooooo aşıyoooor). During the ceremony Atatürk's bust would look at us with frowning eyes. At the end, we would show off the goose bumps on our arms caused by nationalist emotions and the cold morning breezes of central Anatolia.

In the mid-1980s, although many transformations in entertainment had taken place in Turkey, the Republic Day celebrations remained the same. It was difficult for the repetitious celebrations to compete with the programs on multiple private television channels, paparazzi news in colorful magazines, and the affordable prices offered by the newly built holiday villages targeting domestic tourists during off-season. Upper middle-class people used the one-and-a-half-day break to go to beaches in southern Turkey, while others stayed at home and watched movies on private television channels or went out for picnics. The most participatory act many citizens performed for Republic Day was to hang Turkish flags on their balconies. The majority was happy to have another day off work, much like Americans on July 4.

National celebrations changed form for the first time in 1994.[6] After they won a major electoral success in the local elections, the Islamist mayors of the Welfare Party were reluctant to organize Republic Day celebrations. As a reaction, the state-appointed and thus secularist governors decided to organize popularly attended Republic Day festivities. Because the usual stadium celebrations occasioned poor attendance, the governors organized free outdoor concerts with popular singers to attract masses and turn the celebration into entertainment. On October 29, regular stadium activities took place during the day, while at night hundreds of thousands of people filled Taksim Square. Some were there to listen to their favorite pop singers for free, while others wanted to join a demonstration against the Islamists. Citizens were invited to the celebration neither to follow the choreographed activities nor to watch them. For the first time, they could participate by simply attending a concert and yelling slogans.

The slogan of the day seemed quite informal compared with the usual nationalist language used for Republic Day: "I love the Republic and Democracy" ("Cumhuriyeti ve Demokrasiyi Seviyorum"). The previous slogans I had learned in school, such as "Let my existence be a present to the existence of Turks!" ("Varlığım Türk varlığına armağan olsun!"), had shown citizens their lower place in relation to the Turkish state and nation. The new slogan, on the other hand, suggested a more equal relationship. More important, "love" seemed a novel and particularly personal and sentimental concept for talking about political institutions in Turkey. Although it was used commonly during the 1930s in order to define the citizenly commitment to the republic, in the 1990s, the term introduced a new intimacy into the public sphere since it inferred the personal and emotional attachment of individual citizens.

The 1998 seventy-fifth anniversary celebrations took place in a different political atmosphere than those in 1994. What became known as the "February 28 decisions" initiated by the military in 1997 included a series of measures taken to suppress political Islam such as applying strict control on veiled university students, discharging hundreds of officers close to Islamist politics, and closing down middle schools that gave religious education. The same measures also suggested that the seventy-fifth anniversary of the republic should be celebrated by mass participation. Secularist groups and the government working in close collaboration with the army expressed the hope that an active celebration of the seventy-fifth anniversary would raise the people's consciousness as citizens of the Turkish Republic, connect people to Republican ideals, and show to Islamists that people supported the secular ideology of their free will.[7] The organizers of the celebration decided that the old form of the festivities, however, would not create the desired feelings or offer a valid proof of popular support. The new celebration therefore was going to be organized by a civil society organization, rather than the usual state officials, and would be likened to a festival, not a ceremony.

A CIVILIAN ORGANIZATION FOR A CIVILIAN CELEBRATION

In 1998, for the first time in Republican history, the prime ministry transferred resources to an independent nongovernmental organization, the History Foundation. The new political economy of the celebrations reflected a novel understanding of privatization (özelleşme) for the celebrations. This shift in the organization from the state to a nongovernmental organization symbolized the involvement of the civilian initiative not only at the level of participation but also at the level of planning.

The History Foundation was founded in 1991 by two hundred academics and intellectuals, most of whom took a critical stance toward national history writing in Turkey. The founders defined the mission of the foundation as "to develop and spread historical consciousness in Turkey" (Türkiye'de tarih bilincini geliştirip yaygınlaştırmak). The foundation also defined itself in opposition to the Turkish History Institute, which was founded in 1935 to write the official history of the new nation. Following the order of Atatürk, the original institute devoted itself to producing a so-called Turkish History Thesis, which argues that Turks are the ancestors of all civilizations (Copeaux 1998).

In order to differentiate their foundation from the original Turkish History Institute, the founders of the History Foundation emphasized independence from the state. Its first catalogue emphasized the organization's refusal to serve as a mouthpiece for the state: "The History Foundation is unique in terms of its structure and founding process compared to the majority of other foundations in our country. There is no wealthy family, political party, or big business group behind us. The foundation is a civil society organization completely independent from the state."

In its early years the History Foundation displayed not only an independent but also a critical stance toward the Turkish state. During the United Nations Habitat meetings in 1993 in Istanbul, the prime ministry funded the History Foundation for the first time to coordinate the meetings and organize two exhibits, one on the history of Istanbul and another on forms of housing in Anatolia through the ages. During this event, some bureaucrats called for a transfer of funds and responsibility for historical events to a nongovernmental organization, while others opposed it. In the end, although the History Foundation received major funding from the state, the prime ministry did not give them all they promised.

The relationship between the central state and the History Foundation developed further during the seventy-fifth anniversary celebrations. In 1996, the History Foundation prepared a project for the anniversary entitled "Seventy-five Years of the Turkish Republic as a Modernization Project: A Reassessment, 1923–1998" (Bir çağdaşlaşma Projesi Olarak Cumhuriyet'in 75 Yılı: Bilanço 1923–1998) and submitted it to the president, Süleyman Demirel. The proposed project suggested that nongovernmental organizations be involved in the planning and implementation of the celebration. The History Foundation demanded 10 million dollars for the project. The original plan was to distribute some of that money to other civil society organizations. President Demirel was very enthusiastic about the project and wanted to implement it at once. Yet despite his support, some of the more conservative officials opposed handing such a large sum to a nongovernmental organization and also delegating important official business to a nonofficial group. In the end, the Turkish state allocated 10 million dollars for the celebrations, but the History Foundation received only 2 million dollars; the rest of the money was distributed among other state organizations.

The transfer of funds from the state to a civil society organization can be seen as part of ongoing privatization efforts in Turkey. Tensions around this transfer also demonstrate the ambivalence of officials about relinquishing control of their resources. At the time of the celebration, the Turkish state was privatizing state-owned enterprises one after another and trying to move from a state-based economy toward a market-based one (Alexander 2002). Although Turkey was never a socialist country, until the 1980s, some aspects of the economy functioned quite similarly to those in Eastern European countries, with a centrally planned economy and a domestic economy well protected by high tariffs. As Katherine Verdery (1996) describes it for socialist economies, in Turkey, as well, suppliers held more power in their hands than consumers. Prior to 1980, when the primary economic activity in Turkey was import-substitution industrialization, it was the government policies rather than marketing that determined the profits for industry (Keyder 1987). In the transition to a market economy, Turkish and postsocialist states transferred more of their resources to private entities. However, during the process, they still held a strong position as a supplier and even used the privatization process as another resource they could control (Gülalp 2001). More important, they have more say in the now "privatized" matters because the amounts of resources transferred from the state to nonstate bodies has greatly increased. The 2 million dollars spent on the state budget during the "privately celebrated" seventy-fifth anniversary was the highest amount spent for a Republic Day celebration in history.

THE NEW FORM OF THE ANNIVERSARY CELEBRATION

The History Foundation's chair, İlhan Tekeli, introduced the idea of a festival-like celebration. He appealed to the president and suggested a change in celebrations that would allow citizens to express themselves.[8] In the report he prepared for the president, he stated: "[The ongoing] celebrations became a way of giving unidirectional messages to people. In such contexts, which are closed to spontaneity and participation, people cannot express themselves" (Tekeli 1998, 19) According to his definition, "ceremonies are hierarchically organized. They point to an office, respect, and pride rather than a social joy and enthusiasm" (3). He argued that the social situation in Turkey required a change in the nature of celebrations: "Recent threats against the Turkish Republic in terms of its unity and modernization added significance to the celebration of the Republic . . . . Developing innovative celebrations is an urgent necessity in Turkey in order to meet these desires and to provide that celebrations fulfill their social functions" (21). Hence Tekeli suggested that participatory celebrations would prove a powerful statement against the Kurdish uprisings and Islamic politics threatening Turkey's official founding ideologies of national homogeneity and secularism.

The new celebration, Tekeli suggested, would be likened to a festival (şenlik) and be organized around three concepts: mass participation (kitlesel katılım), spontaneity (spontanlık), and enthusiasm (coşku). Through such a conceptual reorganization, the celebration would allow citizens to express their passion for the Turkish state freely. More important, by framing their voice as free and spontaneous, it would give the supporters of the Turkish state legitimacy against the oppositional groups. Pro-government citizens would appear as individual customers choosing to support the official ideology based on their free will rather than as ones forced to take part in a state-planned celebration.

While spontaneity, zeal, and participation appear as new symbols that fit market symbolisms, they also resemble the ones used by the authoritarian single-party officials to define the tenth-anniversary celebrations of 1933. Much like the one for the seventy-fifth anniversary, the tenth-anniversary celebration program predefined the feelings the celebration would generate: "The tenth anniversary of the Ankara Republic will be celebrated for three days and nights enthusiastically [büyük coşkunlukla], sincerely [candan], and collectively [hep beraber]" (Behnan 1934, 6). Later the same program announces that "the first section of the event was completed with an internal desire and enthusiasm. Everyone competed with each other to show their presence in the event" (7). A significant difference between the depiction of the 1933 and 1998 anniversaries was an emphasis on the quiet and orderly nature of the earlier event. In 1933, state officials interpreted "the ubiquitous silence [as] a proof of the orderliness" (5). In the end, both celebrations were preplanned activities that aimed to display popular support for the state ideology and policy.

During my interview with him a year after the celebration, İlhan Tekeli claimed that the most important motive for the seventy-fifth anniversary celebration was to make an anti-Islamist statement. As an answer to why the History Foundation came up with an innovative celebration, he told me that its members thought of this plan when the Islamist Virtue Party and the conservative True Path Party were in coalition in 1996. "As enlightened Turks [Türk aydını]," he said, "we felt responsible for the republic and wanted do something against the religious uprising." They hoped a participatory celebration of the republic would motivate people to express their reaction against the Islamists. The anniversary celebrations, however, also took place in the framework of the February 27 measures that suppressed political Islam. At the time, the Islamist Welfare Party and its leader were banned from politics. In search for symbols of popular support for the new measures, both the president and the army generals were supportive of a festival-like celebration.

It was only Mesut Yılmaz, the center-right prime minister, who objected to a cheerful celebration, arguing that the word *festival* appeared too joyous for a serious event like a national anniversary. While discussing which word to choose, organizers did not really have an event to refer to in Turkish history or tradition. Being a very productive scholar, İlhan Tekeli took the responsibility of preparing a booklet about the history of festivals in the world and Turkey. The president, having difficulties explaining to critical officials like Yılmaz what the History Foundation meant by a festival, urged Tekeli to move swiftly; he also wanted to learn all about the term's history.

In the 1998 booklet, Tekeli argues that festivals have formed an important part of social life because one of the definitions of humans is *homo ludens*, the man who plays. When discussing the tradition of celebrations in Turkey, however, Tekeli does not have much to say. He mentions the sixteenth-century Ottoman festivals in which trade guilds would stage demonstrations for the sultan. This, unfortunately, is a long-dead tradition, accessible only through the Ottoman miniatures made at the time. The actual models for the 1998 celebrations were thus the mass-participatory tenth-anniversary celebrations for the Turkish Republic and contemporary European spectacles such as the Love Parade in Berlin.[9] The revived tenth-anniversary celebration was based on a new temporal and spatial organization that reminded one of the original festivities but also went beyond them.

While describing the changing nature of festivals after the 1789 French Revolution, Mona Ozouf (1988) points out the centrality of space and time in the symbolism of political change. She argues that the new festivals succeeded in conveying a message about the transformation of the political system because they effectively organized time and space. For example, they set up a new calendar and carried the celebrations to open spaces in order to demonstrate that the new political system was based on a new kind of unity. Since 1789, many regimes have established and transformed festivals in order to establish tighter relations with the people they govern. In 1998, Turkish politicians likewise introduced new spatial and temporal dimensions to Republic Day celebrations, which had been limited to stadiums and school yards for several decades. Organizers of the seventy-fifth anniversary hoped that the new dimensions would provoke enthusiasm and reunite the citizens around the founding principles of the republic.

In order to transform the celebration from an official one into a festival, they first moved it out of the confined spaces of the stadiums into city centers. Streets and squares used for the celebration created an aura of freedom and accessibility to anyone on the street. In the streets, crowds could participate and walk without following a line or synchronized steps. Also, more people could watch this kind of parade from their windows even if they did not participate.

Second, the celebration encouraged a change in the form of political expression. In previous celebrations, formulaic nationalist speeches by government officials constituted the culmination point. In 1998, on the other hand, events led to popular music concerts. This not only dramatically increased the number of participants in the event but also allowed these people to "express themselves" through popular music and dance and connect with each other at an emotional level. While listening to political speeches, spectators could not participate in any other way than by applauding. Music and dance in the new celebrations included participants into the event and gave them a limited sphere of self-expression and participation. The participants I interviewed enjoyed the new form more than the earlier one. But they did not necessarily think they had a wider sphere of self-expression in which they could state their views and feelings about the nature of the regime under which they lived.

The new celebration also involved a temporal reorganization. Spontaneity was favored over preplanned and coordinated activities. Instead of having choreographed demonstrations, participants walked and danced as they wished. Moreover, while stadium activities used to take place in the morning, the Republic Day concerts took place at night. This change in temporality disassociated the event from other political events, including protests or political meetings, which always take place during the day and frequently around Taksim Square. As Taksim turns into Istanbul's entertainment district at night, it allowed citizens to unite outside the traditional boundaries of politics.

At first sight, it appears that Turkish celebration organizers adopted a Bakhtinian differentiation of spectacles. In his work on medieval carnivals, Mikhail Bakhtin argues that carnivals and official feasts constitute two radically different kinds of activities. The comic and carnivalesque spectacles were situated outside the political world and "offered a completely different, non-official, extra ecclesiastical and extra political aspect of the world, of man, and of human relation; they built a second world and second life outside officialdom" (1984, 6). The chaotic atmosphere of carnivals, where cultural dichotomies were turned upside down, created a separate world. When the limited time of the carnival was over, people returned to their own regular lives, as well as their normal values. Official feasts, on the other hand, differed dramatically from carnivals because, rather than creating a space of freedom, they reinforced the "existing hierarchy, the existing religious, political, and moral values, norms and prohibitions" (9). Bakhtin believes that only official celebrations, which can clearly be differentiated from the carnivalesque, can have any impact on political life, and only in terms of reproducing it.

In the case of the seventy-fifth anniversary celebrations, Turkish politicians also suggested a division between carnivals and official feasts. However, their aim was not to create chaos or turn things upside down. Rather, they wanted to utilize the enthusiasm and mass participation of carnivals for political purposes—an impossible case in Bakhtinian categorization. As I demonstrate below, politicians and public intellectuals aimed to create a basis for a civilian celebration that would introduce market-based concepts such as participation, spontaneity, and free will to the celebration of the official ideology. Such notions were to emphasize the fact that Turks freely supported the official ideology, rather than being forced to do so. At the same time, many of the concepts they introduced as new were reminiscent of those used by the authoritarian single-party regime to define the tenth-anniversary celebration. In the end, as Bakhtin would have predicted, the 1998 celebrations did not overthrow the existing political hierarchies or create an alternative world of chaos. Yet the seventy-fifth anniversary celebrations introduced new forms and symbolisms of celebrating the state, and they creatively blended the authoritarian symbolism of the single-party regime with that of contemporary market-inspired neoliberal modernity.

A CIVILIAN PARADE

During the 1998 Republic Day celebration, I participated in a local Istanbul parade organized by the Republican Kadiköy municipality on Baghdad Avenue.[10] Kadiköy, located on the Asian side of Istanbul, is a peculiar district housing 3 million mostly middle-class residents. Most important, it is also one of the most secular sections of the city, always voting for secular center-left parties such as the RPP or the DLP (Democratic Left Party). Even during the 1999 elections, when the RPP did not reach the 10 percent barrier necessary in general elections to have representation in parliament, Selami Öztürk from the party was elected as mayor for the third time.

Baghdad Avenue, one of the main arteries of the Kadıköy district, is one of the most European-looking neighborhoods of the city, with outdoor cafes and chic boutiques. My parents are typical residents of this neighborhood and were among those who filled up the wide avenue that night. They live in an apartment on a side street that intersects Baghdad Avenue. They resemble others residing in the same building because they are an upper middle-class, professional family with a secular outlook.

On the evening of October 29, my mother and I walked down from my parents' apartment to the avenue. My father had left several hours earlier to be at the forefront of the parade with the mayor. A three-kilometer long section of Baghdad Avenue was closed to traffic between Bostancı and Göztepe for the parade. Although it was organized as a nonpartisan event, Deniz Baykal, the leader of the RPP, and other party officials also participated. Along with the supporters of the party, the residents joined in the march. When we stepped out, we found ourselves in the middle of individuals carrying Turkish flags or groups of ten carrying giant flags. People wore other paraphernalia such as shirts, hats, and headbands with the Turkish flag, creating a scene similar to a victory celebration for Turkish soccer teams. When we reached Baghdad Avenue, we joined in a crowd of hundreds of thousands of people filling up the four-lane street for several kilometers. That night, our march from Suadiye to Selamiçeşme took three hours, a walk that would take about half an hour at a normal pace. The culmination of the event was a short concert by Zülfü Livaneli, a popular singer who ran as an RPP candidate for parliament in 1994 and 1998.

The crowd was very enthusiastic. Paraders sang the tenth-anniversary march, repeatedly blasted by the five-foot speakers atop the bus leading the parade. Even at the back of the parade, where the sound of the stereo did not reach, the participants were singing the march on their own and yelling slogans. The most popular slogan was one developed after the victory of the Welfare Party in 1994: "Turkey is secular, and it will remain secular!" (Türkiye laiktir laik kalacak!). Other slogans were adopted from soccer games. For example, one group would yell "red," another group would respond, "white," and then all of them would say, "Turkey is the greatest" (En büyük Türkiye). At times, groups of people would stop and sing the national anthem and then continue walking. As the paraders were marching along, thousands of people applauded and waved flags at them from their balconies and windows. The residents of the apartments facing the street had invited guests to watch the parade.

Although from the balconies it probably looked like paraders were united in emotion, at the street level, one could feel the tension between the supporters of the Republican People's Party, who had organized the event, and others. Partisans and nonpartisans had different opinions about the political nature of the event. Some militant members of the RPP, including my mother, wanted to use this opportunity to have an enthusiastic secular crowd for party propaganda. They started to wave the RPP flag instead of the Turkish flag and began to yell slogans for Deniz Baykal: "Baaaaykal, the prime miiiiinister!" (Baaaaykal başbaaaakan!). This made many participants who did not support the RPP quite angry. During the parade, two middle-aged women holding their Turkish flags looked at my mother and her party flag angrily. One of them said loudly to her friend: "Do you see what they are doing? This is really inappropriate." As a devoted party member, my mother snapped back: "The Republican People's Party established the republic. Of course I am going to carry its flag." The second woman, clearly not a supporter of the party, was quick to reply: "We are all here for the republic, but not for the Republican People's Party. You are trying to use us for their political interests." My mother was upset, but when she saw other heads nodding in agreement with the two women, she chose not to reply, and we walked away.

Several days later, when I visited my mother to talk to her about the parade, she repeated her frequent complaint about how she could not understand why secular people were angry with her party, one devoted to secularist politics. She said, "If you ask, everyone in our neighborhood is a Kemalist and anti-Islamist, but no one is willing to come and work for the only party that is committed to secularism. They think politics is a dirty thing and that I am in it for my personal interests." I asked her why she was devoting all her time and energy to the party despite the criticism. She answered, "If we do not engage in politics and tell people what we think is true, how are things going to change in this country? People just want to complain about things, but not do anything for the party."

My mother is the daughter of a parliamentarian and an elementary school teacher born in 1940 during the single-party rule of the Republican People's Party. Raised as an orthodox Kemalist, she is a firm believer in Westernization, secularism, and Turkish nationalism. In her youth in the 1960s, her political beliefs changed parallel with those of the RPP, which became a social democrat party supporting the rights of workers and peasants. Although she always supported the party, she could not be an openly active member because she worked for the national oil company. In 1980, the military junta closed down the RPP, as well as other parties. After the junta, social democrats could not unite and were split up into several parties. In 1992, when one of the social democrat factions reestablished RPP, my mother started to work for the party actively. In the 1990s, the party's and my mother's major political concern became secularism.[11]

I did not have a chance to talk to the women had who expressed their dislike of party politics even though they shared the RPP's political concerns. However, during my fieldwork I met many other secular people who expressed their discontent with party politics. Even those who frequently joined demonstrations against Islamists and made regular donations or worked for secular organizations such as the Support for Modern Living Association or the Atatürkist Thought Association chose not to join the most secular party, and even not to vote for it.[12] They believed that such organizations should appeal to citizens in their totality rather than being partisan and hence divisive. The kind of civilian and personalized enthusiasm they expected the parades to generate was a clearly defined and unifying one, even though the event was organized by the municipality representing a political party.

Such an understanding of a unified society devoid of partisan division has roots in the corporate-solidarist ideology of the single-party era. Based on the writings of Ziya Gökalp, the main theoretician of the single-party regime, Taha Parla defines corporate solidarism in the following words: "As a model of society and economy, corporatism sees society as an organic and harmonious whole consisting of mutually interdependent and functionally complementary parts" (1985, 46). Parla argues that in their application of this ideology, the early Republican leaders conceptualized the single party as the only mechanism that could unify the society and the state (1991, 186). In his numerous speeches, Atatürk underlined the fact that the party did not differentiate among the citizens and considered them a unified whole. One of the famous lines of the tenth-anniversary march also attests to this harmonious understanding of society: "We are a blended mass, lack of classes and privileges" (Imtiyazsız, sınıfsız kaynaşmış bir kütleyiz). The corporatist understanding of society rejected the idea of multiple political parties that would divide the unified nation along artificial lines, such as class and interest. The seventy-fifth anniversary celebrations and many participants aimed to recreate the image of a unified society at the expense of erasing some members from the picture.

THE TURKISH NATION HAND IN HAND

A three-part series of advertisements prepared by the History Foundation and the Lowe advertisement company further elaborated the theme of civilian and national unity around secular Republican values. These advertisements were published in all major newspapers and broadcast on all major television channels. Their main theme was a display of Turkish citizens from all walks of life—including urbanites, peasants, students, and elderly people—holding hands. The pictures were taken in symbolically important locations for Republican history, including major engineering projects such as the Bosphorus Bridge and the Keban water dam, or the beautiful locations of the country such as the grassy fields of the Black Sea region and Cappadocia. All the ads had the same headline, "We Meet in the Republic" (Cumhuriyet'te Buluşuyoruz), indicating that all the citizens come together in Republican ideology.

In all three ads, hundreds of citizens hold hands surrounding a young woman in a white shirt. The first advertisement in the series shows the

8. The official Republic Day posters. The headline reads: "We meet in the Republic. Because we accomplished our modernization with it."

young woman standing still with a bouquet of red and white roses, the colors of the Turkish flag. In the second picture, she runs with her flowers. In the third picture, she puts the flowers on a statue pedestal. Although not represented in the photograph, it is clearly an Atatürk statue since hardly any statue in Turkey depicts anyone else. In the ad, the woman stands for both the Turkish youth to whom Atatürk gave the republic as a present and for the Turkish Republic itself, which Atatürk asked the youth to protect and defend. Clean and innocent in her white shirt, looking simultaneously like a high school student and a bride with a bouquet of flowers, she needs to be protected by all the citizens against threats. Likening the republic to a young woman, or a girl/virgin (kız), constitutes a very powerful trope in Turkey and partakes of what anthropologists define as the honor-and-shame culture of the Middle East and the Mediterranean. In the ad, citizens are urged to protect Republican values just as they would the virginity of their daughters by constantly enforcing externally imposed restrictions.[13] This kind of symbolization of the republic becomes clear if we consider that during the seventy-fifth anniversary, the novel slogan, "Let's be responsible for the Republic" (Cumhuriyet'e sahip çıkalım) was frequently used. Compared to the 1994 Republic Day slogan, "I love the Republic and Democracy," which brought the republic to an equal level with the citizen, the new slogan even lowered the status of the republic. This time, the republic was in need of protection, like a young, unmarried woman, rather than standing as a superior or equal being. Significantly, this time, it was the private citizen's duty to claim ownership of the republic and personalize it through a statement of protection.

It is significant that in the advertisement citizens appear in circle dancing, which establishes a social bond among the group of people and distinguishes them from others outside the dance. Wedding ceremonies and political demonstrations in Turkey thus always end with a circle dance. In this way, participants get both unified and differentiated from others outside the circle. It is thus important to analyze who is included in the circle and who is left out. Although the main purpose of the ad was to show that Turkish citizens from all walks of life stand together, hand in hand, for the Turkish Republic, religious people were excluded from these pictures. In all three ads, all except three women are bareheaded, mostly wearing suits. Discerning eyes could see women in the background wearing the headscarves of a mountain village. These women stood for peasants, their head coverings part of their traditional outfits rather than serving as political statements. Their physical location in the photograph matches their temporal positioning in secularist ideology as belonging to the past. Women in the foreground are always bareheaded and look like secular urbanites.

A walk in the middle-class neighborhoods of Istanbul, however, would make it apparent that the people in the ads did not reflect how Istanbulites look, let alone citizens of Turkey in general. In 1998, many more women than were represented in the ad wore headscarves, and more men had Islamic beards. By depicting only certain kinds of people, the advertisement conveyed the message that only middle-class and secular people were devoted to Republican principles and connected to each other around the Turkish Republic. Moreover, it indicated that only they had the duty and privilege of protecting the republic, not only from external threats but also from the internal challenges posed by religious groups.

Organizers of the seventy-fifth anniversary promised to introduce dramatic changes in the celebration. As opposed to earlier celebrations that put the state at the center, the new celebration would put the people in central position. It would also emphasize their passionate participation in keeping with the shift described in earlier chapters to a more personalized and emotional experience and support of republicanism. The celebrations were coordinated by a civil society organization, participated in by the civilian masses, and seemed genuinely festive and joyous.

One of the ways in which I read the change in the organization and form of the major national day in Turkey is to see it as an effort to incorporate neoliberal market symbolism into the field of state activity. In the post–Cold War era, state planning lost its appeal in every arena, including that of national celebrations. The older anniversaries displayed the power of the state by mass parades organized by the government. Choreographed demonstrations represented how the multitude of the nation's young bodies could turn into a harmonious whole through central coordination and training. In the neoliberal semiotics of legitimacy, however, spontaneity rather than synchrony, market freedom rather than state planning, and civil society organizations rather than government offices gained an upper hand. Thus the new celebration was a festive one organized by a civil society organization and spontaneously enacted by the people. This allowed participants to celebrate the foundational history of their state in a novel way.

While the organization and form of the seventy-fifth Republic Day anniversary diverged from the earlier celebrations of the past few decades, a second reading of its symbolism demonstrates that it also shared striking points with the legendary tenth-anniversary celebration of 1933. Thus I also interpret the same event as a nostalgic recall of the tenth anniversary in 1998. Similar to the one in 1998, the 1933 celebration also emphasized enthusiasm and mass participation. It is significant that both the 1933 and 1998 celebrations took place at a time when state policies needed alternative forms of legitimation. The tenth-anniversary celebration marked the solidification of the authoritarian single-party regime, while the 1998 celebration followed an understated military intervention into politics that suppressed a democratically elected Islamist government. In 1998, internal and external critics of the Turkish state accused the central power of being too directly involved in politics and not allowing citizens any political freedom of choice and expression. In both cases, popular and enthusiastic participation in the Republic Day celebrations legitimated the Republican regimes when electoral votes did not have a determining power.

Equally committed to both of these interpretations, I ask what kind of a discursive or political field made it possible for the seventy-fifth anniversary—or the popular life histories of first-generation Republicans, commercial pictures of Atatürk, and museum exhibits about the family lives of citizens—to appear as a civilian initiative and a tool of the state power at the same time. The conclusion I reach is that the fields of the state, society, and the market are not as contradictory and mutually exclusive as the more optimistic scholars of civil society and the market argue. My analysis takes Charles Taylor's (1990) pessimistic views seriously when he warns that civil society can lead to a Rousseauian understanding. In such a case, civil society sees itself as an expression of the general will and becomes a threat to the freedom of other ideas. The kind of civilian and personalized enthusiasm Republicans aimed to generate in the 1998 parades was a clearly defined and homogenizing one in compliance with the official ideology. Rather than encouraging free and increased political participation, civilian celebrations created space only for limited and carefully crafted kinds of expressions while silencing others.

The state and civil society often merge in more complicated ways in non-Western political contexts than suggested by Taylor. Partha Chatterjee argues that in postcolonial societies like India, civil society creates further political alienation, especially for the masses. He points out that it is only the nationalist elite who organize civil society associations in order to educate the masses and to create "a new ethical life in society, one that conforms to the virtues of the Enlightenment and of bourgeois freedom" (1998, 62). The irony of such institutions, he claims, is that the "actual 'public' will not meet the standards required by civil society, and that the function of civil societal institutions in relation to the public at large will be one of pedagogy rather than of free association" (62). Although Turkey was never formally colonized, the nationalist elite has acted in very similar ways to that of its contemporaries in postcolonial societies and took on a pedagogical civilizing mission of the masses. During the seventy-fifth anniversary as well, the civilian organizers were limited to elite public intellectuals with positions in state institutions such as the universities.

In transition to the market economies, the creation of civil society organizations and privatization function as symbols of a new kind of regime (Verdery 1996). In the post-1980 Turkish case as well, when Turkey began opening itself to the world economy, civil society became a symbol of democracy. Civil society discussions in Turkey, however, have become particularly limited in the alternative venues they create for political participation. In the 1990s, groups in government, or others who wanted to have a position in the government, used "civil-society [as] a symbolic ground on which legitimate state power was going to be based" (Navaro-Yashin 1997, 21). Most of the time groups organized in order to promote the official ideology, and often they were funded by it (Erdoğan 2000).

According to Yael Navaro-Yashin (2002), it is exactly the belief in the distinctiveness of the state and civil society that makes it possible for the state to create and reproduce its power. In her monograph on the production of politics in Turkey, she argues that in the 1990s, state power increasingly produced itself outside of its traditional realms. She suggests that despite predominant cynicism about government functions, the idea of the state remains still alive and well in Turkey because politicians and intellectuals believe that a separation between the state and civil society actually exists. The emphasis on the civilian aspect of the seventy-fifth anniversary celebrations, despite the fact that the History Association was handpicked and funded by the state to organize a mass-participatory celebration, once more proves Navaro-Yashin's point that the state and civil society intermesh. It also demonstrates that the celebration of the state by seemingly nonstate organizations constituted a deliberate strategy to give further legitimacy to the Kemalist state ideology. Yet, at the same time, a close analysis of the seventy-fifth anniversary showed that regardless of its aims, the market-based symbolism did introduce novel forms of political expression and participation, and carried state symbolism into arenas of life considered outside the state, thus making it gain new meanings.

The symbolisms utilized for the seventy-fifth and tenth-anniversary celebrations appear curiously related to each other. Ironically, the seemingly new emphasis on nonstate and market-related concepts such as voluntarism, enthusiasm, and mass participation was indeed invented during the

1933 celebrations in order to demonstrate the all-encompassing power of the authoritarian single-party regime. In that respect, the way Kemalist intellectuals and officials utilize neoliberal discourses in the 1990s reconciles the memory of the single-party regime with the market, rather than preparing grounds for the replacement of the state ideology by the market. At the same time, however, the same Kemalists introduced something totally new that transformed the nature of the political field, rendering the idea of freewill citizen participation crucial for political legitimation.

The next chapter examines how Islamists carved a legitimate space for themselves in the new political field subsumed under freewill and personalized attachments to the symbols of the state and especially to nostalgic depictions of the early Republican era.

CHAPTER 5

Public Memory as Political Battleground

Kemalist and Islamist Versions of the Early Republic

On October 29, 1998, the seventy-fifth anniversary of the Turkish Republic, national newspapers were covered with full-page pictures of Mustafa
Kemal Atatürk, the founding father of Turkey. Sabah published a picture of
him sitting leisurely on a wall in golf pants with his adopted daughter
Sabiha Gökçen, the first woman aviation pilot in the world and thus a
potent symbol of modern Turkey.[1] Milliyet had a picture of the leader in
tuxedo surrounded by Turkish women in Western clothes and hats. Cumhuriyet and Yeni Yüzyıl selected pictures of him looking very charming in a
chic Western hat, elegant coat, and a wooden walking stick, the new kind
of clothes Atatürk required Turkish citizens to wear. Other newspapers
such as Hürriyet and Fanatik used graphic designs in which pictures of
Atatürk were mixed with pictures of contemporary urban youth, pointing
to the future-oriented ideology of the leader.[2] Covering the front pages of
newspapers with pictures of the founding father on Republic Day, and thus
carrying him to the immediacy of the present, is an almost eighty-year-old
tradition. This time, it seemed, newspapers paid particular attention to
display Atatürk in the Western-oriented and secular context he aimed to
create for his citizens, rather than printing isolated portraits of his.

On the same day, the Islamist daily Akit also followed the tradition, but it
published a unique photograph of Atatürk. This one has never appeared in

school textbooks, Atatürk documentaries on the official television channels, or the Republic Day sections of mainstream newspapers. In this photograph taken on October 29, 1923, following the public declaration of the new regime as a republic, Atatürk appears among a group of men on the balcony of the National Assembly building. To Turks, the most striking feature of the photograph is that a religious leader with a white turban stands next to Atatürk. Moreover, everyone in the group, including Atatürk, is praying with their chest-level palms turned upward. Undoubtedly, when they had finished their prayer, they would have rubbed their palms to their faces, saying "amen" and asking God to accept their prayers and protect the new regime.

Akit's editors matched this extraordinary picture with another equally striking but more familiar one on the same page: a policewoman covering the mouth of a veiled university student. Like mainstream newspapers that positioned Atatürk next to images of young women and students, Akit also put a picture of a young Turkish student next to that of the leader. The female student Akit chose to feature as Atatürk's ideal, however, wore a pink headscarf rather than a Western hat or a miniskirt. The picture was taken during the ongoing nationwide protests on university campuses organized by veiled university students after they had learned that they would not be allowed to register in universities for the new academic year unless they unveiled. Hence, by using this picture, Akit's editors indicated that the present Turkish government, rather than religious groups, was contradicting Atatürk's founding principles, which they had defined as Islamic. They were reminding the secularist state officials of the earlier alliance Atatürk made with religious leaders in the country, something forgotten in nationalist history writing and public memory.

During the seventy-fifth anniversary of the Turkish Republic, the memories of the founding years became a way for Islamist and secularist politicians to define their political position and cultural identity in the present. In this chapter I explore how these memories have been deployed, mediated, and managed at an especially charged moment, namely, when the Islamist Welfare Party, which had received the greatest number of votes in the 1995 elections, was closed down in 1997 on grounds of working against the Turkish Republic's principle of secularism.[3] I argue that the officials and supporters of the Virtue Party, which replaced the Welfare Party, attempted to challenge the foundational myths of the Turkish Re-

9. Cover of *Akit* on October 29, 1998.

public, and, more important, tried to reinscribe themselves into the politically legitimate center by revisiting the public memory of the early years. By
choosing memory as one of their sites of political struggle, Virtue Party
activists demonstrated that the representation of the past not only serves as
a ground of cultural reproduction but can also constitute a source of resistance to it.

STRUCTURAL NOSTALGIA FOR THE
FOUNDATIONAL YEARS OF THE REPUBLIC

In the previous chapters I demonstrated how Kemalist citizens and government officials promoted a specific nostalgia for the foundational years of
the republic in order to legitimize their lifestyle and position in society, as
well as to assert a personal and voluntarily engaged-in relationship with
the official ideology. As the above example demonstrates, however, Kema-

lists did not have a monopoly on the memories of the foundational years. Especially toward the end of the 1990s, the Islamist Virtue Party propagated an alternative version of that same period formerly interpreted uniformly in public. Unlike Kemalists, who saw the rise of political Islam as a fundamental threat to the foundational principles of the republic, the Virtue Party and some affiliated Islamist intellectuals emphasized the religious nature of the republic in the 1920s. They argued that the current hardship political Islam and religious Muslims faced constituted a deviation from these original principles. In doing so, they offered a claim to counter the contemporary pressures exerted on them by the contemporary government under the influence of the secular Kemalist army, especially after the February 28 measures.

The Islamist nostalgia for the foundational years—and more specifically, the way it competed with the Kemalist one in public media such as newspapers, political speeches, posters, and banners—further points to the fact that memory is a presentist act that reconfigures contemporary, rather than past, relations and structures of power. Both Islamists and Kemalists utilized the prevailing disappointment about the present situation in Turkey to depict the foundational years as a time during which a perfect harmony and unity existed between the state and its citizens. The nature of that past unity that would offer the blueprint to transform the present was, however, hotly contested. Whereas the Virtue Party activists saw religion as the basis of harmony, for Kemalists the unifying force came in the form of secularity and a Westernized lifestyle. Both camps claimed that their own interpretation of the past should determine the nature of legitimate politics in contemporary Turkey. In other words, as both parties used a nostalgic representation of the past as a blueprint to transform the present, the representation of the past became an arena for struggle over political legitimacy and domination.

Nostalgia can become a political battleground for people with conflicting interests. What is most interesting for our purposes is that a shared understanding of the past as an unspoiled time, what Michael Herzfeld (1997) calls "structural nostalgia," can serve as a resource for the marginalized. By creating alternative representations of an already glorified past, they can make a claim for themselves in the present. It is this kind of a presentist negotiation that the Virtue Party administration sought by redefining the foundational past and, more important, by establishing an exclusive relation to it. By publishing a religious image of Atatürk next to the image of a contemporary veiled student being harassed by the police, the editors of Akit brought the contestation of foundational history and present politics back to the public. The privatization of Turkey's foundational history through the celebration of Republic Day by nongovernmental organizations (chapter 4), the commodification of Atatürk imagery (chapter 3), and the attention paid to the individual life histories of first-generation Republicans (chapters 1 and 2) has excluded contemporary religious people from a national history that is supposed to be shared and celebrated collectively. Thus, as Virtue Party officials unsettled the conventional memory of the foundational past, they also challenged the exclusionary characteristics of a privatized history. The subversive recall of the founding moment proved influential in moving the party from the margins of the political system to its center.

ISLAMIC REPRESENTATION OF THE EARLY REPUBLIC

As Kemalist officials and intellectuals attempted to monopolize the legitimate grounds of politics and its celebration in 1998, Islamist politicians engaged in creative methods to include themselves in the political center from which they had been excluded. The banned Welfare Party reemerged with a new name (Virtue Party) and a new leader (Recai Kutan). Even though the party organization and membership had remained practically the same, Kutan drew a conciliatory portrait and adopted a moderate political discourse. He abandoned the earlier Islamist, anti-Western, and countercapitalist platform in favor of a conservative and center-right one. One interesting strategy the new party embraced was to celebrate the seventy-fifth anniversary of the republic wholeheartedly. This constituted a novel approach; earlier Welfare Party officials notoriously refused to participate in the national celebrations, not singing the national anthem or visiting Atatürk's mausoleum. When they celebrated Republic Day, the Virtue Party leadership contested depictions of the early republic as strictly secular and redefined it as Islamic. By doing so, partisans were able to critique contemporary secularist officials as departing from the foundational principles and thus wrongly marginalizing Islamists both from the past and the present of the Turkish Republic.

Prior to the seventy-fifth anniversary celebrations in 1998, many of the prominent Islamists showed greater interest in commemorating the Ottoman past than the Republican regime, which had erased the imperial legacy alongside its memory. Promoters of neo-Ottomanism had a rather flattened sense of the seven-hundred-year rule of the Ottomans and saw the empire as proof of the superior achievements of a Turkish state that accepted Islam as its official religion. Ottomanism became especially popular among the newly rising Islamist elite who advocated a consumerist taste that marked both their political identity and their class position (Navaro-Yashin 2002; White 2002). Neo-Ottomanism found nonconsumerist political expressions among the public as well. When the Welfare Party won the local elections in Istanbul, the municipality organized mass celebrations for the previously unpopular anniversary of the conquest of Constantinople on May 29, 1453, by the Ottoman sultan Mehmed IV (Bora 1999; Çınar 2001). Alternative Islamic commemorations for Istanbul Day, Alev Çınar argues, "serve to construct an alternative national identity which is Ottoman and Islamic, evoking a civilization centered in the city of Istanbul, as opposed to the secular, modern Turkish Republic centered in the capital city of Ankara" (2001, 365).

In 1998, after the Welfare Party was banned and reincarnated as the Virtue Party, it adopted a new political strategy in relation to history-based identity. Party activists publicly embraced the memory of the republic, yet without letting go of their Ottomanism. Unlike Kemalist officials and activists, who see the rise of political Islam as a fundamental threat to the secular principles of the republic, Virtue Party officials and some likeminded Islamist intellectuals emphasized the religious origins of the republic. By resurrecting forgotten aspects of Republican history, the Virtue Party countered the contemporary pressures exerted on them by the secular government. More important, they aimed to create a legitimate space for themselves in the political center, which is defined through commitment to the foundational principles of the Turkish Republic.

A close look at the early years of the republic provided Virtue Party activists with numerous Atatürk images and sayings in favor of Islam. Even though Atatürk became less and less tolerant toward religion in the 1930s, during the early 1920s, he worked with some religious leaders and mobilized them for the national uprising between 1919 and 1922. During this era, he gave many speeches in favor of Islam, the caliphate, and veiling.[4]

He publicly prayed, accepted sacrifices of sheep, and visited tombs of religious leaders. In this period, Atatürk also formed alliances with some Kurdish tribes in the southeastern region of the country. Once he established the Turkish Republic, consolidated the single-party regime, and defeated his political rivals, Atatürk delivered a marathon speech to parliament in 1927 in order to leave behind an official narrative of the foundation of the new regime (Parla 1991). In this narrative, he denounced a great majority of his earlier alliances. It is the later approaches and policies of the leader that have defined the predominant public memory about the early republic as uniformly secular and nationalist.

The memory of religious oppression during the single-party regime remains vivid among many religious groups in contemporary Turkey. Undoubtedly, not all religious groups hold fond memories of early Republican policies. Some Islamist Web sites condemn Atatürk for being a drunk, a womanizer, and an enemy of Muslims.[5] Other Islamist intellectuals, such as Ahmet Kabaklı, recognize him as a great military leader who saved the country from foreign powers, but argue that he is only one of many military heroes in Turkish and Islamic history and should be treated accordingly (Kabaklı 1998). Thus it would be erroneous to generalize the nostalgic claims of the Virtue Party and its affiliated intellectuals to include the entire, and very diverse, Islamist movement in Turkey.[6] It is also important to recognize that some religious groups were only loosely connected with the Welfare and Virtue Parties, while others still support different center-right political parties. What I do want to suggest, however, is that the unusual history campaign led by the Virtue Party during the seventy-fifth anniversary constituted a well-planned rhetorical strategy that aimed to critique the past and present pressures against Islamists, and also to create a space for Islam in the politically legitimate center.

THE ISLAMIST SUBVERSION OF THE REPUBLICAN NOSTALGIA

As I showed in chapter 3, Atatürk constitutes the central focus of the political sphere in Turkey, both from the perspective of the political elite and from that of the masses. Nazlı Ökten argues that Atatürk is "a common point of reference that guarantees identification with the masses" and that for others "who are deprived of the means of efficient participation in the public sphere, he is an intermediary medium" (forthcoming). The political elite often utilizes Atatürk to delineate the boundaries of legitimacy; he stands for the state, the nation, and the public.[7] For example, prosecutors of the court case against the Welfare Party in 1998 made frequent references to sayings of Atatürk that were critical of Islam in order to prove that the party contradicts the state's foundational principles (Koğacıoğlu 2003). In this tightly demarcated arena of political legitimacy, Virtue Party activists utilized the medium of Atatürk to gain access to the legitimate public sphere from which they had been banned.

On Republic Day, the headline in Akit, located just above the picture of Atatürk praying, reads, "It Started Like This" (Böyle Basladi). Another, smaller, headline next to the picture of the arrested veiled student contrasts "And It Became Like That" (Ve Böyle Oldu). The captions to the pictures pointed to the divergence between the foundational years and the present: "Seventy-five years ago, when Mustafa Kemal Atatürk established the republic, there were religious leaders in their turbans next to him. And they were all praying together"; and, "Seventy-five years later, this picture is a proof against the claims that the republic brought freedom." Even though the pictures and their captions made a strong statement, Akit provided a more elaborate version of the newspaper's Islamic interpretation of the foundational years in an editorial:

> The republic that was founded seventy-five years ago following the War of Liberation was fought by the whole nation, which included the veiled, the bearded, and the baggy-panted.[8] It was declared with the prayers and the affirmation of the greatness of God. Seventy-five years ago on this day, the enemies were kicked out of the country, the French soldiers who tried to unveil our women were killed by those like Sütçü İmam; the Greek army had to leave the way it came. And seventy-five years ago today, Atatürk declared the republic next to turbaned religious leaders. And again seventy-five years ago, [the constitution] declared that "the religion of the Turkish state is Islam" in accordance with the beliefs of the people. In those days, there was no such concept as "secularism" used as a tool of oppression. The republic that was established by blood is celebrated today with whiskey. . . . It was declared that with the republic, people would be freer. But today, the grandchildren of the people who established the republic are not allowed in the universities; their right to education is taken away from them. (Akit, October 29, 1998)

The above narrative presents an unusual portrait of the foundational moment and defines it as Islamic. By doing so, it turns the tables, casting Islamists as the true Republicans and secularists as people who diverge from the original aims of the republic. The editors of the newspaper claim that it is the religious Muslims who saved the country from the Allies and the Greeks and allowed a new republic to be born. In those days, they argue, Islam was central to the newly founded state, but today, oppressive state officials have diverged from the foundational spirit. After redefining the foundational intent and equating themselves with the founders, the Akit editors accuse contemporary Turkish officials for being the real counter-Republicans who disrespect the religious principles on which the republic was founded.

On the anniversary of Atatürk's death the same year (November 10), Milli Gazete, another Islamist daily closely associated with the Virtue Party, printed a similarly nostalgic approach to Atatürk and his era. That day, the newspaper sported the headline, "We Wish You Had Lived" ("Keşke yaşasaydın"). Under this call was a picture of Atatürk with his then wife, Latife Hanım, in her black veil. Atatürk had been married to this woman for a brief period in 1924 before he launched his secularization reforms. Even though the French-educated Latife Hanım wore Western garb and let her hair show at other times, she wore a black veil when she accompanied her husband through Anatolia. The section under the veiled picture of the first lady next to her husband reads as follows:

> Mustafa Kemal, the founder of the republic, at the seventy-fifth anniversary of your creation and at the sixtieth anniversary of your death, we are faced with a group who torture our nation. This group does not consider the villagers, whom you called the masters of the nation, as humans. They betray you by calling anyone who resists their torture enemies of Atatürk. This group, which is responsible for fulfilling the goals you showed [us], created the following scene: the literacy rate is below the rate in the rest of the world, the per capita income is painful. . . . At the anniversary of your death we recall your sayings about veiling to those who could not learn them during the past seventy-five years: "It is not an issue for us to make changes in how women dress. We are not obliged to teach our nation new things on this issue. As individuals, we can use all kinds of dress accord-

ing to our taste, our desire, and our education and economic level"; and, "The veil recommended by our religion suits both life and *virtue* well. Those who imitate European women in their dresses should consider that every nation has its own traditions and national particularities. No nation should be an imitator of another." (From the speech delivered by Atatürk on March 21, 1923). (Milli *Gazete*, November 10, 1998; emphasis mine)

Here Milli *Gazete* adopted the secularist strategy of talking and complaining to Atatürk, especially during his death anniversary, as if he were alive and contemplating the state of his country. The Islamist editors blamed the officials for not being respectful of the traditions of the Anatolian people, whom Atatürk labeled "masters of the nation" (köylü milletin efendisidir). They claimed that when government officials denied veiled students the right to an education and to work in government offices, they degraded traditional values and even called people who observed them "enemies of Atatürk" (Atatürk düşmanları). They also accused officials of misinterpreting Atatürk and abolishing veiling in his name. By publishing Atatürk's words in favor of veiling uttered in 1923 several months before he declared the new regime, Milli *Gazete* demonstrated that the contemporary officials were acting against the leader's teachings. Because they were so far away from the foundational intents and principles of the great leader, editors argued, present government officials were incapable of administering the country properly.

During the 1999 election campaign six months after the seventy-fifth anniversary, the Virtue Party administration emphasized its exclusive connection to the foundational intent once more. Party activists covered practically every single corner of Istanbul with a simple banner bearing one short sentence, "The Republic Is Virtue" (Cumhuriyet Fazilettir), followed by the familiar signature of Atatürk. Atatürk had pronounced this during the initial years of the republic while telling people how good a regime a republic is. By choosing this saying as a slogan for their party, the Islamist politicians both declared themselves loyal followers of Atatürk and the only true Republicans to whom the leader had bequeathed the nation. Through this slogan, they once more challenged secularists who accused them of being Atatürk's enemies and wanted to exclude them from politics.

During the same election campaign, the Virtue Party reemphasized its

10. Mustafa Kemal Atatürk with his then wife Latife Hanım.

11. The Virtue Party's election poster. The caption reads: "The Republic was born in the hands of mothers and will grow up in their hands."

appreciation of Atatürk, as well as his reverence for religion, with a powerful poster. In the background was a black-and-white picture of Atatürk's mother, Zübeyde Hanım, and her adopted son, Abdurrahim Tunçak.[9] In the picture, Zübeyde Hanım sits on a chair, her hair loosely covered with a white headscarf. Abdurrahim Tunçak, his face only partly exposed, is respectfully bowing down to kiss her hand, which she keeps at the level of her chin as she proudly looks at the camera.[10] In the poster, Abdurrahim Tunçak looks just like Atatürk.[11]

Any Turkish citizen who finished elementary school would have learned that Zübeyde Hanım was a religious woman. First-graders learn that Atatürk was born in a pink house in Salonika to Zübeyde Hanım and Ali Rıza Bey. They also learn that at age seven, his parents had an argument about what kind of school little Mustafa should attend. Zübeyde Hanım wanted to send him to a religious school in the neighborhood, but his father wanted to send him to a European-style school. In the end, Mustafa went to the religious school for one year, but because he did not like it there, his father switched him to the progressive one the following year. Soon after the incident, Mustafa's father died and his mother raised him, but she was unable to further influence his education. In fact, it was not necessary to know these historical facts in order to receive the poster's message. The poster appears to show that Mustafa Kemal Atatürk used to bow down in front of his mother in her headscarf. It also reminded viewers that the person who gave birth to and raised the father of the Turkish Republic was a religious woman.

The second image in the poster was also a powerful and carefully chosen one. A smaller color picture appears in the lower right corner of the poster, one in which a woman is holding a small child in her arms. Like Zübeyde Hanım, this woman also wears a white headscarf. Her loose head cover and simple flowery dress mark her as a peasant or a squatter. The slogan on the poster reads: "The Republic was born to [veiled] mothers and is growing up in their hands." The poster narrated continuity from Zübeyde Hanım and Atatürk to contemporary veiled religious mothers and their babies. By doing so, it includes veiling, the most potent symbol of a religious lifestyle, in nationalist symbolism.

The choice of these two veiled women in this poster involves another strategic political move. The secularist army and judicial authorities often argue that political Islam introduced a novel, foreign-inspired, and politically motivated practice by veiling. This kind of veiling, associated mostly with university students or other young urbanites, involves wrapping a wide headscarf around the head in a particular way and attaching it with pins.[12] The fact that Zübeyde Hanım and peasant women also have headscarves highlights the fact that veiling has historical and traditional roots in Turkey and is a nonpolitical practice that forms part of everyday life.

In addition to creating a new representation of the Kemalist past as Islamic, some pro–Virtue Party intellectuals also subverted the common accusation that they are reactionary (irticacı). This is an old concept used since the nineteenth century by modernist Ottoman and Turkish intellectuals to accuse religious people of hindering Turkey from its intended unilinear path toward progress and Westernization.[13] In 1998, during the political campaign in which the Virtue Party attempted to associate itself with the republic and rescue it from the monopoly of the secularists, its members turned the reactionary accusation around and used it against the secularists who were becoming increasingly nostalgic for the foundational years. Two weeks before Republic Day, the editor of Milli Gazete accused the secularists of being backward:

Ten to fifteen years ago, covered women who worked in the fields were accused of being reactionary because they were reluctant to send their daughters to school. Now, the same women face political accusations because their daughters go to school with their headscarves. The leftists, who are a continuation of the "single-party" ideology, cannot realize that in real Republican systems, it is the people that count. . . . Does the republic mean the people, or does it mean Ecevit and Baykal [leaders of the two main secularist parties at the time, both derived from the Republican People's Party]? These men, who are trying to bring back the darkness of the 1940s, will not be able to gain anything by pointing to the nation who founded the republic as the enemies of the republic. (*Milli Gazete*, October 14, 1998)

Here the editor made a subversive move by saddling the very people who accused Islamists of being backward with the same label. He inversely argued that Islamists were not reactionary but, rather, progressive, even by Kemalists' own criteria. They want to send their daughters to school, but the reactionary secular state officials prohibit them by not allowing veiled students to enroll. He accused the two leaders of the center-left secularist parties, Bülent Ecevit, of the Democratic Left Party and Deniz Baykal, of Atatürk's Republican People's Party, of wanting to return the country to the "dark" days of the single-party regime, when people's demands were not taken seriously. Even the choice of the adjective *dark* to define those days subverts the secularist association of religious people with darkness and of modernization with enlightenment.

In this piece, the editor clearly named only the 1940s as the "dark ages of the single-party regime," excluding the 1920s and 1930s. By doing so, he disassociated Atatürk, who died in 1938, from the oppression of the single-party regime and held only İsmet İnönü, who succeeded the leader after his death and ruled the country until 1950, responsible for the severe measures against Islam.[14] Although many anti-Islamic measures were taken during Atatürk's time, the editor strategically found an Islamic basis for the foundational intent of Atatürk. This enabled him to go along with the familiar nostalgic narrative of deterioration since Atatürk's death.

The novel turn of the Virtue Party toward the foundational past had a particular impact on the present. As Kemalist activists were organizing an anti-Islamist Republic Day celebration in 1998, the Kemalist judiciary discussed the possibility of banning the Virtue Party as well. Opponents of the group argued that the Virtue Party was a direct continuation of the Welfare Party and thus a threat to the fundamental principles of the Turkish Republic.[15] By redefining the foundational past as Islamic, the Virtue Party officials emphasized their respect for the founding principles of the republic, as well as for its founding leader. Rather, they claimed, it was the secularist parties in coalition that diverged from Atatürk's teachings. Thus they attempted to demonstrate to voters from diverse sections of society that they were the most appropriate party for ruling the country.

AN ALTERNATIVE PUBLIC GATHERING OF HOLDING HANDS

The public memory of foundational history was not the only political site the Virtue Party challenged to make it inclusive of Islam. The other symbolically powerful site they chose was the Republic Day celebrations in 1998. During the seventy-fifth anniversary celebration, Virtue Party supporters organized an alternative gathering that subverted the official messages of national unity. The gathering made a reference to and at the same time challenged the official anniversary advertisement prepared by the History Foundation depicting citizens from all walks of life holding hands, excluding, however, religious people (see chapter 4).

On October 11, almost three weeks before Republic Day, Virtue Party officials organized a nationwide gathering that challenged the Republic Day advertisement. The initial aim of the gathering was to protest increasing pressures against Islamists in general, and veiled university students in particular. Following the banning of the Welfare Party on February 28, 1997, university administrators were ordered to keep veiled students off campuses for the 1998–99 school year. The protest against the new policies was named Hand in Hand: A Human Chain for Humanistic Respect and Freedom of Thought and took place simultaneously in more than twenty cities. In each city, protestors formed kilometer-long human chains, holding hands or holding the ends of ribbons to prevent unmarried men and women from holding hands. The chain consisted almost exclusively of veiled women and bearded men.

Following the Islamist gathering of holding hands, Islamist intellectuals and politicians argued that people in the Republic Day advertisements did not represent the real Turkish people. They claimed that only the ones who

12. Hand in Hand for the Headscarf Freedom, October 13, 1998, Milliyet

joined the alternative gathering did. Moreover, they asserted, that Hand in
Hand constituted the only true Republic Day celebration since the chain
included all groups of society without excluding the religious. A day after
the protest, İhsan Karahasanoğlu, a columnist for the Islamist daily Akit,
argued, for example, that the meeting united the people marginalized by
the secular state:

> Television channels broadcast an advertisement for the seventy-fifth anni-
> versary. . . . In the advertisement young and old people from all kinds of
> backgrounds hold hands. The only missing people are the ones with
> headscarves and beards. What we see as the people are only the bareheaded
> ones. In the advertisement, holding hands symbolizes the celebration of
> the seventy-fifth anniversary. On October 11 [during the human chain],
> people with and without beards, with or without headscarves were holding
> hands. Although the message of the advertisement talks about equality, it
> does not take an important section of the people into consideration. On
> October 11, people were in the streets just in the way it was originally meant
> in the advertisement. But when the real people [gerçek halk] held hands,
> some claimed that they were resisting the republic. If the Republic brought
> equality, peace, and freedom, why are the people who hold hands on
> October 11 not equal to other citizens? (Akit, October 30, 1998)

As Republic Day was approaching, the Virtue Party printed an alternative
poster to the Republic Day advertisements. The poster was very similar to

the Republic Day ad in the sense that large groups of people were standing next to each other, but instead of all being secular urbanites, the crowd was dominated by veiled and bearded individuals. On top of the picture, "They Met in Virtue" (Fazilette Buluştular) replaced the phrase "They Met in the Republic" (Cumhurlyette Buluştular). By printing this advertisement, Virtue Party officials declared their commitment to a Republican public sphere while at the same time expressing a desire to redefine it as for and populated mainly by religious people.

Despite their opposition to the exclusionary nature of the secularist definition of Republican principles, Islamic intellectuals shared the secularists' understanding of civilian participation in politics. Like secularist officials they believed in a single unitary will of the Turkish nation to be represented by only one group. For example, Sadık Albayrak wrote the following in the daily Milli Gazete: "The first thing to do at the seventy-fifth anniversary is to find out where the national will, which founded the republic, lies. After that, we need to discuss the principles that will be claimed by the whole nation, which will bring together the nation on every single issue" (Milli Gazete, October 15, 1998).

Albayrak, much like other İslamist and secular intellectuals, saw the Turkish nation as a holistic entity, one that could come together on every issue. In negating differences and conflicting interests, Albayrak painted a corporatist picture of society similar to the one promoted by the single-party regime in the 1930s. This ideology took shape under the influence of the Durkheimian concept of an organic society and contemporary authoritarian regimes (Parla 1985). Kemalist corporatism assumed that Turkish society was exempt from interest conflicts and that status differences helped it to function like a harmonious machine working to realize the nationally shared goals. Instead of emphasizing the legitimacy of their different yet marginalized interests in the political public sphere, post-1997 Virtue Party–affiliated activists and intellectuals chose to redefine a unitary national will and history as Islamic.

USING NOSTALGIA TO SILENCE THE OPPOSITION

So far, I have discussed recent Islamist attempts at creating a space for themselves in the legitimate public sphere of the post-1997 era through making alternative references to Republican history. In the following section I will describe the secularist counterattempts that directly intended to monopolize the public. By doing so, I aim to demonstrate that the secularist intellectuals did not abandon the public sphere as they adopted new practices that privatized Republican history and ideology. Rather, when they felt threatened by the appearance of counter-Republican ideologies and symbols in the public sphere, they did not hesitate to utilize the early Republican symbols such as the tenth-anniversary march and the Atatürk statues to silence oppositional voices in the public. Potent symbols of the early republic became tools both to privatize and to publicize the Republican ideology in an exclusionary manner.

During the seventy-fifth anniversary, one of the most noticeable signs of nostalgia was the revival of the tenth-anniversary march. The march became so fashionable that its popularity exceeded that of the national anthem. Some Turkish intellectuals explained the new popularity of the march by its emphasis on nationalism, as compared to the national anthem, which incorporated religious symbolism into nationalism (Bora 2004). Although this may be a viable explanation, I suggest that the popularity of the march also lay in its direct reference to the authoritarian modernism of the 1930s. The quasi-militaristic march was composed in 1933 and taught to the whole nation in schools and through the single-party organization. Many of the elderly vividly remembered when they spent months learning the march and teaching it to others. They saw learning the march as a national duty, a sign of loyalty to the new regime. The lyrics of the march are as follows:

> We ended every war proud in the past ten years
> *Çıktık açık alınla on yılda her savaştan*
> We created 15 million youth of all ages in ten years
> *On yılda onbeş milyon genç yarattık her yaştan*
> The whole world respects our leader and commander in chief
> *Başta bütün dünyanın saydığı başkumandan*
> We knitted all four corners of the motherland with railroad tracks
> *Demir ağlarla ördük anayurdu dört baştan*
> We are Turks of the republic; our chest is a bronze shield
> *Türküz cumhuriyetin göğsümüz tunç siperi*
> The Turk does not stop; the Turk is at the front. Forward Turk!
> *Türk'e durmak yaraşmaz, Türk önde, Türk ileri.*

The tenth-anniversary march was rediscovered in the 1990s, and this time it was carried to nonofficial realms such as the commercial music market and social gatherings. Following the political victory of the Islamic Welfare Party in the mid-1990s, the song became a popular expression of resistance toward Islamists and of nostalgia for the early days of the republic. Several famous pop singers quickly made Kemalist albums consisting of songs with lyrics glorifying Atatürk and containing remixes of nationalist marches. Kenan Doğulu, for example, recorded a lively commercial remix of the tenth-anniversary march. The piece starts with the voice of a young boy saying, "He was born like the sun," referring to Atatürk. The voice is reminiscent of a preschool child learning how to recite Atatürk poetry. It is followed by Atatürk's voice from a well-known recording of the speech he delivered for the tenth-anniversary celebrations in 1933, saying: "My citizens, we accomplished a great deal in such a short period of time" (Yurttaşlarım, az zamanda cok işler başardık). These two familiar voices, which bring the child/citizen and the father/state/leader together, are immediately followed by a lively disco rhythm.

The lively rhythm of the remix distanced the march from its customary contexts of school yards and brought it to Istanbul's giant discos and nightclubs. Hence the most important march of the Turkish Republic was desacralized and made into something people could dance to. During the mid-1990s, deejays played this piece over and over again to their rich, young customers who felt threatened by the rising power of political Islam and have become increasingly nationalist throughout the nineties. Thousands of students attending universities in the United States during the school year and returning to Turkey for their summer vacation crowded the outdoor nightclubs and sang along to the tenth-anniversary march at the top of their lungs, jumping repeatedly as was the fashion during the time. In the hot summer nights of Istanbul—especially on Wednesdays, Fridays, and Saturdays—the clubs blasted the tenth-anniversary march to compete with the increasing volume of the call to prayer following the victory of the Islamist party. The last notes of music coming from the nightclubs merged with the sound of the first call to prayer at dawn.

In 1998, both the remix and the original tenth-anniversary march became popular in wider circles than ever go to nightclubs. Especially during the mass gatherings for the seventy-fifth anniversary, Doğulu's remix was played over and over again to middle-aged, middle-class participants. At other times, in less crowded gatherings such as the fund-raising lunches of Kemalist organizations and sometimes even during home gatherings among friends, people sang the original tenth-anniversary march or clapped along as a form of protest against Islamists.

Despite the popularity of the march, the lyrics remained surprisingly unfit for the social and economic context of 1998. During the seventy-fifth anniversary, Turks were no longer proud of their population as they had been proud of reaching 15 million at the tenth anniversary. On the contrary, social analysts suggested that the growing population of 70 million was one of the reasons why Turkey could not develop. A large population, they argued, caused unemployment, lower income per capita, and poor quality in state services. The fourth line of the march refers to the early Republican project of covering the country with railroads. In 1998, this was irrelevant. Turkey stopped building railroads in 1950 when the Marshall aid arrived with strong recommendations for allocating resources to building highways for automobiles. Finally, at the end of the twentieth century, Turkey had no hope for going forward as the fifth and sixth lines called for. Singing the march was a nostalgic act, filled with despair toward the future rather than hope. The new singers of the march were aware of the misfit between the lyrics and the present day. What they longed for was not a bigger population or longer railways, but the kind of hope and pride the march aimed to create for Turkish citizens in 1933.

Even though the literal meaning of the tenth-anniversary march did not translate to the social and economic context of 1998, it was in line with the desire to recreate the political aura of the early days. The martial lyrics, Atatürk as the commander in chief, the citizens as bronze shields, and the military command of "Forward Turk" reflect the authoritarian and militaristic attitude of the 1930s. The march suited well the support the military received during the late 1990s when it fiercely opposed the Islamist Welfare Party. During the same period, the army also had the full support of nationalist Turks because they were proving successful in battling Kurdish guerillas and actually captured Abdullah Öcalan, the leader of the PKK (Kurdish Workers Party) guerilla movement, shortly after the seventy-fifth anniversary. When the army participated in the people's marches on Republic Day in major cities around Turkey in their uniforms, civilian participants applauded and greeted them with slogans of "The Army and the People Are Hand in Hand," just as they were during the early days of the Republic.[16]

In 1998, the revival of the tenth-anniversary march and the fact that no new march was created for the seventy-fifth anniversary became an issue of public debate. A belated competition for the seventy-fifth anniversary march took place. Neither the competition nor the winning piece, however, received much public attention. The new march was played several times a day on the state channels, but no one learned it, and I never heard it sung in the dozens of Republic Day gatherings in which I participated. Instead, celebrators of the seventy-fifth anniversary insisted on clinging to the tenth-anniversary march because they considered it full of enthusiasm and, as a pharmacist friend in his fifties told me, because it helped them forget their pessimism for a moment.

At the time, some saw the revival of the tenth-anniversary march as a very positive development and a sign of contemporary public enthusiasm for Kemalist principles. Others, however, found it sad that people could not come up with a new march. A politically active musician, Zülfü Livaneli, for example, argued that the inability to popularize a new march was indicative of the current moral pollution of the country.

You remember the discussions around the march ordered for the seventy-fifth anniversary. The march could not even survive until Republic Day because this is an issue of heart, not of music. Even if music experts such as Bach, Beethoven, Mozart, Itri, Dede Efendi came together, they would not be able to compose a march that would replace the tenth-anniversary one because during its tenth anniversary, the republic was clean, pure, full of belief, heroic, and moralistic. It was the song of those who "got out of each war proud in the past ten years." That is why it still touches us in our hearts despite the epic words in it. . . . The situation we are in today is pitiful. On the one hand, we march in Republican celebrations; on the other hand, we are covered with Mafia links. Two days prior to the Republic Day celebrations, the prime minister organizes a meeting with the Mafia. Bribery and lawlessness surround us like cancer.[17] The grandchildren of those who gave their lives in Gallipoli and the liberation war are only concerned about being rich. (Sabah, October 29, 1998)

Livaneli believes that music, especially marches, reflects the period in which it was composed. The positive, pure, and moralistic aura of the 1930s created the tenth-anniversary march, which still spoke to the hearts of secularist modernists. On the seventy-fifth anniversary, however, he supposed that even the best musicians of the West and the East would not be able to compose a march because the whole of Turkey was morally polluted with corruption, Mafia links, and lawlessness. Citizens, and especially state officials, did not think of the interests of their country, but only of themselves. Since marches came out of pure hearts, it would logically be impossible to compose a march during the seventy-fifth anniversary.

Under such a pessimistic outlook, when Republican citizens could not make themselves learn the seventy-fifth anniversary march because it did not reflect a real emotion, Kemalists kept singing the tenth-anniversary march. They used it to voice their ideal, if not real, state in order to attack and silence the voices opposing the foundational principles. One of the most spectral practices of singing the tenth-anniversary march took place in the square facing Atatürk's mausoleum. A chorus consisting of five thousand singers sang the march under the direction of Hikmet Şimşek, one of the most well-known classical music conductors of the present day. Şimşek himself is one of the first classical music conductors trained as a result of the Westernization project of the early republic.[18] He claimed that the tenth-anniversary march was a form of political protest against the counter-Republicans, meaning Islamists and Kurdish guerillas, as well as the corrupt state officials. He and like-minded officials gathered in chorus to sing the march to the leader in the name of the whole nation to assure Atatürk that his followers were still following his path and desired that his principles take over the contemporary state. They also wanted to sing it loudly and in unison through the mouths of thousands of people so that it would silence the voices of oppositional groups who wanted to take control of the state.

Three months after the celebrations, a group of secular singers had an opportunity to use the tenth-anniversary march to physically silence an opposing voice—that of someone who supports Kurdish political autonomy, though he is not an Islamist. In February 1999, the Magazine Journalists' Association hosted an award ceremony and gave prizes to singers, comedians, news reporters, and others. As I watched on TV, I noticed that one of the prizewinners was Ahmet Kaya, a radical singer who became famous in the 1980s for making leftist protest music. During the ceremony Kaya made a short speech, saying, "I am receiving this prize in the name of the Human Rights Association, Mothers of the Disappeared (Cumartesi Anneleri), and the labor of journalist friends." To name oppositional groups such as the Human Rights Association and the Mothers of the Disappeared was already sufficient to make many uncomfortable, but the real trouble started when he stated that he had included a Kurdish folk song on his new album and would make a video for it. He said, "I know that there are many courageous people in our country who will broadcast this video. I also know that if they do not, they will have to explain this to the Turkish nation." At this moment, other prizewinners in their tuxedos and formal outfits walked over to confront him—to beat him up, actually—while others threw their forks, knives, and plates, swearing at the famous singer. Everyone in the room started screaming, "Get out of here," and, "There is no such thing as a Kurd." At this point the police escorted Kaya out of the room.[19]

The angry crowd of celebrities did not calm down even after Kaya left the ceremony. Further motivated by the presence of television cameras, the group continued their protests and competed with each other trying to demonstrate their patriotism. Right after Kaya was escorted out, Serdar Ortaç, a famous pop singer, stood in front of all the guests already standing up and yelling at Kaya and said, "No one is a sultan in this world. We are next to Atatürk, and this country is ours," leading the guests in singing the tenth-anniversary march. In Ortaç's view, any individual saying anything supposedly contradictory to the interests of the Turkish state completely denies it and wants to abolish the Republican regime Atatürk founded. Although Kaya's position had nothing to do with the nature of the political regime, especially in relation to being a monarchy or a republic, Ortaç accused him of being a monarchist and even himself wanting to be the sultan. Ortaç delegitimated and silenced Kaya's position by declaring him an enemy of the republic and united the other celebrities by inviting them to sing the tenth-anniversary march together against the "enemy."

Following Ortaç's lead, Reha Muhtar, an infamous broadcaster, had the same crowd sing a song called "My Homeland" ("Memleketim"). Thus he indicated that by singing a Kurdish song, Kaya was siding with the Kurdish guerilla movement, which many perceive as the enemy of Turkey. This event, which took place in the presence of many cameras, was shown multiple times on numerous television channels. In these programs, the newscasters, who usually report the news with overt emotional expressions, gave an approving smirk as they related the protest against Kaya. The tenth-anniversary march sung by celebrities became proof that the whole nation was willing to silence oppositional voices and save the republic their ancestors had founded.

Discussions about the tenth-anniversary march and the ways it has been used demonstrate the meanings the Kemalists have associated with it. In a situation in which the corrupt Turkish state seemed illegitimate to its citizens, the two could not unite through a march. Republican citizens did not learn or sing the new march composed for the seventy-fifth anniversary because they did not associate themselves with the contemporary state. Rather, they kept singing the tenth-anniversary march, expressing a desire for the authoritarian, strong, and ideal state of the 1930s. Ironically, being critical of the present state and longing for the foundational years was something they shared with the Islamists. In 1998, Kemalists preferred to use the voice of the founding state they imagined in order to silence oppositional voices, including those of Islamists and the Kurds. Throughout the seventy-fifth anniversary, Kemalist Republicans sang this march over and over again, getting louder and louder so that metaphorically, or as in the case of Ahmet Kaya, literally, no other voices could be heard.

THE STATUE FOR THE PRINCIPLES OF ATATÜRK, THE REPUBLIC, AND DEMOCRACY

The tenth-anniversary march was not the only way Kemalist citizens used nostalgia for the foundational days to silence or overshadow other positions. The seventy-fifth anniversary monument built in Istanbul had a similar purpose. Shortly before the general and municipal elections in April 1999, Ayfer Atay, the secularist mayor of Beşiktaş and a member of the Republican People's Party, decided to fund a major monument for Atatürk, the republic, and democracy. Beşiktaş, the crossroads on the European side of the city, constituted one of the few districts of Istanbul with a non-Islamist municipality.

Atay chose the small plaza of Beşiktaş in a densely crowded historical neighborhood for the monument. The rising metal cylinder at the heart of

Beşiktaş aroused much curiosity among the residents. Passersby debated whether it was a pylon for a third bridge across the Bosporus, a water dam, or even a monument to high-rises in the area. After several months, it became clear that the construction was a monument named "Democracy, Republic, and the Principles of Atatürk." The statue ended up being a twenty-meter high, partly red, partly silver cylinder covered with a mirrorlike material. The monument was completed by a two-dimensional relief of Atatürk facing the sea, reading his most famous speech to the Turkish youth, and standing before a map of Turkey.

The huge and shiny structure is easily visible to the 1 million people who pass through Beşiktaş by land and sea everyday. The size of the statue is its most striking feature, reflecting the Republicans' fear that Kemalist social values are being lost. When viewed from the sea, the statue appears to be a little taller than the minaret of the sixteenth-century Sinan Paşa Mosque, built in the classical period of the Ottoman Empire and located right across the street from the statue, and it is tempting to think that the planners created this impression intentionally. Currently, the most prominent structure in Beşiktaş is this statue, rather than an Ottoman tomb built by the most famous Ottoman architect, Sinan.

The primary concerns about this huge statue were made clear by the artist, Tamer Başoğlu, in the interviews he gave to journalists. When he was asked how he made the statue, he answered: "The mayor is a progressive person. I am also a progressive person. That is why they asked me, and I made it." In reply to a question regarding the size of the statue, he answered: "In our country, many forces have come together to belittle Atatürk and his principles. They try to pull secularism and democracy backward by reactionary activities. The mayor Atay—who is a democrat, secularist, and Republican—and I asked ourselves what kind of a project we could do" (Radikal, January 20, 2000). Finally, the secularist mayor and the artist agreed on building an enormous monument in order to counter the belittling of Atatürk and his principles. Başoğlu's interview makes it clear that the size of the statue was deliberately planned as a statement against the Islamists. The monument aimed to reinscribe the Kemalist ideology onto the historical landscape of Beşiktaş and render it beyond challenge.

If one way to interpret the main purpose of the statue is for it to overshadow any other building around it, including the historical mosque, another interpretation is to suggest that the monument aimed to carry the struggle over the Turkish Republic back to the public sphere again. The privatized relation to Republican ideology had also feminized it. Newly popular phrases such as "protecting the republic" or "claiming it" (sahip çıkmak) referred to a feminized conceptualization of the Turkish state that required the kind of privatized protection women would need. The massive monument was a nostalgic reference to times when the secular state was the only source of authority, one not in need of protection but, rather, able to threaten and discipline its citizens. Its public presence served to remind of a masculine spirit that chose to publicly compete with the Islamist challenge.

CONCLUSION

In the 1990s, when Kemalist politicians and citizens developed a nostalgic longing for the early days of the republic, Islamist political activists reacted in two different ways. In the early 1990s, they took an alternative approach to memory-based politics and yearned for the Ottoman period when Islam was the official religion of the state. In the late 1990s, however, when the February 28 measures against political Islam limited the legitimate boundaries of politics in Turkey, officials of the new Islamic party, the Virtue Party, turned toward the Republican past. By highlighting the Islamic aspects of the foundational moment, they tried to include themselves in the politically legitimate sphere from which they were excluded. While nostalgia for the early republic helped Kemalists establish a new and private relationship with the official state ideology, a parallel but subversive nostalgia allowed Islamist Virtue Party activists to have access to the dominant political field.

The Virtue Party's alternative reading of the past challenged the secularist monopoly over this moment and created a legitimate space for Islamist politics. Even if many partisans did not personally embrace the memory of the founding father in their private lives, publicly evoking the memory of the founding moment and Atatürk indicated that the party was moving from its marginal position toward the center. This trend became more apparent in an alternative celebration of Republic Day that made a reference to the central nationalist symbol of the people. In their interpretation of the event, Virtue Party–affiliated intellectuals reproduced the dominant image of a homogenous—and exclusively Islamic—nation, undivided along lines of class, ethnicity, and religiosity. Despite its attempts at moving toward the center, the Virtue Party was banned from politics in 1999 on the basis of being a direct continuation of the Welfare Party (Koğacıoğlu 2003). Yet as this book was being written, the Justice and Development Party, which is an offshoot of the Virtue Party, held the majority of seats in parliament and was implementing a center-right, pro–European Union, and pro-IMF political agenda adopting neoliberal structural adjustment policies with an increasingly less religious discourse and avoiding conflict with the secularist Turkish army.

Kemalist reactions to the new actor in the legitimate political sphere making subversive claims about the foundational past tell us once more that nostalgia is far from being only an imagining of the past. Rather, it is a powerful and versatile way of relating to and transforming the present. Kemalist attempts to reclaim public history, as well as to monopolize the public sphere, also tell us that nostalgia is not merely a personal engagement with the past either. Kemalists were aware of the public and political implications of alternative readings of the past, and they were willing to struggle for them in public. At the same time, this reaction showed that the Kemalist nostalgia for the early republic was also very real in the sense that it expressed an appreciation for a period in which Kemalism dominated the public sphere, a kind of control that no longer exists.

Conclusion

In *The Future of Nostalgia* Svetlana Boym (2001) claims that "the twentieth century began with a futuristic utopia and ended with nostalgia" (xiv). The founding generation of the Turkish Republic experienced all stages of this process. Its members were born in an age when it was considered shameful and degrading to long for the past. As this book was written, they were completing their lives with a deep nostalgia for their days of contentment with the present and of anticipation for the future. Boym also suggests that the millennial nostalgia came in two forms: restorative and reflexive. In her typology, "restorative nostalgia stresses *nostos* and attempts a transhistorical reconstruction of the lost home. Reflective nostalgia thrives in *algia*, the longing itself, and delays the homecoming" (xviii). Nationalist and religious revivalist movements with a single plot belong to the former type, while the homesickness of exiles who do not plan to return are of the second type.

Although helpful conceptually, a purely restorative nostalgia, as the nostalgia for the single-party regime of the early republic demonstrates, proves difficult to maintain, especially if it is experienced by individuals, rather than circulated in political pamphlets. At first sight, the new Kemalist nostalgia appears closer to a restorative one in the sense that it "evokes national past and future" (49), "gravitates towards collective pictorial symbols and oral culture" (49), and suggests a unique truth. Despite these characteristics, however, neither the narrators nor the circulators of the Kemalist memory aim, or believe that it was even possible, to transhistorically restore an early Republican past. On the contrary, the circulation of such nostalgic positionings attests to the fact that the single-party regime and its supposedly heavenly qualities belong to the past and are lost for forever. In that sense, much like reflective nostalgia, they "delay the homecoming" and even mark the loss of such a possibility. By doing so, Kemalist nostalgia marks the present as distinct from the past, and hence as something new.

In this manuscript I explored how nostalgia for the single-party era is indicative of a *new* kind of relationship citizens have established with the founding principles of the Turkish Republic, one that manifests itself in affective, domestic, and otherwise private realms generally considered outside the traditional field of politics. The Turkish case I studied here demonstrates that liberalism in its latest phase has become not only manifest but also possible through a new set of everyday practices, affective expressions, and ideological imaginaries that define themselves in the private but are also intimately connected to the formal political field. My analysis of the transformation of the secularist etatist state ideology of Kemalism attests to the fact that the new set of idealized relations between the state and the citizen go much beyond the privatization of state services and property, something many scholars of neoliberalism concentrated on in their research.

In that sense my analysis of the privatization of state ideology and symbolism in Turkey confirms Katherine Verdery's insightful observation about "privatization as an arena of state formation, in which one can look for contradictory destatizing and restatizing processes" (1996, 210). In her research on postsocialist transformation in Eastern Europe, Verdery demonstrates that transferring property rights from the state to private individuals does not make the state smaller. On the contrary, privatization turns state officials into central actors who behave like feudal lords in controlling the newly regulated market relations. In this study I took this discerning point one step further and argued that parallel processes of destatization and restatization can take place outside the field of property relations, such as in the decoration of the domestic sphere, the organization of lifehistory narratives, and the celebration of national holidays. But the political and sentimental privatization of the official ideology I describe in Turkey did not eradicate the political field either. Rather, the novel practices of carrying state symbolism to areas considered outside the control of state officials became a revivalist attempt seeking to reconcile the etatist memory of the founding days with market-inspired neoliberal symbolism.

Privatizing state symbolism and ideology makes for an especially loaded act at a time when market ideologies are imported into formerly second and third world countries with the alleged intention of minimizing supposedly inefficient and cumbersome states. The commercialization of the most potent symbol of the state in Turkey demonstrates that being enmeshed in market symbolism neither eradicates nor democratizes state politics. The most important aspect this phenomenon reveals is that market behavior does not easily dominate the fields left vacant by the withdrawing governments. Rather, some private citizens take on the responsibility for defending and disseminating state ideology, personalize it, and hence create a new type of connection between the state and the citizen. In their novel way of connecting with state symbolism, citizens utilize market-inspired concepts such as free will or choice that emphasize voluntarism or emotions underlying personalized connection.

The novel appearance of the political and the public in the private has come with a new perception and definition of the areas of life considered most intimate. The sociologist Nilüfer Göle has argued that the Turkish public sphere does not fit the Habermasian model of an organically formed arena that expands out of and completes a particular form of domestic culture. Rather, it "provides a stage for the didactic performance of the modern subject in which the nonverbal, corporeal, and implicit aspects of social imaginaries are consciously and explicitly worked out" (2002, 177). Nostalgic Kemalism of the turn of the millennium demonstrates that recently the private sphere has also turned into a didactic sphere of neoliberal modernity in which individual citizens need to perform their voluntary commitment to Republican values in order to give legitimacy to it. In that sense, what has been happening in Turkey cannot be seen as a colonization of the public sphere by private concerns; rather, it is the old public ideologies and symbolisms finding themselves new homes in the personal, domestic, market-related, and civic arenas—transforming them in the process. It is in these new spheres that the authoritarian Kemalist modernization project established new expressions and connections to neoliberalism and at the same time accommodated resistance to it by using its discourse for its own ends.

Ideas about privacy and domesticity have long been deeply intermeshed with Turkish perceptions of the public sphere. Early Kemalist government officials and contemporary public intellectuals perceived private lives as appropriate sites of direct control and manipulation necessary for shaping public behavior and creating ideal citizens. Late Kemalist intellectuals, on the other hand, promote a perception of the private as a voluntary site outside the authority of the state. To counter the increasing critiques of Turkish modernization as externally imposed by the state, public intellectuals who are anti-Islamist and pro–European Union are fashioning a history of the Turkish Republic that is Habermasian in its assumption that an authentically modern public sphere must be related to an authentically intimate private sphere.

Kemalist citizens who exported Republican rituals and symbolism from inside the conventional boundaries of the state seemed quite aware of the implications of their actions. For example, artists coloring black-and-white pictures of Atatürk for the market told me that they were doing so to enable Atatürk and his ideology to compete with other attractive images available to youngsters. One photo studio owner told me, "We need to make sure that Atatürk looks better than all these new images out there. I am coloring his old photographs to make them attractive for the young and the children." Another store owner, who purchased one of those colored photographs for his rug store, told me that his intention was to show Islamists that Atatürk's ideology was not forced on people, but that people like him willingly embraced the leader's image and ideology. Producers and consumers of pictures of Atatürk; organizers and participants of the Republic Day celebrations arranged by civil society organizations; narrators and circulators of the life-history narratives of individuals who transformed their lives as a result of the Kemalist reforms; and producers and listeners of the pop music albums that remixed the tenth-anniversary march originally made in 1933 all had similar aims. They wanted to protect the memory of the Kemalist modernization project from the recent attacks of Islamists, Kurdish nationalists, and European Union officials by carrying it from a public sphere—where things and images belong to everyone and thus to no one—to sentimental, personal, domestic, and civilian spheres. In these private spheres they didactically performed to an imaginary public their voluntary engagement with the memory of the ideology of the founding father.

The new voluntaristic models of national identification that privatize the official ideology must thus also be understood as reactions to contemporary Islamist, Kurdish, and liberal critiques of the Turkish state, all of which define the state's modernization policies as externally imposed and, therefore, oppressive and inauthentic. Circulators of early Republican life histories, private exhibit organizers, and civilian celebrators of the Turkish state who display a secular, modern Turkish domesticity to the public emphasize that Turkish citizens have voluntarily and intimately internalized Republican principles, even in areas of private life that remain outside state authority. Because organizers are nongovernmental, their involvement in Republic Day celebrations also served as proof of deliberate, unprompted support for the modernist principles of the Turkish state.

The new choice-based and affective engagement with Kemalist representations and ideology defied the unquestionable dominance of the founding ideology in Turkey. Simultaneously, these very same acts carried the state-related ideology, imagery, and practice to previously unvisited spheres, hence making them even more ubiquitous. The new circulation of the Turkish state symbolism as a part of market principles points to the end of corporatist and etatist Kemalism and revives it in a new form. I named the new ideology nostalgic Kemalism, but it can also be called neo-Kemalism. In its nostalgic vision, it constitutes a novel political model neither fully etatist nor completely market-dominated, but rather state-centric and at the same time prone to market symbolism. Nostalgic Kemalism masks the prominence of brute state power with market-related behavior and symbolism, as well as with sentimental attachment to the memory of the founding years. The new consumption patterns and privatization attempts, however, carry state symbolism into new spheres such as homes, markets, and personal identities. The new legitimacy of the political actors now depends on the symbolic manifestations of free will and personalized citizen support, rather than on politicians' mere ability to represent the people in their collectivity.

Notes

Introduction

1   *Zeybek*, one of the terms of endearment used for Atatürk, is translated by the Redhouse dictionary as "swashbuckling village lad of southwestern Anatolia."

2   My use of the concept of the political field is inspired by Pierre Bourdieu's (1993) definition of the field in cultural production. I take the political field as a relatively autonomous but also as a dynamic structure that is prone to change as the position of individual agents or other related fields alter.

3   I follow Edmund Amann and Werner Baer (2002) in defining neoliberalism and explaining its emergence in Turkey as parallel to those they observed in Latin America: "The old paradigms of development through import substitution industrialization (ISI), in a closed economy setting, with a large role for the state, were jettisoned in favor of an open economy for the state, with an exit of the state through massive privatization and predominance of market forces. The convergence of the region within the neo-liberal paradigm can only partially be attributed to a general recognition of the inefficiencies associated with ISI. In addition, the adoption of the new policy framework was the result of a comprehensive shift in international relations power relationships. With Latin American economies desperately in need of capital inflows following the debt crisis of the early 1980s, policy makers in the region found themselves under unprecedented pressure to accept the prescriptions of multilateral international financial institutions, backed by the major industrial countries and the principal creditors of the region" (Amann and Baer 2002, 945). In

this book I do not focus on structural readjustment policies, but rather on how neoliberal symbolism travels into fields outside the economy and shapes the everyday understandings and practices of politics and citizenship.

4   In their work on the postcommunist regimes of Eastern Europe, Johanna Bockman and Gil Eyal (2002) ask a parallel question about the rapid acceptance of neoliberalism in Eastern Europe after the fall of the Berlin Wall.

5   Turkey was one of the first countries to receive the World Bank's structural adjustment loans. The World Bank named Turkey as one of the very few successful adopters of the adjustment policies (Shaker 1995).

6   Here I do not wish to suggest that the public sphere equals state authority. Scholars have successfully demonstrated the complex and conflictual ways in which the public sphere is understood and works in diverse settings (Nuhoğlu Soysal 2002). My observations are limited to Turkish citizens' observations of this sphere in the late 1990s.

7   Yael Navaro-Yashin (1997) successfully repudiates this local understanding and demonstrates that many fields considered as part of civil society, and hence nonstate arenas, are actually funded and supported by the state organization, leaving the distinction between the state and civil society meaningless on the ground.

8   At the turn of the millennium Kemalism was not the only form of nostalgia in Turkey. Rather, the public culture seemed saturated with numerous engagements with the past, often in nostalgic notes. See Neyzi 1999 and Özyürek 2006.

9   Hegel defined it as "the most recent age" (qtd. in Habermas 1990, 7), Charles Baudelaire as "the transient, the fleeting, [and] the contingent" (1964, 403), and Peter Osborne as "a form of historical time which valorizes the new as the product of a constantly self-negating temporal dynamic" (1995, xii), or as an experience of "permanent transition" (14).

10   The "Regular Report from the European Commission on Turkey's Progress towards Accession" in 1998 makes the following statement: "The army is not subject to civil control and sometimes even appears to act without the government's knowledge when it carries out certain large scale repressive military actions. The judicial system includes emergency courts (the state security courts) which are not compatible with a democratic system and run counter to the principles of the European convention on human rights. Major efforts need to be made to ensure the real independence of the judiciary and to give judicial system the human and material resources it needs to operate in a manner consistent with the rule of law" (European Commission 1998, 14).

11   According to the IMF "Memorandum of Economic Policies" of June 26, 1998, Turkish authorities launched an economic program to decline inflation following the advice of the IMF officials. The main elements of the program included: (1) a large and sustained improvement in the primary budget balance to narrow the large public sector deficits that lie at the heart of the inflation process; (2) the

adjustment of public-sector wages and agricultural support prices in line with targeted inflation to minimize inflation inertia; (3) structural reforms to ensure a lasting strengthening of public finances; (4) stepped-up privatization to enhance economic efficiency and lower the domestic borrowing requirement; (5) measures to strengthen the banking sector; and (6) limits on the expansion of the central bank's net domestic assets to ensure the consistency of overall policies. According to the "Concluding Statement of February 1999, IMF Staff Visit to Review the Staff Monitored Program" of February 8, 1999, the IMF staff found the program very successful. In 2001, two years after this assessment, the Turkish economy faced the largest crisis in its history, raising questions about the soundness of the IMF advice.

12 Tanıl Bora (2000) gives a telling account of the changing reactions toward Europe by following Turkish soccer fans. He notes that until the 1980s, fans and sports journalists interpreted the Turkish teams' participation in international games as a sign of being part of the civilized world. In the 1990s, however, such games became places where the soccer fans could express Turkey's frustrations with Europe in a way that Turkish diplomats could not. Turkish fans generated obscene and violent slogans against a homogenized Europe, which they believed sided with the Kurdish guerrilla movement. At other times, they expressed their support for teams from countries that they believed supported the Turkish cause.

13 Other examples of self-initiated modernization projects include China, Japan, and the Soviet Union.

14 Brian Silverstein (2003) persuasively disagrees with scholars who call this process Westernization. He argues that the European provinces of the Ottoman Empire were of central importance, hence not leaving the Ottomans outside the West; the Ottomans did not see these reforms as Westernization but rather as an adoption of technical matters that would make them superior to their enemies; and finally, the Ottomans did not differ from the Russians, Greeks, or Spaniards who also sent commissioners to Paris, London, and Berlin to learn about the latest military and administrative developments.

15 Benjamin Fortna (2002) argues that Ottomans introduced their own approach to Western education by Islamizing it.

16 Similarly to Mardin, Michael Meeker (2002) also argues that the transition from the Ottoman Empire to the Turkish Republic involved more continuities than ruptures. Based on his study on the notables of the Black Sea town of Of, he demonstrates that since the nineteenth century, provincial notables had participated in imperial institutions and adopted "universal standards of social thinking and practice in the course of bringing themselves into alignment with the imperial system" (xx). While doing so, they defined their own local traditions as corrupt and degenerate. According to Meeker, both the Ottoman and the Republican central government officials utilized such nonofficial social oligarchies to supplement government

hierarchy. Because the Republican regime used the same networks of ruling elites, the same families in Of have emerged as notables in both the Ottoman and Republican periods.

17 The Soviet model of modernization proved as influential as the West European model for the first generation administrators of the young Turkish Republic (Walstedt 1980, 65–70). The nationalist state officials critical of the liberal economic models and class conflicts adopted an etatist and corporatist model of economic development. In 1932, the vice president İsmet İnönü visited the Soviet Union and was impressed by its planned economy and industrialization. Following the visit, Soviet officials helped Turkey to develop its first five-year economic plan. The Soviets also assisted the young republic in establishing its first major factories, including the steel and aluminum plants in İskenderun and Seydişehir. The state-planned economic development and an emphasis on industrialism have proven so influential that even the governments following the single-party regime further expanded the role of state enterprises.

18 Parla 1992 argues that the Kemalist ideology was developed in the 1920s and defined in the party program in 1931 without being given a name. Therefore, he argues, the claims that Kemalism turned into ideology under the influence of fascist Germany do not have a historical basis.

19 The socialist intellectual Ömer Laçiner (1995) provides an enlightening genealogy of the use of Kemalist ideology by different groups who wanted to claim the state. He notes that in 1950 the Democrat Party, which replaced the single-party regime, followed the Kemalist idea of economic progress. However, as it urged the bourgeoisie to increasingly improve economic development, the bureaucrats and the army who considered Kemalism their monopoly felt threatened and conducted a military coup in 1960. Throughout Republican history, the Turkish armed forces have seen themselves as "the guardians of the State, as established and maintained according to Atatürk's principles" (Karaosmanoğlu 1993, 28) and have not hesitated to intervene in politics if they considered either Atatürk's principles or their leading role in protecting them threatened. The 1960 military coup brought a more democratic constitution; however, it also ensured that only the state was responsible for bringing progress and modernization to the country. It also marked a starting point in a series of interventions by the army. Subsequently, there were military coups in 1971 and 1980, as well as a military intervention into politics in 1997. In each of these episodes the political autonomy of the army (Cizre 1997) and its desire to monopolize the Turkish understanding of modernity increased.

20 After forty years of give and take, the European Union gave an official date to start formal open-ended negotiations for Turkey's full membership on December 17, 2004.

21 Islamism in Turkey is diverse and has a complex history. The first Islamist party,

the National Salvation Party (MSP), was established in 1970 and entered coalitions in parliament through the 1970s. Although the party initially was more supportive of small businesses and a conservative lifestyle, it became more radical following the 1979 revolution in Iran. The 1980 military junta closed down this party, as well as all others. When the party was reemerged in 1983 as the Welfare Party (RP), it incorporated a younger and more radical body of activists. The party won major victories in the 1994 local elections and became the first party to receive 21 percent of the votes in the 1995 general elections, but it had to enter into a coalition with the center-right True Path Party (DYP). The party resigned from government following the 1997 recommendations of the Turkish army. In 1998 the Welfare Party was closed down on the basis of violating the secularism principle of the Turkish Republic and was replaced by the Virtue Party (FP). Although the latter was more moderate than the first one, it caused a major political scandal as one of the parliamentarians elected for parliament in the 1999 elections was a veiled woman, Merve Kavakci (Özyürek 2000). When this party disbanded, it was replaced by the Justice and Development Party, which adopted a pro-capitalist and pro-Western policy and came to power in the 2002 elections, receiving 34 percent of the votes. Along with the political parties, which have a pretty conservative and moderate approach to politics, a loosely defined Islamist movement in Turkey includes a multitude of religious orders (Houston 2001b; Turam 2004), as well as armed groups such as the Islamic Great Eastern Raiders Front (IBDA-C). For a history of Islamism in Turkey, see Çakır 1990, Gülalp 1999, Yıldız 2003.

22 Economic historians of the early Republican regime state that civil servants, along with the intelligentsia and the army, prospered through an increase in their real income between 1929 and 1940 (Balazs 1990). Çağlar Keyder (1987) argues that Turkish etatism involved a coalition between the political elite and the bourgeoisie in which they "joined forces to isolate a national economic space for themselves in which heavy oppression of the working class and exploitation of the agricultural sector would allow for rapid accumulation—all this achieved under an ideology of national solidarity, more or less xenophobic, which denied the existence of conflicting class interests in favor of a corporatist model of the society" (107). He observes that this coalition would start breaking in the 1950s when the local bourgeoisie claimed independence from bureaucracy and their relation became formulated in terms of a mass-elite opposition.

23 Organizations such as the Atatürkist Thought Association (Atatürkçü Düünce Derneği) and the Support for Modern Living Association (Çağdaş Yaşamı Destekleme Derneği) were established in the 1990s and attracted members from diverse backgrounds around the country including small business owners and homemakers (Erdoğan 2000).

24 All translations are mine unless otherwise noted.

25 Scholars have demonstrated how modernity takes unique shapes in France (Rabinow 1989), Greece (Faubion 1993), or Ethiopia (Donham 1999), thus making it impossible to uniformly define it.

26 Here I do not mean to imply that political science is limited to these kinds of studies. These studies, however, have certainly dominated the field.

27 For a discussion of the changing nature of political engagement in the United States, see Putnam 2000.

28 For a review of this literature, see Gledhill 2000.

29 For an excellent and exhaustive review of this literature, see Stoler and Cooper 1997.

30 Timothy Mitchell's work on the British colonization of Egypt (1988) and Partha Chatterjee's work on colonial and postcolonial India (1993) have proven very influential among these anthropologists.

31 For a review of this literature, see Hansen and Stepputat 2001, and for significant representatives, see Taussig 1993, Gupta 1995, Coronil 1997, and Trouillot 2001.

32 Here I share George Steinmetz's (1999) assessment of the changing role of the state at the turn of the twenty-first century: "Even if the present-day state has lost some of its erstwhile importance, it can hardly be said to be 'withering away.' The state may have relinquished some of its earlier capacity to control the movement of capital across its own borders, but it is still the key actor in a number of arenas, including the definition of access to citizenship and its benefits, the control and production of violence, and the meta-coordination of the discursive nongovernmental institutions involved in 'governance'" (11).

33 One of the most innovative studies on the production of the state outside its traditional boundaries is based on ethnographic research on the Turkish public sphere. In her perceptive study on the rituals and fantasies of the Turkish state, Yael Navaro-Yashin (2002) demonstrates that the state has effectively withstood its recent deconstruction. She argues that despite predominant cynicism the idea of the state is still alive and well in Turkey because politicians and intellectuals believe that a misleading separation between the state and civil society actually exists. That is why more rituals of the state, such as farewell ceremonies to soldiers, campaigns for buying Turkish flags, or the commodification of Atatürk pictures are increasingly practiced as if they existed outside the state. She states, "It has recently proven more effective for state power to reproduce itself, not by enforcing narcissistic rituals, but by enabling certain groups outside the center of state practice, to produce in-and-of-themselves . . . rituals of thralldom for the state" (119). Navaro-Yashin's argument is discerning, but she fails to ask why the reproduction of state power moved outside the state at this particular moment in history. In the present study, I aim to understand the changing symbolism of the state and its circulation in relation to the new transnational hegemony of post–Cold War liberalism, which encourages the privatization of state enterprises and celebrates the market.

34 After I had completed most of my research, my father was elected to the parliament as a member of the Republican People's Party in the 2002 general elections.

1. The Elderly Children of the Republic: The Public History in the Private Story

1 Most of the popular books sell between ten and twenty thousand copies. Each printing consists of two thousand units.

2 Yael Navaro-Yashin argues that the "oral history of Kemalist women, who survived the early republican reforms" have been a "counterpoint to Islamist women as an object of social science" (2002, 67).

3 The Social and Economic History Association and the Women's Works Library (Durakbaşa and İlyasoğlu 2001) conducted extensive oral history projects with the first generation of the Turkish Republic. Public and private television channels broadcasted numerous documentaries about the lives of first-generation Republicans including *Protectors of the Republic (Cumhuriyet'e kanat gerenler)* and *Imaginations of the Republic (Cumhuriyet'in Hayalleri)*.

4 The term "second Republicanist" is used to refer to a particular group of liberal intellectuals of the 1990s who suggested that the foundational principles of the Turkish Republic reflect its original times. Hence some of its principles, such as national economy, strict secularism, and Turkish nationalism, should be abandoned.

5 Nilüfer Gürsoy had this interview for the documentary "Imaginations of the Republic."

6 For the ideology and accomplishments of this generation, see Mardin 1962, Ahmad 1969, Kayalı 1997, and Hanioğlu 2001.

7 By "Anatolian notables" he refers to local notables or merchants from the provinces of Anatolia who migrated to and became powerful in major cities starting in the 1950s and thus curtailed the elite and urban modernization project of the young republic.

8 Based on thirteen life-history interviews she conducted with first-generation Republican women, Funda Şenol Cantek also argues that these women either worked as teachers or wished they had had a chance to (2003, 334). In a 2001 book entitled *The Generation of the Tenth Anniversary*, sixteen of the twenty individuals Firdevs Gümüşoğlu interviewed are also teachers. Not all, but a great proportion of the first-generation teachers of the Turkish Republic were women.

9 There is a rich body of literature that discusses the formation of the new Turkish female body as publicly visible yet sexually unnoticeable, as well as the Turkish female mind that needs to be educated in order to render the women enlightened mothers and wives (Kandiyoti 1987; Kadıoğlu 1998; Göle 1996; Durakbaşa 1998, Z. Arat 1998; Navaro 2000).

10 All names used in the text are pseudonyms to protect the anonymity of the research subjects.

11 The interviews quoted in the text were all conducted between the fall of 1998 and the winter of 1999.

12 This practice is an extension of the respect paid to religious teachers. Tapper and Tapper 1991 demonstrate that despite the major changes in the Republican education system, most of the key concepts and methods of the education system have been appropriated from the Ottoman-Islamic tradition.

13 At the time she published this book, consisting of twenty interviews with members of the first generation of the Turkish Republic, Firdevs Gümüşoğlu was a PhD student in the political science department of Istanbul University. In the preface she defines her aim in compiling this book as an effort to understand the passion and excitement of the Turkish generation who founded a new country. What motivated her to publish the interviews as a book was a desire to pass these stories on to the younger generations so as to "enlighten their future" and instill in them the founding passions (2001, 9).

14 Turn-of-the-twentieth-century Turkish nationalist love novels idealize a new woman who knows that the happiness of her nation and homeland comes before her individual happiness. These novels also emphasize the importance of establishing nuclear conjugal families based on mutual respect and understanding to form the basis of a new nation (Kandiyoti 1987; Sirman 2000, 2002). The new educated women of the young republic, such as Meliha, grew up reading such nationalist novels and internalizing this ideal, at least at the representational level.

15 Navaro-Yashin 2000 describes the rationalization of housework through Taylorist principles of calculation and measurement during the early Republican era. Meliha's narrative makes clear that a new emphasis on calculation also formed the basis of new marriages.

16 Andrew Davison (1998) argues that early republican officials both aimed to suppress religious practices (i.e., secularization) and take religion under state control (i.e., laicization).

17 Bruce Mannheim and Denis Tedlock argue that narrative and ethnography are formed dialogically where "a narrative told to an ethnographer is a joint construction of the ethnographer and the storyteller" (1995, 13). At the same time, it is a part of the larger world in which this interaction takes place. Mannheim and Tedlock assert "even the simplest conversation is constructed jointly by its participants, including bystanders and eavesdroppers, and who signal acquiescence to their positions in the emerging interaction" (9).

18 Zehra Arat (1998), who interviewed the first-generation teachers merely to learn about the education they received, also notes that every single teacher she talked to complained about recent times, especially the recent increase in veiling.

19 For a discussion of the central role veiling has played in the imagination of Turkish modernization, see Göle 1996.

20 Yael Navaro-Yashin defines claims made by both secularist and Islamist activists in the 1990s about what kind of outfit or lifestyle is really a local practice in Turkey as debates of "nativeness" (2002, 19–22).

21 Based on their interviews with the same generation of women, Ayşe Durakbaşa and Aynur İlyasoğlu (2001, 200) argue that in the new social organization, where old rules of sex segregation were not applied, it was on women's shoulders to follow strict social conduct that prevented any sexual implication. They had to look modest but not appear timid either. One of their interviewees gave the following account of how she felt when she was invited to go to a trip with her male and female classmates in college: "I could have been considered quite a pretty woman in my youth. If a few people looked at me with attention, I would feel responsible. Not that they were interested in my beauty, but I felt shy about whether they felt encouraged by my facial expression or behavior. I had extreme pride. Naturally, I did not want to reject either. I told my father and my father said: 'I believe in your strong character and mind, if you think it is proper to go, you can go.' These words of my father have always backed me"(200).

22 Nevzat Tandoğan, the high-powered governor and mayor of Ankara between 1929 and 1946, implemented radical measures in the new capital. Tandoğan paid utmost attention to regions of the city Atatürk frequently passed through, namely Çankaya and Ulus, and made sure that anything that would appear ugly in the leader's eyes was demolished, displaced, or carefully cleaned. Such efforts included keeping older city residents, peasants, or workers from the newly built boulevards of the capital; not allowing journalists to report on burglaries or murders in the city; and giving the police unlimited power to provide order. For Tandoğan's policies, see Şenol Cantek 2003, 218–24.

23 Funda Şenol Cantek notes that in those years, the Ankara police would drive the drunks they ran into on the street up to distant neighborhoods and drop them there. They figured that the drunks would sober up and realize their mistake while walking back to their homes (2003, 220).

24 The Action Army headed by Mustafa Kemal came to Istanbul from Thrace in 1909 to subdue the anticonstitutional rebellion known as the Affair of March 31.

25 Probably because I looked upset with the idea that I would not be able to use some of the material we recorded, she added: "But you can use whatever you want."

26 Ferhunde Özbay (1996) argues that as Turkish residents applied modern concepts in their household, the female and male sections of the houses were transformed into living rooms and guest rooms. In the new guest rooms, women and men began to spend time together, and during the daytime, these rooms hosted women's gatherings during which women talked about the modern ways of living, their topics ranging from good manners to fashion, from child raising to marriages. She argues that living rooms served as a space for women to take part in the public sphere at home.

2. Wedded to the Republic: Displaying Transformations in Private Lives

1 Beşiktaş is one of the oldest, most central, and overpopulated parts of Istanbul. Two million middle- and upper middle-class inhabitants live in this residential and business district of the city.

2 Republican reformers chose the Swiss Civil Code because at the time it was the most recently revised one (Berkes 1988).

3 People who are married through an Islamic marriage are not penalized on that basis, but they are not legally considered married and cannot receive benefits such as inheritances from a spouse.

4 The civil marriage is so central to the Republican reforms that during the tenth-anniversary festivities in 1933 the celebration committee prepared a building-size billboard in Ankara contrasting the old form of marriage with the new one (Behnan 1934, 4).

5 Ali Bulaç based this argument on an agreement the Prophet Muhammad made with three Jewish tribes in Medina.

6 In Turkey it is common for banks to fund cultural events such as exhibits, concerts, and plays. Yapı Kredi not only funds a number of such cultural events but also has its own publishing house. This bank is also very active in supporting exhibits about important historical and contemporary events.

7 In her work on architecture during the early Republican period, Sibel Bozdoğan demonstrates how the modernist cubic architecture and interior design of the 1930s became "visual markers of thoroughly transformed, Westernized, and secularized lifestyle" (2001, 197).

8 In their extensive study of Istanbul households between 1880 and 1940, Cem Behar and Alain Duben (1991) make evident that ideals of the European bourgeois family such as conjugal companionship, the nuclear domestic unit, and an emphasis on the quality upbringing of children had become a popular trend among the upper classes even prior to the establishment of the Turkish Republic.

9 According to Habermas, the intimate emotional structure of the bourgeois family played a decisive role in the formation of a "rational-critical public sphere" in early modern Europe. By the eighteenth century, Habermas argues, the conjugal patriarchal unit had become the dominant household form in Europe. Ownership of domestic property and a claim to familial intimacy made the bourgeois man feel like an independent and equal human being who could participate in the public arena regardless of his social status. Such feelings, appropriate to the private man, did not develop just because domestic units became smaller in size. Rather, it was the specific condition of experiencing emergent forms of conjugal intimacy as qualities oriented toward an external audience that made man feel part of a new public. In Habermas's words, the "sphere of public arose in the broader strata of the bourgeoisie as an expansion and at the same time completion of the intimate sphere of the family" (1989, 50).

10 A total of seventy thousand people visited Three Generations of the Republic in Istanbul and Ankara. The majority of the visitors were students on school tours. Although there is no available data on what kinds of people visited the exhibits, research conducted by the History Foundation on another exhibit about the history of Istanbul displayed at the Mint Building proves informative. According to this research, the majority of the visitors to the Istanbul exhibit had high levels of education and income and defined themselves as people who have a habit of visiting museums. In other words, visitors to such exhibits have the Western living standards and habits that Kemalist reforms tried to create. In these exhibits, they had a chance to see and celebrate how their ideology came into being. Most of the visitors to To Create a Citizen, on the other hand, were curious pedestrians who ran into it. There was a greater variety in their backgrounds and approach to Republican ideology.

11 It is customary to capitalize all the first letters of phrases that refer to Atatürk. This practice marks his superiority to all other human beings, implying his omnipotence and omnipresence.

12 There were surprisingly few notes that spoke critically of the Kemalist reforms or the exhibit itself. It is most likely that people who would be critical simply did not visit the exhibit or did not take the time to write in the notebooks. One comment written to the organizers criticized the overemphasis on Westernization. "It is not possible for a postwar nation to be so rich and joyful. Here we do not see any representation of Anatolian people. What we see is a society consisting of degenerate and rich people. Individuals and societies do not change that rapidly. We are Turks and are proud of our Turkishness and Atatürk. But it is clear that the exhibit does not reflect the Turkish society." Another note disapproved of the exaggerated veneration of Atatürk: "Dear general Atatürk. We love and respect you. But we do not worship you. We worship only God. You are just another slave of God. Muslim Youth." Despite the very moderate tone of critique, writers of both notes avoided to sign their full names. The author of the first note signed only with her first name, while the second one did not put down any name, but drew three crescents, the symbol of the ultranationalist National Action Party.

13 Hatice, who comes from a farming family in central Anatolia, was in her mid-thirties at the time of the interview and worked as a sociologist for a research institute. She has strong Republican values and voted for the nationalist and the center-left Democratic Left Party in the 1999 elections, and for the secularist and social democrat Republican People's Party in the municipal elections.

14 It is common for middle- to lower-class men to grow a mustache when they establish their own families and are free of their father's authority. Yet over the past few decades it has become more fashionable and a sign of modernity to have a bare upper lip.

15 This part of the exhibit consisted of twenty different panels exploring how the

Turkish Republic and its modernization project transformed different aspects of life. The exhibit displayed the complete transformation the Republican regime caused in individual lives by concentrating on divergent fields including political organization, gender relations, the construction of the modern body, art, agricultural transformation, urban planning, and the social imagination. These panels were organized by eight academics; Ali Akay, Feride Çiçekoğlu, Akile Gçekoğlu, Akile Gürsoy, Nükhet Sirman, Arzu Öztürkmen, Uğur Tanyeli, Füsun Üstel, and Hakan Yılmaz.

16 For the history of the two corporations and autobiographies of Vehbi Koç and Sakıp Sabancı, see Buğra 1994.

3. Miniaturizing Atatürk: The Commodification of State Iconography

1 The Turkish army officially intervened in politics in 1960, 1971, and 1980. The 1980 intervention was followed by a deadlock in the parliament over forming a coalition and widespread political violence in the country. At the time, the import-substitution industrialization policies were no longer working due to structural deadlocks inherent in the system and changing economic policies worldwide. The junta abolished the parliament, put extreme political pressure on the political left, and adopted the restructuration policies of the International Monetary Fund. In order to legitimate their rule and unite what they saw as a divided nation, the military junta heavily relied on the cult of Atatürk.

2 One of the most striking of Atatürk's statues decorates the center of the provincial town of Afyon. Sculpted in 1936 by Heinrich Krippel, this statue depicts Atatürk standing up naked with his hands up about to hit the fallen Greek enemy—also naked—for the last time.

3 In the 1990s, religious commodities were common and shared many characteristics with those in places such as Cairo, as discussed by Starrett 1997.

4 For the Ottoman political aesthetics of representation, see Necipoğlu 2000, Renda 2000, and Çağman 2000.

5 In her analysis of the same event, Yael Navaro-Yashin (2002) argues that the main symbolic importance of the phenomenon lies in the fact that Yukarı Gündeş is located in a predominantly Kurdish area. This interpretation may be correct for Turks who live outside the area. During my interviews with the predominantly Alevi residents of Yukari Gündeş in Damal, however, it became clear to me that they have utilized the event to assert their identity against the Turkish government, which prioritizes Sunni beliefs and practices.

6 I went to Damal quite skeptical about the shadow. I was surprised when the image suddenly appeared as the clouds blocking the sun moved close to sunset. Needless to say, one could liken the image to many other individuals. The villagers themselves were joking that after ten minutes the image would have a longer nose

and look like Alpaslan Türkeş, the deceased ultranationalist leader of the Nationalist Action Party.

7 The law of last names was one of the modernizing reforms of the Kemalist regime.
This law, which assigned each nuclear family an official last name, divided larger
families into nuclear units and helped the new government to Turkify the names
people carry. Before this law, individuals were named after their fathers, and large
families had their own, unofficial names.

8 For almost a hundred years, Ottomans paid the Western press to promote a positive image first of their empire and then that of the republic (Deringil 1998).

9 Neither these nor other works that concentrated on the private life of Atatürk,
however, explore the nature of his relationship with the numerous daughters
whom he adopted after his divorce (Özverim 1998; Sönmez 1998; Deliorman 1999).

10 After he married Latife, Atatürk sent Fikriye to a sanatorium in Europe. Extremely
hurt by the arrangement, Fikriye committed suicide. After he divorced Latife,
Atatürk never remarried but adopted numerous daughters. It is widely accepted
that Afet İnan, whom he adopted at the age of seventeen, was his surrogate wife,
and it is quite possible that he had relationships with some of his other adopted
daughters as well.

11 Documentaries made in the early years of the Republic include *In the Paths of Victory*
(*Zafer Yollarinda*) by Fuat Uzkınay (1934) and two other documentaries by Soviet
directors: *Ankara, Heart of Turkey* by Sergey Yutkevic and Lev Oskarovic (1934) and
Forward Steps in the Turkish Revolution (*Türk Inkılabında Terakki Hamleleri*) by Ester Shub
(1937).

12 Afet İnan defended a PhD thesis in 1939 at the University of Genova based on this
survey. A Turkish translation of this dissertation was published later (Afetinan
1947).

13 I considered pictures of Atatürk's mausoleum, the pictures of the houses he stayed
in, and his museums as pictures of Atatürk. Although many other pictures were
related to him, such as the ones titled "Women of Atatürk" or "Youth of Atatürk," I
did not count these pictures. One hundred and nineteen of these images were
included in the four Atatürk albums published by the newspaper. Even if we
exclude these pictures where Atatürk's image does not appear, there was one
Atatürk picture for every single other image in the newspaper.

14 Following the economic liberalization program of the 1980s, the advertisement
sector in Turkey grew dramatically. In the 1990s, advertising companies in Turkey
discovered that ads based on local characters and values proved more successful
than the old kind advertisements that replicated European ads. For a very interesting discussion of the way the Indian advertisement sector brought together global
and local concerns in the mid-1990s, see Mazzarella 2003.

15 It is important to note that it is not the Mitsubishi company but local Mitsubishi
distributors who funded this advertisement.

1 Turgut Özakman told these memories during an interview for the documentary entitled *Imaginations of the Republic*.

2 The 1925–26 Law on the Maintenance of Order had suppressed the entire opposition. In 1931 there was a short-lived experiment of establishing a docile opposition party. When the party received unexpected public support, Atatürk closed it down. Other social organizations and periodicals not directly related to the party were also shut down at the time (Zürcher 1998, 184–89).

3 *Gazi*, an Islamic military term meaning "veteran," is one of the commonly used titles of Mustafa Kemal Atatürk.

4 Brownell (1995) discusses how the People's Republic of China similarly utilizes the disciplined bodies of athletes and mass sports events to demonstrate its power.

5 Liisa Malkki (1997) lays out the historical connection nationalist projects established between people living in a nation-state and their land. She argues that this connection is now perceived as so commonsensical that it is difficult to realize its constructed nature. Similarly, Carol Bardenstein (1999) demonstrates how Israelis attempt to establish a naturalized connection between themselves and the soil of Israel through planting trees in their new country.

6 I was not in Turkey during that time. My description of the event relies on newspaper accounts of the event and Yael Navaro-Yashin's (2002, 146–52) discussion.

7 A news article of February 24, 1998, in the daily *Yeni Yüzyıl* reports that one of the measures the army took to fight against political Islam was to "give meaningful messages to anti-Republicans during the seventy-fifth anniversary celebrations."

8 İlhan Tekeli is a professor of urban planning at the Middle East Technical University in Ankara. His report was published as a 1998 booklet with the title *Republican Parades and Festivals: Ankara; Seventy-Fifth-Year Project*.

9 For an interesting analysis of the Love Parade as a new form of political engagement, see Borneman and Senders 2000.

10 This avenue gets its name from being, for centuries, the starting point of the road that goes from Istanbul to Baghdad.

11 For a history of the Republican People's Party, see Bila 1999.

12 During the general elections in 1998, the RPP received 8 percent of the votes nationwide and could not pass the national barrier to have members in the parliament. In the 1970s, the RPP, which was then a social democratic party, used to receive as much as 40 percent of the votes. After the party was closed down in 1980, the social democrats split up, none of them any longer being able to garner such a high ratio of votes.

13 According to Delaney 1991, Muslim societies perceive the function of the woman as the field and of the man as the seed during procreation. In this framework, a strict control of the field guarantees the legitimacy of the man's seed.

5. Public Memory as Political Battleground:
Kemalist and Islamist Versions of the Early Republic

1   For the symbolic importance of Sabiha Gökçen in Turkish nationalism, see Altınay 2000.

2   Of these newspapers, *Sabah*, *Yeni Yüzyıl*, *Milliyet*, and *Hürriyet* have mainstream, liberal, nationalist, and secularist outlooks. *Fanatik* is a popular sports newspaper. *Cumhuriyet* is a left-wing Kemalist daily.

3   For an analysis of the constitutional court cases that banned the Welfare Party and the pro-Kurdish People's Labor Party (HADEP), see Koğacıoğlu 2003.

4   For example, on April 24, 1920, right after the photograph of him among religious leaders was shot, Atatürk made the following speech to the nation as the president of the National Assembly: "We, your deputies, swear in the name of God and the Prophet that we claim that we are rebels against the sultan and the caliph is a lie. All we want is to save our country from sharing the fate of India and Egypt" (qtd. in Mango 1999, 278).

5   Because of the Turkish law against insulting Atatürk, anti-Kemalist individuals and groups use cyberspace to disseminate their ideas. For an example of such a site founded by people of Turkish descent living in Germany, see www.mustafa kemal.de.

6   For an account of the ideological, class-, and ethnicity-based diversity of the Islamist movement in Turkey, see Houston 2001b.

7   Such a close association of political legitimacy with the legacy of a deceased leader contradicts Claude Lefort's definition of modern power. He argues that contrary to the premodern world, where authority was invested in the sacralized body of the king, in the modern world political power remains disembodied. He argues that in modern society, "people experience a fundamental indeterminacy as to the basis of power, law, and knowledge" (1986, 19). I suggest that in the Turkish case, the locus of legitimate power, law, and knowledge ceases to be under the monopoly of a certain individual or group particularly because it is represented by the deceased body of Atatürk.

8   The visible signs of religious Muslims and those of rural background.

9   In later stages of his life, Abdurrahim Tunçak declared that he was Atatürk's illegitimate child and that that was why Zübeyde Hanım raised him. Although Sabiha Gökçen, one of Atatürk's adopted daughters, denied this statement, the similarity of Abdurrahim Tunçak's features with those of Atatürk seems striking.

10 For Atatürk's biography, see Kinross 1965, Volkan and Itzkowitz 1984, and Mango 1999. In their famous biography of Atatürk, Volkan and Itzkowitz used the same picture, but the note under the image says: "A grateful nation pays homage to Atatürk's mother. An unidentified Turk kisses Zübeyde Hanım's hand" (1984, 16).

11 I asked numerous people in Turkey to identify the man and the woman in this picture. They all thought the two were Atatürk and Zübeyde Hanım, his mother.

12 About the politics of wrapping the headscarf in different ways, see Özdalga 1998 and White 1999 and 2002.

13 For a discussion of the history of this concept in Turkey since the nineteenth century, see Özipek 2004.

14 For İsmet İnönü's era, see Heper 1998.

15 In the end, the party was disbanded. For a discussion of recent party closures in Turkey, see Koğacıoğlu 2003.

16 Taha Parla (1991) argues that early Republican ideology was based on the unity of the Turkish army and the nation. He analyzes Atatürk speeches in which the leader makes frequent references to the idea that the Turkish army realized the common wishes and aspirations of the Turkish nation.

17 Here Livaneli is making a reference to the increased power of Mafia organizations and corruption in the country.

18 For the single-party regime's efforts toward Westernizing Turkish music, see Stokes 1992.

19 After this event, Kaya moved to Germany, waiting for the anger against him to subside. He was, however, never able to return to Turkey and died of a heart attack in 2001.

References

Abadan-Unat, Nermin. 1996. *Kum Saatini İzlerken.* Istanbul: İletişim Yayınları.

Abrams, Philip. 1977. "Notes on the Difficulty of Studying the State." *Journal of Historical Sociology,* no. 1: 58–89.

Abu-Lughod, Janet. 1987. "The Islamic City: Historical Myth, Islamic Essence, and Contemporary Relevance." *International Journal of Middle East Studies* 19 (2): 155–76.

Abu-Lughod, Lila. 1998. "Introduction: Feminist Longings and Postcolonial Conditions." In *Remaking Women: Feminism and Modernity in the Middle East,* ed. Abu-Lughod, 3–31. Princeton, NJ: Princeton University Press.

Ahmad, Feroz. 1969. *The Young Turks: The Committee of Union and Progress in Turkish Politics, 1908–1914.* Oxford: Clarendon Press.

Akar, Rıdvan. 1992. *Varlık Vergisi: Tek Parti Rejiminde Azınlık Karşıtı Politika Örneği.* Istanbul: Belge Yayinlari.

Akat, Asaf Savaş. 1993. "Sivil Toplum İnanılmaz Hızla Güçleniyor." In *İkinci Cumhuriyet Tartışmaları,* ed. Metin Sever and Cem Dizdar, 115–32. Istanbul: Başak Yayınları.

Akkad, Moustapha, dir. 1976. *The Message (Al risalah).* 177 min. Hollywood: Filmco International Productions.

Aksan, Doğan. 2001. *Cumhuriyet'in Çocukluk Gençlik Günleri ve Bugün: Cumhuriyet'in 78. Yıl Dönümüne Armağan.* Ankara: Bilgi.

Akşura, Yusuf. [1904] 1994. "Üş Tarz-ı Siyaset." *Türkiye Günlüğü,* no. 31: 9–18.

Aktar, Ayhan. 1992. *Varlık Vergisi ve Türkleştirme Politikalari.* Istanbul: İletişim Yayınları.

Alexander, Catherine. 2002. *Personal States: Making Connections between People and Bureaucracies in Turkey*. New York: Oxford University Press.

Altınay, Ayşe Gül. 2000. "Ordu-Millet-Kadınlar: Dünyanın Ilk Kadın Savaş Pilotu Sabiha Gökçen" In *Vatan Millet Kadınlar*, ed. Altınay, 246–79. Istanbul: Iletişim Yayinlari.

———. 2004. *The Myth of the Military-Nation: Militarism, Gender, and Education in Turkey*. Palgrave Macmillan.

Amann, Edmund, and Werner Baer. 2002. "Neoliberalism and Its Consequences in Brazil." *Journal of Latin American Studies*, no. 34: 945–59.

Anderson, Benedict. 1991. *Imagined Communities: Reflections on the Origin and Spread of Nationalism*. London: Verso.

Appadurai, Arjun. 1986. "Introduction: Commodities and the Politics of Value." In *The Social Life of Things: Commodities in Cultural Perspective*, ed. Appadurai, 3–63. Cambridge: Cambridge University Press.

———. 1996. *Modernity at Large: Cultural Dimensions of Globalization*. Minneapolis: University of Minnesota Press.

Arat, Yesim. 1999. "Democracy and Women in Turkey: In Defense of Liberalism." *Social Politics* 6 (3): 370–87.

Arat, Zehra F. 1998. "Educating the Daughters of the Republic." In *Deconstructing Images of "the Turkish Woman,"* ed. Arat, 157–82. New York: St. Martin's.

Araz, Nezihe. 1993. *Mustafa Kemal'le 1000 Gün*. Istanbul: Apa Ofest.

———. 1994. *Mustafa Kemal'in Ankarası*. Istanbul: Apa Ofset.

Aretxaga, Begona. 2000. "A Fictional Reality: Paramilitary Death Squads and the Construction of State Terror in Spain." In *Death Squad: The Anthropology of State Terror*, ed. Jeffrey A. Sluka, 46–69. Philadelphia: University of Pennsylvania Press.

Atay, Tayfun. 2004. *Din Hayattan Çıkar: Antropolojik Denemeler*. Istanbul: İletişim.

Austin, John L. [1962] 1975. *How to Do Things with Words*. New York: Oxford University Press.

Aydın, Suavi. 2001. "Cumhuriyet'in İdeolojik Şekillenmesinde Antropoloji'nin Rolü: Irkçı Paradigmanin Yükselişi ve Düşüşü." In *Modern Türkiye'de Siyasi Düşünce: Kemalizm*, 2: 344–69. Istanbul: İletişim.

Azak, Umut. 2000. "İslami radyolar ve türbanlı spikerler." In *İslamın kamusal yüzleri*, ed. Nilüfer Göle, 93–109. Istanbul: Metis.

Bakhtin, M. M. 1981. *The Dialogic Imagination: Four Essays*. Ed. Michael Holquist. Trans. Caryl Emerson and Holquist. Austin: University of Texas Press.

———. [1968] 1984. *Rabelais and His World*. Trans. Helene Iswolsky. Bloomington: Indiana University Press.

Bakker, Karen. 2003. "A Political Ecology of Water Privatization." *Studies in Political Economy*, no. 70: 35–59.

Balazs, Judit. 1990. *Lessons of an Attempt at Stabilization: Turkey in the 1980s*. Budapest: Hungarian Scientific Council for World Economy.

Bali, Rıfat. 2000. *Cumhuriyet Yıllarında Türkiye Yahudileri: Bir Türkleştirme Serüveni, 1923–1945*. Istanbul: İletişim.

Baran, Zeyno. 2000. "Corruption: The Turkish Challenge." *Journal of International Affairs* 54 (1): 127–46.

Bardenstein, Carol. 1999. "Trees, Forests, and the Shaping of Palestinian and Israeli Collective Memory." In *Acts of Memory: Cultural Recall in the Present*, ed. Mieke Bal, Jonathan Crewe, and Leo Spitzer, 148–68. Hanover, NH: University Press of New England.

Barkey, Henri. 2000. "The Struggles of a 'Strong' State." *Journal of International Affairs* 54 (1): 87–105.

Bartu, Ayfer. 1999. "Who Owns the Old Quarters? Rewriting Histories in a Global Era." In *Istanbul: Between the Global and the Local*, ed. Çağlar Keyder, 31–46. Lanham, MD: Rowman and Littlefield.

Baudelaire, Charles. 1964. *The Painter of Modern Life and Other Essays*. Ed. and trans. Jonathan Mayne. London: Phaidon.

Bauman, Zygmunt. 2001. *The Individualized Society*. Oxford: Blackwell.

Beck, Ulrich. 1997. *The Reinvention of Politics: Rethinking Modernity in the Global Social Order*. Trans. Mark Ritter. Cambridge, MA: Blackwell.

Behar, Cem, and Alain Duben. 1991. *Istanbul Households: Marriage, Family, and Fertility, 1880–1940*. Cambridge: Cambridge University Press.

Behnan, Enver. 1934. *Cumhuriyet'in Onuncu Yıldönümü Nasıl Kutlandı, 1923–1933*. Ankara: Hakimiyeti Milliye Matbaası.

Bektan, Ali. 1998. *Atatürk'ün Kehanetleri*. Istanbul: Sınır Ötesi Yayınları.

Benett, Tony. 1995. *The Birth of the Museum: History, Theory, Politics*. London: Routledge.

Benhabib, Seyla. 1998. "Models of Public Space: Hannah Arendt, the Liberal Tradition and Jürgen Habermas." In *Feminisim: The Public and the Private*, ed., Joan B. Landes, 65–99. New York: Oxford University Press.

Berdahl, Daphne. 1999. *Where the World Ended: Re-unification and Identity in the German Borderland*. Berkeley: University of California Press.

Berkes, Niyazi. [1964] 1988. *The Development of Secularism in Turkey*. New York: Routledge.

Berlant, Lauren. 1997. *The Queen of America Goes to Washington: Essays on Sex and Citizenship*. Durham, NC: Duke University Press.

Bhabha, Homi K. 1990. *Nation and Narration*. London: Routledge.

———. 1994. *The Location of Culture*. London: Routledge.

Bila, Hikmet. 1999. CHP Tarihi: 1919–1979. Ankara: Deruk Matbaacılık Sanayii.

Bilici, Mücahit. 2000. "İslamın Bronzlaşan Yüzü: Caprice Hotel Örnek Olayı." In *İslamın Kamusal Yüzleri*, ed. Nilüfer Göle, 216–36. Istanbul: Metis.

Bockman, Johanna, and Gil Eyal. 2002. "Eastern Europe as a Laboratory for Economic Knowledge: The Transnational Roots of Neoliberalism." *American Journal of Sociology* 108 (2): 310–52.

Bora, Tanıl. 1999. "Istanbul of the Conqueror: The 'Alternative Global City' Dreams of Political Islam." In *Istanbul Between the Global and the Local*, ed. Çağlar Keyder, 47–58. Lanham: Rowman and Littlefield.

——. 2000. "Türkiye'de Futbol ve Milliyetçilik." In *Türkiye'de Sivil Toplum ve Milliyetçilik*, 559–84. Istanbul: İletişim.

——. 2004. "Laik bir dua: Onuncu; Yıl Marşı." *Milliyet Popüler Kültür*. 30: 15.

Bora, Tanıl, and Ümit Kıvanç. 1995. "Yeni Atatürkçülük." *Yüzyıl Biterken Cumhuriyet Dönemi Türkiye Ansiklopedisi*, no. 13: 777–80.

Bora, Tanıl, and Yüksel Taşkın. 2001. "Sağ Kemalizm" In *Modern Türkiye'de Siyasi Tarih: Kemalizm*, 2: 529–45. Istanbul: İletişim.

Borneman, John. 1998. *Subversions of International Order: Studies on Political Anthropology of Culture*. Albany: State University of New York Press.

Borneman, John, and Stephan Senders. 2000. "Politics without a Head: Is the 'Love Parade' a New Form of Political Identification?" *Cultural Anthropology* 15 (2): 294–317.

Bourdieu, Pierre. 1993. *The Field of Cultural Production: Essays on Art and Literature*. Ed. Randal Johnson. New York: Columbia University Press.

Boym, Svetlana. 2001. *The Future of Nostalgia*. New York: Basic Books.

Bozdoğan, Sibel. 2001. *Modernism and Nation Building: Turkish Architectural Culture in the Early Republic*. Seattle: University of Washington Press.

Bozdoğan, Sibel, and Reşat Kasaba, eds. 1997. *Rethinking Modernity and National Identity in Turkey*. Seattle: University of Washington Press.

Brenner, Suzanne April. 1998. *The Domestication of Desire: Women, Wealth, and Modernity in Java*. Princeton, NJ: Princeton University Press.

Brownell, Susan. 1995. *Training the Body for China: Sports in the Moral Order of the People's Republic*. Chicago: University of Chicago Press.

Buğra, Ayşe. 1994. *State and Business in Turkey: A Comparative Study*. Albany: State University of New York.

Bulaç, Ali. 1992. "Medine Vesikası Hakkında Bazı Bilgiler." *Birikim*, no. 38–39: 102–11.

——. 1993. "Medine Vesikasi Üzerine Tartışmalar." *Birikim*, no. 47, 40–46.

Çağman, Filiz. 2000. "Istanbul Sarayının Yorumu: Üstad Osman ve Dizisi." In *Padişahin Portresi: Tesavir-i Al-i Osman*, ed. Selmin Kangal, 164–87. Istanbul: İş Bankası Yayınları.

Çakır, Ruşen. 1990. *Ayet ve Slogan: Türkiye'de İslami Oluşumlar*. Istanbul: Metis.

Cam, Surham. 2002. "Neo-liberalism and Labor within the Context of an 'Emerging Market.'" *Capital and Class*, no. 77: 89–114.

Carrier, James G. 1997. "Introduction." In *Meanings of the Market: The Free Market in Western Culture*, ed. James G. Carrier, 1–67. Oxford: Berg.

Casanova, José. 1994. *Public Religions in the Modern World*. Chicago: Chicago University Press.

Celarier, Michelle. 1997. "Privatization: A Case Study in Corruption." *Journal of International Affairs* 50 (2): 531–44.

Çelik, Zeynep. 1986. *The Remaking of Istanbul: Portrait of an Ottoman City in the Nineteenth Century*. Seattle: University of Washington Press.

Chang, Ha-Joon. 2002. "Breaking the Mould: An Institutionalist Political Economy Alternative to the Neo-Liberal Theory of the Market and the State." *Cambridge Journal of Economics* 26(5): 539–59.

Chatterjee, Partha. 1993. *Nationalist Thought and the Colonial World: A Derivative Discourse*. Minneapolis: University of Minnesota Press.

——. 1998. "Beyond the Nation? Or Within?" *Social Text* 16 (3): 57–69.

Çınar, Alev. 1997. "Refah Party and the City Administration of Istanbul: Liberal Islam, Locality, and Hybridity." *New Perspectives on Turkey* 16 (3): 23–40.

——. 2001. "National History as a Contested Site: The Conquest of Istanbul and Islamist Negotiations of the Nation." *Comparative Studies in Society and History* 43 (2): 364–91.

Cizre, Ümit. 1997. "The Anatomy of the Turkish Military's Political Autonomy." *Comparative Politics* 29 (2): 151–66.

Cohen, Jean, and Andrew Arato. 1992. *Civil Society and Political Theory*. Cambridge, MA: MIT Press.

Comaroff, John, and Jean Comaroff. 2000. "Millennial Capitalism: First Thoughts on a Second Coming." *Public Culture* 12 (2): 291–343.

Connerton, Paul. 1989. *How Societies Remember*. Cambridge: Cambridge University Press.

Copeaux, Etienne. 1998. *Türk Tarih Tezinden Türk-İslam Sentezine*. Istanbul: Türk Tarih Vakfı Yurt Yayınları.

Coronil, Fernando. 1997. *The Magical State: Nature, Money, and Modernity in Venezuela*. Chicago: University of Chicago Press.

Coşkun, Can Aktan. 1997. "Turkey: From Etatism to a More Liberal Economy." *Journal of Social, Political, and Economic Studies* 22 (2): 165–85.

Courbage, Youssef, and Philippe Fargues. 1997. *Christians and Jews under Islam*. Trans. Judy Mabro. London: I. B. Tauris.

Crouch, Colin, Klaus Eder, and Damian Tambini. 2001. "Introduction: Dilemmas of Citizenship." In *Citizenship, Markets, and the State*, ed. Crouch, Eder, and Tambini, 1–22. Oxford: Oxford University Press.

Das, S. K. 2001. *Public Office, Private Interest: Bureaucracy and Corruption in India*. Oxford: Oxford University Press.

Davison, Andrew. 1998. *Secularism and Revivalism in Turkey: A Hermeneutic Reconsideration*. New Haven, CT: Yale University Press.

Delaney, Carol. 1991. *The Seed and the Soil: Gender and Cosmology in Turkish Village Society*. Berkeley: University of California Press.

——. 1995a. "Father State, Motherland, and the Birth of Modern Turkey." In *Naturalizing Power: Essays in Feminist Cultural Analysis*, ed. Sylvia Yanagisako and Carol Delaney, 177–200. New York: Routledge.

———. 1995b. "Untangling the Meaning of Hair in Turkish Society." In *Off with Her Head! The Denial of Women's Identity in Myth, Religion, and Culture*, ed. H. Elberg-Schwartz and W. Woniger. 53–75. Berkeley: University of California Press.

Deliorman, Altan. [1961] 1999. *Atatürk'ün Hayaindaki Kainlar*. Istanbul: Toplumsal Dönüşüm Yayınları.

Demir, Hülya, and Rıdvan Akar. 1994. *İstanbul'un Son Sürgünleri: 1964'te Rumların Sınırdışı Edilmeleri*. Istanbul: İletişim.

Demirel, Ahmet. 1995. "Atatürk Döneminde Kemalizm." *Yüzyıl Biterken Cumhuriyet Dönemi Türkiye Ansiklopedisi* 13: 766–770. Istanbul: İletişim.

Denktaş, İbrahim. 1998. *Başöğretmenli Yıllar*. Istanbul: İnkılap.

Deringil, Selim. 1998. *The Well-Protected Domains: Ideology and the Legitimation of Power in the Ottoman Empire, 1876–1909*. London: I. B. Tauris.

Donham, Donald. 1999. *Marxist Modern: An Ethnographic History of the Ethiopian Revolution*. Berkeley: University of California Press.

Duara, Prasenjit. 1995. *Rescuing History from the Nation: Questioning Narratives of Modern China*. Chicago: University of Chicago Press.

Dündar, Can. 1998. 12th edition. *Sarı Zeybek: Atatürk'ün Son 300 Günü*. Istanbul: Milliyet Yayınları.

Durakbaşa, Ayşe. 1988. "Cumhuriyet Döneminde Kemalist Kadın Kimliğinin Oluşumu." *Tarih ve Toplum* 9 (52): 167–71.

———. 1998. "Cumhuriyet Döneminde Modern Kadın ve Erkek Kimliklerinin Oluşumu: Kemalist Kadın Kimliği ve Münevver Erkekler." In *75: Yılda Kadın ve Erkekler*, ed. Ayşe Hacımirzaoğlu. 29–50. Istanbul: Tarih Vakfı.

Durakbaşa, Ayşe, and Aynur İlyasoğlu. 2001. "Formation of Gender Identities in Republican Turkey and Women's Narratives as Transmitters of 'Herstory' of Modernization." *Journal of Social History* 35 (1): 195–203.

Eickelman, Dale. 1974. "Is There an Islamic City? The Making of a Quarter in a Moroccan Town." *International Journal of Middle East Studies* 5 (3): 274–94.

Elibal, Gültekin. 1973. *Atatürk, Resim ve Heykel*. Istanbul: İş Bankası Yayınları.

Elyachar, Julia. 2002. "Empowerment Money: The World-Bank, Non-Governmental Organizations, and the Value of Culture in Egypt." *Public Culture* 14(3): 493–513.

Erdoğan, Necmi. 2000. "Kalpaksız Kuvvacılar: Kemalist Sivil Toplum Kuruluğları." In *Türkiye'de Sivil Toplum ve Milliyetcilik*, ed. Stefanos Yerasimos. 235–64. Istanbul: İletişim.

———. 2001. "Neo-Kemalizm, Organik Bunalım ve Hegemonya." In *Modern Türkiye'de Siyasi Düşünce: Kemalizm*, ed. Ahmet İnsel, 2: 584–91. Istanbul: İletişim.

Ergun, Perihan. 1997. *Cumhuriyet Aydınlanmasında Öncü Kadınlarımız*. Istanbul: Tekin Yayınevi.

Erikson, Richard, Dean Barry, and Aaron Doyle. 2000. "The Moral Hazards of Neo-Liberalism: Lessons from the Private Insurance Industry." *Economy and Society* 29(4): 532–58.

European Comission. 1998. Regular Report from the European Comission on Turkey's Progress towards Accession. Brussels: European Comission.

Evren, Kenan. 1990. Kenan Evren'in Anıları. Istanbul: Milliyet Yayınları.

Fabian, Johannes. 1983. Time and the Other: How Anthropology Makes Its Object. New York: Columbia University Press.

Falasca-Zamponi, Simonetta. 1997. Fascist Spectacle: The Aesthetics of Power in Mussolini's Italy. Berkeley: University of California Press.

Faubion, James D. 1993. Modern Greek Lessons: A Primer in Historical Constructivism. Princeton, NJ: Princeton University Press.

Fortna, Benjamin. 2002. Imperial Classroom: Islam, the State, and Education in the Late Ottoman Empire. New York. Oxford University Press.

Foucault, Michel. 1979. Discipline and Punish: The Birth of the Prison. Trans. Alan Sheridan New York: Vintage.

———. 1991. "Governmentality." In The Foucault Effect: Studies in Governmentality, ed. Graham Burchell, Colin Gordon, and Peter Miller, 87–104. Chicago: University of Chicago Press.

Fourcade-Gourinchas, Marion and Sarah L. Babb. 2002. "The Rebirth of the Liberal Creed: Paths to Neoliberalism in Four Countries." American Journal of Sociology 108(3): 533–79.

Fraser, Nancy. 1999. "Rethinking the Public Sphere: A Contribution to the Critique of Actually Existing Democracy." In Habermas and the Public Sphere, ed. Craig Calhoun, 109–42. Cambridge, MA: MIT Press.

Fujitani, Takashi. 1996. Splendid Monarchy: Power and Pageantry in Modern Japan. Berkeley: University of California Press.

Gal, Susan. 2002. "A Semiotics of the Public/Private Distinction." Differences 3 (1): 77–95.

Gal, Susan, and Gail Kligman. 2000. The Politics of Gender after Socialism: A Comparative-Historical Essay. Princeton, NJ: Princeton University Press.

Gills, John R. 1994. "Memory and Identity: The History of a Relationship." In Commemorations: The Politics of National Identity, ed. Gills, 3–26. Princeton, NJ: Princeton University Press.

Gledhill, John. 2000. Power and Its Disguises: Anthropological Perspectives on Politics. 2d. ed. London: Pluto.

Göçek, Fatma Müge. 1987. East Encounters West: France and the Ottoman Empire in the Eighteenth Century. New York: Oxford University Press.

———. 1998. "From Empire to Nation: Images of Women and War in Ottoman Political Cartoons, 1908–1923." In Borderlines: Genders and Identities in War and Peace, 1870–1930, ed. Billie Melman, 47–72. New York: Routledge.

Gökçen, Sabiha. 1994. Atatürk'le Bir Ömür. Istanbul: Altın Kitaplar.

Göle, Nilüfer. 1994. "Toward an Autonomization of Politics and Civil Society in Turkey." In Politics in the Third Turkish Republic, ed. Metin Heper and Ahmet Evin, 213–22. Boulder, CO: Westview.

———. 1996. *The Forbidden Modern: Civilization and Veiling*. Ann Arbor: University of Michigan Press.

———. 2001. *İslamın Kamusal Yüzleri*. Istanbul: Metis.

———. 2002. "Islam in Public: New Visibilities and New Imaginaries." *Public Culture* 14 (1): 173–90.

Grant, Bruce. 2001. "New Moscow Documents; or, States of Innocence." *American Ethnologist* 28 (2): 332–62.

Gülalp, Haldun. 1999. "Political Islam in Turkey: The Rise and Fall of the Refah Party." *Muslim World* 89 (1): 22–41.

———. 2001. "Globalization and Political Islam: The Social Bases of Turkey's Welfare Party." *International Journal of Middle East Studies* 33 (3): 433–48.

———. 2005. "Enlightenment by Fiat: Secularization and Democracy in Turkey." *Middle Eastern Studies* 41 (3): 351–73.

Gümüşoğlu, Firdevs. 2001. *Cumuhuriyet'te İz Bırakanlar: 10; Yıl Kuşağı*. Istanbul: Kaynak Yayınları.

Günal, Asena. 2001. "Mine G. Kırıkkanat ve Beyaz Türk Oryantalizmi." *Birikim*, no. 144, 66–73.

Gupta, Akhil. 1995. "Blurred Boundaries: The Discourse of Corruption, the Culture of Politics, and the Imagined State." *American Ethnologist* 22 (2): 375–402.

Gür, Faik. 2001. "Atatürk heykelleri ve Türkiye'de resmi tarihin görselleşmesi." *Toplum ve Bilim*, no. 90: 147–66.

Habermas, Jürgen. 1987. *The Philosophical Discourse of Modernity: Twelve Lectures*. Trans. Frederick G. Lawrence. Cambridge, MA: MIT Press.

———. 1989. *The Structural Transformation of the Public Sphere: An Inquiry into a Category of Bourgeois Society*. Trans. Thomas Burger, with the assistance of Frederick Lawrence. Cambridge, MA: MIT Press.

Hale, William. 1994. *Turkish Politics and the Military*. London: Routledge.

Haley, Alex. 1973. "Black History, Oral History, and Genealogy." *Oral History Review*, no. 1: 1–17.

Hanioğlu, Şükrü. 1995. *Young Turks in Opposition*. New York: Oxford University Press.

———. 2001. *Preparation for a Revolution: The Young Turks, 1902–1908*. Oxford: Oxford University Press.

Hann, Chris, and Elizabeth Dunn, eds. 1996. *Civil Society: Challenging Western Models*. London: Routledge.

Hansen, Bent. 1991. *The Political Economy of Poverty, Equity, and Growth: Egypt and Turkey*. Oxford: Oxford University Press.

Hansen, Thomas Blom, and Finn Stepputat. 2001. "Introduction: States of Imagination." In *States of Imagination: Ethnographic Explorations of the Postcolonial State*, ed. Hansen and Stepputat, 1–40. Durham, NC: Duke University Press.

Hart, Kimberly. 1999. "Images and Aftermaths: The Use and Contextualization of

Atatürk Imagery in Political Debates in Turkey." *Political and Legal Anthropology* 22 (1): 66–84.

Heper, Metin. 1998. *İsmet İnönü: The Making of a Turkish Statesman*. Leiden, Netherlands: Brill.

Herzfeld, Michael. 1980. "Honor and Shame: Problems in the Comparative Analysis of Moral Systems." *Man*, no. 15: 339–51.

———. 1987. *Anthropology Through the Looking Glass: Critical Ethnography in the Margins of Europe*. Cambridge: Cambridge University Press.

———. 1997. *Cultural Intimacy: Social Poetics in the Nation-State*. London: Routledge.

Hill, Jane. 1992. " 'Today There Is No Respect': Nostalgia, 'Respect,' and Oppositional Discourse in Mexicano (Nahuatl) Language Ideology." *Pragmatics* 2 (3): 263–80.

Hoberman, John M. 1984. *Sport and Political Ideology*. Austin: University of Texas Press.

Houston, Christopher. 2001a. "Brewing of Islamist Modernity: Tea Gardens and Public Space in Istanbul." *Theory, Culture, and Society* 18 (6): 77–97.

———. 2001b. *Islam, Kurds, and the Turkish Nation State*. Oxford: Berg.

Hunt, Lynn. 1992. *The Family Romance of the French Revolution*. Berkeley: University of California Press.

Huyssen, Andreas. 1995. *Twilight Memories: Marking Time in a Culture of Amnesia*. London: Routledge.

Iğsız, Aslı. 2001. "Memleket, Yurt ve Coğrafi Kardeşlik: Arşivci Kültür Politikaları." In *Hatırladıkları ve Unuttuklarıyla Türkiye'nin Toplumsal Hafızası*, ed. Esra Özyürek, 153–82. Istanbul: İletişim Yayınları.

İnan, Afet. 1947. *Türk Halkının Antropolojik Karakteri ve Türkiye Tarihi*. Ankara: Türk Tarih Kurumu.

International Monetary Fund. 1999. *Concluding Statement of February 1999*, IMF Staff Visit to Review the Staff Monitored Program.

Ivy, Marilyn. 1995. *Discourses of the Vanishing: Modernity, Phantasm, Japan*. Chicago: University of Chicago Press.

Jameson, Fredric. 1991. *Postmodernism; or, The Cultural Logic of Late Capitalism*. Durham, NC: Duke University Press.

Jayawardena, Kumari. 1986. *Feminism and Nationalism in the Third World*. London: Zed Books.

Jessop, Bob. 1999. "Narrating the Future of the National Economy and the National State: Remarks on Remapping Regulation and Reinventing Governance." In *State/Culture: State-Formation after the Cultural Turn*, ed. George Steinmetz, 378–405. Ithaca, NY: Cornell University Press.

Kabaklı, Ahmet. 1998. "Atatürk ve Atatürkçüler" *Yeni Türkiye*, no. 23–24: 679–85.

Kadıoğlu, Ayşe. 1998. *Cumhuriyet İdaresi Demokrasi Muhakemesi*. Istanbul: Metis.

Kandiyoti, Deniz. 1987. "Emancipated but Unliberated? Reflections on the Turkish Case." *Feminist Studies* 13 (2): 317–38.

——. 1991 "End of Empire: Islam, Nationalism, and Women in Turkey." In *Women, Islam and the State*, ed. Kandiyoti, 22–47. Philadelphia: Temple University Press.

Kansu, Aykut. 2001. "Türkiye'de Korporatist Düşünce ve Korporatizm Uygulamaları." In *Modern Türkiye'de Siyasi Düşünce: Kemalizm*, ed. Tanil Bora and Gültekingil, 2: 253–67. Istanbul: İletişim.

Karaosmanoğlu, Ali L. 1993. "Officers: Westernization and Democracy." In *Turkey and the West: Changing Political and Cultural Identities*, ed. Metin Heper, Ayşe Öncü, and Heinz Kramer, 19–34. London: I. B. Tauris.

Kasaba, Reşat. 1997. "Kemalist Certainties and Modern Ambiguities." In *Rethinking Modernity and National Identity in Turkey*, ed. Sibel Bozdoğan and Kasaba, 15–36. Seattle: University of Washington Press.

Kaufmann, Daniel, and Paul Siegelbaum. 1997. "Privatization and Corruption in Transition Economies." *Journal of International Affairs* 50 (2): 419–58.

Kayalı, Hasan. 1997. *Arabs and Young Turks: Ottomanism, Arabism, and Islamism in the Ottoman Empire, 1909–1918*. Berkeley: University of California Press.

Kayra, Cahit. 2002. *38 Kuşağı Anılar*. Istanbul: İş Bankası Yayınları.

Kazancigil, Ali. 2001. "Anti-emperyalist Bağımsızlık İdeolojisi ve Üçüncü Dünya Ulusçuluğu Olarak Kemalizm." In *Modern Türkiye'de Siyasi Düşünce: Kemalizm*, ed. Tanil Bora and Murat Gültekingil, 235–46. Istanbul: İletişim.

Keyder, Çağlar. 1987. *State and Class in Turkey: A Study in Capitalist Development*. London: Verso.

Keyman, Fuat. 1997. "Kemalizm, Modernite, Gelenek." *Toplum ve Bilim*, no. 72: 84–99.

King, Desmond S. 1987. *The New Right: Politics, Markets, and Citizenship*. London: MacMillan.

Kinross, Patrick Balfour. 1965. *Atatürk: A Biography of Mustafa Kemal, Father of Modern Turkey*. New York: W. Morrow.

Koç, Vehbi. 1983. *Hayat Hikayem*. Istanbul: Çeltüt Matbaacılik.

Koğacıoğlu, Dicle. 2003. "Political Party Dissolutions by the Constitutional Court of Turkey: Judicial Delimiting of the Political Domains." *International Sociology* 18 (1): 258–76.

Köker, Levent. 2001. "Kemalizm/Atatürkçülük: Modernleşme, Devlet ve Demokrasi." In *Modern Türkiye'de Siyasi Düşünce: Kemalizm*, ed. Tanil Bora and Murat Gültekingil, 97–118. Istanbul: İletişim.

Korkut, Sinem Barkin. 1998. "O'nun Kadar Şık" *Aktüel*, no. 378: 212–13.

Kuhn, Annette. 1995. *Family Secrets: Acts of Memory and Imagination*. London: Verso.

Laçiner, Ömer. 1995. "1960 Sonrasi Kemalizm." *Yüzyil Biterken Cumhuriyet Dönemi Türkiye Ansiklopedisi*, 13: 771–76. Istanbul: İletişim.

Lambek, Michael. 1996. "The Past Imperfect: Remembering as Moral Practice." In *Tense Past: Cultural Essays in Trauma and Memory*, ed. Paul Antze and Lambek, 235–54. New York: Routledge.

Lan, David. 1985. *Guns and Rain: Guerillas and Spirit Mediums in Zimbabwe*. London: James Currey.

Landes, Joan B. 1998. Introduction to *Feminism: The Public and the Private*, ed. Landes, 1–20. Oxford: Oxford University Press.

Lefort, Claude. 1986. *The Political Forms of Modern Society: Bureaucracy, Democracy, Totalitarianism*. Ed. John B. Thompson. Cambridge, MA: MIT Press.

Lemon, Alaina. 2000. *Between Two Fires: Gypsy Performance and Romani Memory from Pushkin to Postsocialism*. Durham, NC: Duke University Press.

Lerner, Daniel. 1958. *The Passing of a Traditional Society*. New York: Free Press.

Lewis, Bernard. 1961. *The Emergence of Modern Turkey*. Oxford: Oxford University Press.

Linde, Charlotte. 1993. *Life Stories: The Creation of Coherence*. New York: Oxford University Press.

Lowenthal, David. 1985. *The Past Is a Foreign Country*. Cambridge: Cambridge University Press.

Malkki, Liisa H. 1995. *Purity and Exile: Violence, Memory, and National Cosmology among Hutu Refugees in Tanzania*. Chicago: University of Chicago Press.

———. 1997. "National Geographic: The Rooting of Peoples and the Territorialization of National Identity among Scholars and Refugees." In *Culture, Power, Place: Explorations in Critical Anthropology*, ed. Akhil Gupta and James Ferguson, 52–74. Durham, NC: Duke University Press.

Mango, Andrew. 1999. *Atatürk*. London: John Murray.

Mannheim, Bruce, and Dennis Tedlock. 1995. Introduction to *The Dialogic Emergence of Culture*, ed. Tedlock and Mannheim, 1–32. Urbana: University of Illinois Press.

Marcus, George. 1989. "Imagining the Whole: Ethnography's Contemporary Efforts to Situate Itself." *Critique of Anthropology* 9 (3): 7–30.

———. 1991. "Past, Present, and Emergent Identities: Requirements for Ethnographies of Late Twentieth-Century Modernity Worldwide." In *Modernity and Identity*, ed. Scott Lash and Jonathan Friedman, 309–30. Oxford: Blackwell.

———. 1995. "Ethnography in/of the World System: The Emergence of Multi-sited Ethnography." *Annual Review of Anthropology*, no. 24: 95–117.

———. 1998. *Ethnography through Thick and Thin*. Princeton, NJ: Princeton University Press.

Marden, Peter. 2003. *The Decline of Politics: Governance, Globalization, and the Public Sphere*. Burlington, VT: Ashgate.

Mardin, Şerif Arif. 1962. *The Genesis of Young Ottoman Thought: A Study in the Modernization of Turkish Political Ideas*. Princeton, NJ: Princeton University Press.

———. 1997. "Projects as Methodology: Some Thoughts on Modern Turkish Social Science." In *Rethinking Modernity and National Identity in Turkey*, ed. Sibel Bozdoğan and Reşat Kasaba, 64–80. Seattle: University of Washington Press.

Mazzarella, William. 2003. *Shoveling Smoke: Advertising and Globalization in Contemporary India*. Durham, NC: Duke University Press.

McClintock, Anne. 1995. *Imperial Leather: Race, Gender, and Sexuality in the Colonial Context.* New York: Routledge.

McMichael, Philip. 1998. "Development and Structural Adjustment." In *Virtualism: A New Political Economy*, ed. James Carrier and Daniel Miller, 95–116. Oxford: Berg.

Meeker, Michael. 1976. "Meaning and Society in the Middle East: The Black Sea Turks and the Levantine Arabs." *International Journal of the Middle East Studies*, no. 7: 243–70.

———. 2002. *A Nation of Empire: The Ottoman Legacy of Turkish Modernity.* Berkeley: University of California Press.

Messick, Brinkely. 1993. *The Calligraphic State: Textual Domination and History in a Muslim Society.* Berkeley: University of California Press.

Mitchell, Timothy. 1988. *Colonizing Egypt.* Cambridge: Cambridge University Press.

———. 1999. "Society, Economy, and the State Effect." In *State/Culture: State-Formation after the Cultural Turn*, ed. George Steinmetz, 76–97. Ithaca, NY: Cornell University Press.

———. 2000. "The Stage of Modernity." In *Questions of Modernity*, ed. Mitchell, 1–34. Minneapolis: University of Minnesota Press.

Moran, Tatyana. 2000. *Dün, Bugün.* Istanbul: İletişim.

Mosse, George. 1985. *Nationalism and Sexuality: Middle-Class Morality and Sexual Norms in Modern Europe.* Madison: University of Minnesota Press.

Müftüler, Meltem. 1995. "Turkish Economic Liberalization and Economic Integration." *Middle Eastern Studies* 31 (1): 85–104.

Musah, Abdel-Fatau. 2002. "Privatization of Security, Arms Proliferation and the Process of State Collapse in Africa." *Development and Change* 33(5): 911–33.

Nagel, Joanne. 1998. "Masculinity and Nationalism: Gender and Sexuality in the Making of Nations." *Ethnic and Racial Studies* 21(2): 242–69.

Najmabadi, Afsaneh. 1997. "The Erotic Vatan (Homeland) as Beloved and Mother: To Love, to Possess, and to Protect." *Comparative Studies in Society and History* 39 (4): 442–67.

Navaro-Yashin, Yael. 1997. "Uses and Abuses of 'State and Civil Society' in Contemporary Turkey." *New Perspectives on Turkey*, no. 18: 1–22.

———. 1999. "The Historical Construction of Local Culture: Gender and Identity in the Politics of Secularism versus Islam." In *Istanbul: Between Global and Local*, ed. Çağlar Keyder, 59–76. Lanham, MD: Rowman and Littlefield.

———. 2000. "Evde Taylorizm: Cumhuriyet'in İlk Yıllarında Ev İşinin Rasyonelleşmesi." *Toplum ve Bilim*, no. 84: 51–74.

———. 2002. *Faces of the State: Secularism and Public Life in Turkey.* Princeton, NJ: Princeton University Press.

Necipoğlu, Gülru. 2000. "Osmanlı Sultanlarinin Portre Dizilerine Karşılastırmalı bir Bakış." In *Padişahın Portresi: Tesavir-i Al-i Osman*, ed. Selmin Kangal, 22–61. Istanbul: İş Bankası Yayınları.

Neyzi, Leyla. 1999. İstanbul'da Hatırlamak ve Unutmak: Birey, Bellek, ve Aidiyet. Istanbul: Tarih Vakfı Yurt Yayınları.

———. 2001. "Object or Subject? The Paradox of 'Youth' in Turkey." *International Journal of Middle East Studies* 33 (3): 411–32.

Nora, Pierre. 1996. *Realms of Memory: Rethinking the French Past.* Translated by Arthur Goldhammer. New York: Columbia University Press.

Nuhoğlu Soysal, Yasemin. 2002. "Locating Europe." *European Societies* 4 (3): 265–84.

Ökten, Nazlı. 2006. "An Endless Death and an Eternal Mourning: November Ten in Turkey." In *Politics of Public Memory: Production and Erasure of the Past in Turkey,* ed. Esra Özyürek. Syracuse: Syracuse University Press.

Omae, Ken'ichi. 1995. *The End of the Nation-State: The Rise of Regional Economies.* New York: Free Press.

Öncü, Ayşe. 1995. "Packaging Islam: Cultural Politics on the Landscape of Turkish Commercial Television." *Public Culture* 8 (1): 51–71.

Öniş, Ziya. 1997. "The Political Economy of Islamic Resurgence in Turkey: The Rise of the Welfare Party in Perspective." *Third World Quarterly* 18 (4): 743–66.

———. 2000. "Neoliberal Globalization and the Democracy Paradox: The Turkish General Elections of 1999." *Journal of International Affairs* 54 (1): 283–306.

Osborne, Peter. 1995. *The Politics of Time: Modernity and Avant-Garde.* London: Verso.

Özbay, Ferhunde. 1996. "Evler, Kadınlar ve Evkadınları." In *Diğerlerinin Konut Sorunları,* ed. E. M. Komut. 52–64. Ankara: TMMOB Odası Yayınları.

Özbudun, Ergun. 2000. *Contemporary Turkish Politics: Challenges to Democratic Consolidation.* Boulder, CO: Lynne Rienner.

Özdalga, Elisabeth. 1998. *The Veiling Issue: Official Secularism and Popular Islam in Modern Turkey.* Richmond, UK: Curzon.

Özipek, Bekir Berat. 2004. "İrtica Nedir?" In *İslamcılık: Modern Türkiye'de Siyasi Düşünce: Kemalism,* ed. Tanil Bora and Murat Gültekingil. 6: 236–44. Istanbul: İletişim.

Ozouf, Mona. 1988. *Festivals and the French Revolution.* Cambridge, MA: Harvard University Press.

Öztan, Ziya, dir. 1998. *Cumhuriyet.* 150 min. Ankara: Turkish Radio and Television.

Öztürkmen, Arzu. 2001. "Celebrating National Holidays in Turkey: History and Memory." *New Perspectives on Turkey,* no. 25: 47–75.

Öztürkmen, Neriman Malkoç. 1999. *Edibeler, Sefireler, Hanımefendiler: İlk Nesil Cumhuriyet Kadınlariyla Söyleşiler.* Istanbul: Retyo Matbaacılık.

Özverim, Melda. 1998. *Mustafa Kemal ve Corinne Lütfü: Bir Dostluğun Öyüusü.* Istanbul: Milliyet Yayınları.

Özyürek, Esra. 2000. "Mecliste Başörtusu Düğümü" In *Vatan, Millet, Kadınlar,* ed. Ayşe Gül Altınay, 339–57. Istanbul: İletişim.

———. 2006. *Politics of Public Memory: Production and Erasure of the Past in Turkey.* Syracuse, NY: Syracuse University Press.

Paley, Julia. 2001. *Marketing Democracy: Power and Social Movements in Post-Dictatorship Chile*. Berkeley: University of California Press.

Parla, Taha. 1985. *The Social and Political Thought of Ziya Gökalp, 1876–1924*. Leiden, Netherlands: Brill.

———. 1991. *Türkiye'de Siyasi Kültürün Resmi Kaynakları*. Vol. 1. Istanbul: İletişim.

———. 1992. *Türkiye'de Siyasi Kültürün Resmi Kaynaklari: Kemalist Tek Parti İdeolojisi ve CHP'nin Alti Oku*. Vol 3. Istanbul: İletişim.

Passerini, Lois [1979] 1998. "Work Ideology and Consensus under Italian Fascism." In *Oral History Reader*, ed. Robert Perks and Alistair Thomson. London: Routledge.

Pateman, Carole. 1988. *The Sexual Contract*. Stanford: University of California Press.

Peirce, Leslie. 1993. *The Imperial Harem: Women and Sovereignty in the Ottoman Empire*. Oxford: Oxford University Press.

Personal Narratives Group, ed. 1989. *Interpreting Women's Lives: Feminist Theory and Personal Narratives*. Bloomington: Indiana University Press.

Phillips, Joan. 1988. *Policing the Family: Social Control in Thatcher's Britain*. London: Junius.

Plummer, Ken. 2003. *Intimate Citizenship: Private Decisions and Public Dialogues*. Seattle: University of Washington Press.

Portelli, Alessandro. 1991. *The Death of Luigi Trastulli and Other Stories: Form and Meaning in Oral History*. Albany: State University of New York Press.

Povinelli, Elizabeth. 2002. *The Cunning of Recognition: Indigenous Alterities and the Making of the Australian Multiculturalism*. Durham: Duke University Press.

Putnam, Robert D. 2000. *Bowling Alone: The Collapse and Revival of American Community*. New York: Simon and Schuster.

Rabinow, Paul. 1989. *French Modern: Norms and Forms of the Social Environment*. Cambridge, MA: MIT Press.

Rankin, Katharine. 2001. "Governing Development: Neo-liberalism, Micro-credit, and Rational Economic Woman." *Economy and Society* 30(2): 18–37.

Renda, Günsel. 2000. "Portrenin Son Yüzyılı." In *Padişahin Portresi: Tesavir-i Al-i Osman*, ed. Selmin Kangal, 442–543. Istanbul: İş Bankası Yayınları.

Rıza, Enis. 1998. *Cumhuriyetin Hayalleri*. VTR Araştırma Yapım Yönetim.

Robins, Kevin. 1996. "Interrupting Identities Turkey/Europe." In *Questions of Cultural Identity*, ed. Stuart Hall and Paul du Gay, 61–86. London: Sage.

Rofel, Lisa. 1999. *Other Modernities: Gendered Yearnings in China after Socialism*. Berkeley: University of California Press.

Rosaldo, Renato. 1989. *Culture and Truth: The Remaking of Social Analysis*. Boston: Beacon.

Rowbotham, Sheila. 1973. *Hidden from History*. London: Pluto.

Roy, Oliver. 1994. *The Failure of Political Islam*. Cambridge, MA: Harvard University Press.

Saba, Roberto Pablo, and Luigi Manzetti. 1996. "Privatization in Argentina: Corruption." *Crime, Law, and Society* 25 (4): 353–69.

Sakallıoğlu, Ümit Cizre. 1996. "Parameters and Strategies of Islam-State Interaction in Republican Turkey." *International Journal of Middle East Studies* 28 (2): 231–51.

Sarıdoğan, Neşe. 1998. "Siyasiler 75: Yılı Nasil Değerlendirdiler?" *Nokta* 17 (873): 15.

Sassen, Saskia. 1996. *Losing Control? Sovereignty in an Age of Globalization*. New York: Columbia University Press.

Schedler, Andreas. 1997. "Introduction: Antipolitics—Closing and Colonizing the Public Sphere." In *The End of Politics? Explorations into Modern Antipolitics*, ed. Schedler, 1–20. New York: St. Martin's.

Şenol Cantek, Funda. 2003. *Yabanlar ve Yerliler: Başkent Olma Sürecinde Ankara*. Istanbul: İletişim.

Şerifsoy, Selda. 2000. "Aile ve Kemalist Modernizasyon Projesi, 1928–1950." In *Vatan Millet Kadınlar*, ed. Ayşe Gül Altınay, 155–88. Istanbul: İletişim.

Seufert, Gunter. 2000. "Milliyetçi Söylemlerin Sivil Toplum Üzerindeki Etkileri." In *Türkiye'de Sivil Toplum ve Milliyetçilik*, ed. Stefanos Yerasimos. 25–44. Istanbul: İletişim.

Shaker, Sallama. 1995. *State, Society, and Privatization in Turkey, 1979–1990*. Washington, DC: Woodrow Wilson Center Press.

Shryock, Andrew and Sally Howell. 2001. "Ever a Guest in Our House: The Emir Abdullah, Shaykh Majid Al-Adwan, and the Practice of Jordanian House Politics as Remembered by Umm Sultan, the Widow of Majid." *International Journal of Middle East Studies* 33(2): 247–69.

Silverstein, Brian. 2003. "Islam and Modernity in Turkey: Power, Tradition, and Historicity in the European Provinces of the Muslim World." *Anthropological Quarterly* 76 (3): 497–517.

Silverstein, Michael, and Greg Urban. 1996. "The Natural History of Discourse." In *Natural Histories of Discourse*, ed. Silverstein and Urban, 1–20. Chicago: University of Chicago Press.

Sirman, Nükhet. 1989. "Feminism in Turkey: A Short History." *New Perspectives on Turkey* 3 (1): 1–34.

———. 1990. "State, Village, and Gender in Western Turkey." In *Turkish State, Turkish Society*, ed. Andrew Finkel and Sirman, 21–51. London: Routledge.

———. 2000. "Writing the Usual Love Story: The Fashioning of Conjugal and National Subjects in Turkey." In *Gender, Agency, and Change: Anthropological Perspectives*, ed. Victoria Ana Goddard. 250–72. London: Routledge.

———. 2002. "Kadınların Milliyeti." In *Modern Türkiye'de Siyasi Düşünce: Milliyetçilik*, ed. Tanıl Bora and Murat Gültekingil, 226–44. Istanbul: İletişim.

Somel, Selçuk Akşin. 2001. *The Modernization of Public Education in the Ottoman Empire, 1839–1908: Islamization, Autocracy, and Discipline*. Leiden, Netherlands: Brill.

Somers, Margaret R. 1999. "The Privatization of Citizenship: How to Unthink a Knowledge Culture." In *Beyond the Cultural Turn: New Directions in the Study of Society and Culture*, ed. Victoria E. Bonnell and Lynn Hunt, 121–61. Berkeley: University of California Press.

Sommer, Doris. 1991. *Foundational Fictions: The National Romance of Latin America*. Berkeley: University of California Press.

Sönmez, Cemil. 1998. *Atatürk'ün Annesi Zübeyde Hanım*. Ankara: Atatürk Araştırma Merkezi.

Sontag, Susan. 1977. *On Photography*. New York: Farrar, Ştraus and Giroux.

Starrett, Gregory. 1997. "The Political Economy of Religious Commodities in Cario." *American Anthropologist*, no. 1: 51–68.

Steinmetz, George. 1999. "Introduction: Culture and the State." In *State/Culture: State-Formation after the Cultural Turn*, ed. Steinmetz, 1–49. Ithaca, NY: Cornell University Press.

Stewart, Kathleen. 1988. "Nostalgia—A Polemic." *Cultural Anthropology* 3 (3): 227–41.

Stewart, Susan. 1993. *On Longing: Narratives of the Miniature, the Gigantic, the Souvenir, the Collection*. Durham, NC: Duke University Press.

Stokes, Martin. 1992. *The Arabesk Debate: Music and Musicians in Modern Turkey*. Oxford: Oxford University Press.

Stoler, Ann Laura, and Frederick Cooper. 1997. "Between Metropole and Colony: Rethinking a Research Agenda." In *Tensions of Empire: Colonial Cultures in a Bourgeois World*, ed. Cooper and Stoler. Berkeley: University of California Press.

Stoler, Ann Laura, and Karen Strassler. 2000. "Castings for the Colonial: Memory Work in 'New Order' Java." *Comparative Studies in Society and History* 42 (1): 4–48.

Suad, Joseph. 1997. "The Public/Private: The Imagined Boundary in the Imagined Nation/State/Community; The Lebanese Case." *Feminist Review*, no. 57: 73–92.

Tangri, Roger, and Andrew Mwende. 2001. "Corruption and Cronyism in Uganda's Privatization in the 1990s." *African Affairs* 100 (398): 117–33.

Tanyeli, Uğur, ed. 1998. *Üç Kuşak Cumhuriyet*. Istanbul: Türkiye Ekonomik ve Toplumsal Tarih Vakfı.

Tapper, Richard. 1991. Introduction to *Islam in Modern Turkey: Religion, Politics, and Literature in a Secular State*, ed. Tapper, 1–27. London: I. B. Tauris.

Tapper, Richard, and Nancy Tapper. 1991. "Religion, Education, and Continuity in a Provincial Town." In *Islam in Modern Turkey: Religion, Politics, and Literature in a Secular State*, ed. R. Tapper, 56–83. London: I. B. Tauris.

Taussig, Michael. 1993. "Maleficium: State Fetishism." In *Fetishism as Cultural Discourse*, ed. Emily Apter and William Pietz, 217–50. Ithaca, NY: Cornell University Press.

——. 1997. *The Magic of the State*. London: Routledge.

Taylor, Charles. 1990. "Modes of Civil Society." *Public Culture* 3 (1): 95–118.

Tekeli, İlhan. 1998. *Ankara, Istanbul, İzmir için Cumhuriyet Geçitleri ve Şenlikleri: Kuramsal Hazirlik ve Tasarim Calışması*. Istanbul: Tarih Vakfı Yayınları.

Terkel, Studs. 1970. *Hard Times: An Oral History of the Great Depression*. New York: Pantheon.

Thompson, Paul. 1978. *The Voice of the Past: Oral History*. Oxford: Oxford University Press.

Thomson, Alistair. 1990. "Anzac Memories: Putting Popular Memory Theory into Practice in Australia." *Oral History* 18 (2): 25–31.

Togan, S., and V. N. Balasubramanyam, eds. 1996. *The Economy of Turkey since Liberalization*. New York: St. Martin's.

Toprak, Binnaz. 1981. *Islam and Political Development in Turkey*. Leiden, Netherlands: Brill.

Trouillot, Michel-Rolph. 2001. "The Anthropology of the State in the Age of Globalization." *Current Anthropology* 42 (1): 125–33.

Tuğal, Cihan. 2002. "The Islamist Movement in Turkey: Beyond Instrument and Meaning." *Economy and Society* 31 (1): 85–111.

Tumarkin, Nina. 1983. *Lenin Lives! The Lenin Cult in Soviet Russia*. Cambridge, MA: Harvard University Press.

Turam, Berna. 2004. "The Politics of Engagement between Islam and the Secular State: Ambivalences of 'Civil Society.' " *British Journal of Sociology* 55 (2): 259–81.

Turan, Hesabali. 1993. *Bir Eğitimcinin Öyküsü*. Istanbul: Yapı Kredi.

Turan, İlter. 1991. "Religion and Political Culture in Turkey." In *Islam in Modern Turkey: Religion, Politics, and Literature in a Secular State*, ed. Richard Tapper, 31–55. London: I. B. Tauris.

Türkmen, Buket. 2000. "Laikliğin dönüşümü: Liseli gençler, türban ve Atatürk rozeti." In *İslamın kamusal yüzleri*, ed. Nilüfer Göle, 110–47. Istanbul: Metis.

Uçuk, Cahit. 1995. *Bir İmparatorluk Çökerken*. Istanbul: Yapı Kredi Yayınları.

Ünder, Hasan. 2001. "Atatürk İmgesinin Siyasi Yaşamdaki Rolü." In *Modern Türkiye'de Siyasi Düşünce: Kemalizm*, ed. Tanil Bora and Murat Gültekingil, 2: 138–55. Istanbul: İletişim.

Urgan, Mina. 1998. *Bir Dinazorun Anıları*. Istanbul: Yapı Kredi Yayınları.

Verdery, Katherine. 1996. *What Was Socialism and What Comes Next?* Princeton, NJ: Princeton University Press.

Verkaik, Oskar. 2001. "The Captive State: Corruption, Intelligence Agencies, and Ethnicity in Pakistan." In *States of Imagination: Ethnographic Explorations of the Postcolonial State*, ed. Thomas Blom Hansen and Finn Stepputat, 345–64. Durham, NC: Duke University Press.

Volkan, Vamık D., and Norman Itzkowitz. 1984. *The Immortal Atatürk: A Psychobiography*. Chicago: Chicago University Press.

Walstedt, Bertil. 1980. *State Manufacturing Enterprise in a Mixed Economy: The Turkish Case*. Baltimore, MD: Johns Hopkins University Press.

Warner, Michael. 2002. "Publics and Counterpublics." *Public Culture* 14 (1): 49–90.

Wedeen, Lisa. 1999. *Ambiguities of Domination: Politics, Rhetoric, and Symbols in Contemporary Syria*. Chicago: University of Chicago Press.

White, Jenny. 1999. "The Islamic Chic." In *Istanbul: Between the Global and the Local*, ed. Çağlar Keyder, 77–94. Lanham, MD: Rowman and Littlefield.

———. 2002. *Islamist Mobilization in Turkey: A Study in Vernacular Politics*. Seattle: University of Washington Press.

Williams, Brackette. 1995. "Classification Systems Revisited: Kinship, Caste, Race and

Nationality as the Flow of Blood and the Spread of Rights." In *Naturalizing Power: Essays in Feminist Cultural Analysis*, eds. Sylvia Yanagisako and Carol Delaney, 201–38. New York: Routledge.

Williams, Raymond. 1977. *Marxism and Literature*. Oxford: Oxford University Press.

Williamson, Judith. 1986. *Consuming Passions: The Dynamics of Popular Culture*. London: M. Boyars.

Yanagisako, Sylvia, and Carol Delaney. 1995. "Naturalizing Power." In *Naturalizing Power: Essays in Feminist Cultural Analysis*, ed. Yanagisako and Delaney, 1–24. New York: Routledge.

Yang, Mayfair Mei-hui. 1994. *Gifts, Favors, Banquets: The Art of Social Relationships in China*. Ithaca, NY: Cornell University Press.

Yavuz, Hakan. 1999. "The Assassination of Collective Memory: The Case of Turkey." *Muslim World* 89 (3–4): 193–213.

———. 2000. "Cleansing Islam from the Public Sphere." *Journal of International Affairs* 54 (1): 21–42.

Yeğen, Mesut. 2001. "Kemalizm ve Hegemonya." In *Modern Türkiye'de Siyasi Düşünce: Kemalizm*, ed. Tanil Bora and Murat Gültekingil. Istanbul: İletişim.

Yeşilyurt, Süleyman. 1997. *Atatürk'ün Gönül Galerisi*. Istanbul: Yeryüzü Yayınevi.

Yıldız, Ahmet. 2001. *"Ne Mutlu Türküm Diyebilene:" Türk Ulusal Kimliğinin Etno-Seküler Sınırları (1919–1938)*. Istanbul: İletişim Yayınları.

———. 2003. "Politico-religious Discourse of Political Islam in Turkey: The Parties of National Outlook." *The Muslim World* 93 (2): 187–209.

Yúdice, George. 1995. "Civil Society, Consumption, and Governmentality in an Age of Global Restructuring: An Introduction." *Social Text* 14 (4): 1–25.

Žižek, Slavoj. 1999. *The Ticklish Subject: The Absent Centre of Political Ontology*. London: Verso.

Zürcher, Erik Jan. 1998. *Turkey: A Modern History*. London: I. B. Tauris.

Index

Private life: displaying transformations in, 65–92; elderly Republicans framing, through public events, 56–62 (*see also* Elderly Republicans; Life-history narratives); exhibits on, 69

Private sphere: definitions of, 7; displays of, for political purposes, 6–7; impact of emphasis on, 22–23; Kemalism moving to, 2–5; in life-history narratives, 39 (*see also* Life-history narratives); meanings of, 7–8; and perceptions of the public sphere, 2, 90–91, 181; state ideology in, 3. *See also* Public sphere

Privatization, 179–180; citizens' using, to promote "original" ideology, 17–18; as driving force behind neoliberal ideology, 8; and the History Foundation, 136; of Kemalism, 179

Prophecies of Atatürk (Bektan), 118

Protests, 165–166

Public sphere: definitions of, 7; and domesticity, 181; elderly Republicans framing private lives through, 56–62; in life-history narratives, 39 (*see also* Life-history narratives); meanings of, 7–8; nostalgia transforming, into personalized commodities, 9–10; and perceptions of the private sphere,, 2, 181; shared, concept of, 5–6. *See also* Private sphere

Putnam, Robert, 6, 21

Rankin, Katharine, 21

Religion, elderly Republicans on, 46–47. *See also* Elderly Republicans; Islamists; Life-history narratives

Remix, of tenth anniversary march, 169–170

Republic, Turkish: and family, 90 (*see also* Domesticity, and the public sphere; Family); as "family," 71–72; foundation of, 25, 41–42; history of, as told in life-history narratives, 41–42, 56–62; and Islamists, 151–177 (*see also* Islamists); and Kemalists, 151–177 (*see also* Kemalists); march of, 168–169; and national unity, 144–146; official ideology of, 25; private self in the public history of, 38–47; rule of, and Atatürk's gaze, 116–117; tenth anniversary celebration as establishing, 128; and world economy, integration with, 15–16. *See also* Early Republic; Republic Day celebrations; Seventy-fifth anniversary celebration; Tenth anniversary celebration

Republic, The, 109–111

Republican People's Party, 142–143. *See also* Kemalists

Republicans, elderly. *See* Elderly Republicans

Republic Day celebrations, 26–27; change in, after 1994, 133; images of Atatürk in, 151; Islamists participation in, 155–156, 158, 166–167, 176–177; official posters for, 145; organized by civilians, 125–150; sameness of, 132–133; in schools, 132; slogans for, 142, 146; symbolism of, 149–150; and tenth anniversary march, 170–171. *See also* Seventy-fifth anniversary celebration; Tenth anniversary celebration

Robins, Kevin, 14

Rofel, Lisa, 8, 31, 35

Rosaldo, Renato, 31

Roy, Oliver, 8

Sabah (newspaper), 119–120

Sabancı family, 88

Saraç, Faruk, 120

Saridoğan, Neşe, 94

Sarran, Nephan, 51

ESRA ÖZYÜREK is an assistant professor of anthropology at the University of California, San Diego. She is the editor of The Politics of Public Memory in Turkey.

Library of Congress Cataloging-in-Publication Data

Öyürek, Esra.

Nostalgia for the modern :

state secularism and everyday politics in Turkey / Esra Özyürek.

p. cm.—(Politics, history, and culture)

Includes bibliographical references and index.

ISBN-13: 978-0-8223-3879-6 (cloth : alk. paper)

ISBN-10: 0-8223-3879-3 (cloth : alk. paper)

ISBN-13: 978-0-8223-3895-6 (pbk. : alk. paper)

ISBN-10: 0-8223-3895-5 (pbk. : alk. paper)

1. Turkey—Politics and government—20th century. 2. Kemalism.

3. Islam and secularism—Turkey. 4. Islam and politics.

I. Title. II. Series.   DR576.099 2006

956.1′02—dc22   2006010435